I AM MAROON

I AM MAROON

The True Story of an American Political Prisoner

RUSSELL SHOATZ

with Kanya D'Almeida

BOLD TYPE BOOKS

NEW YORK

Bold Type Books
Hachette Book Group
1290 Avenue of the Americas, New York, NY 10104
www.boldtypebooks.org
@BoldTypeBooks

Printed in the United States of America

First Edition: September 2024

Published by Bold Type Books, an imprint of Hachette Book Group, Inc.
Bold Type Books is a co-publishing venture of the Type Media Center and Perseus Books.

The Hachette Speakers Bureau provides a wide range of authors for speaking events. To find out more, go to hachettespeakersbureau.com or email HachetteSpeakers@hbgusa.com.

Bold Type books may be purchased in bulk for business, educational, or promotional use. For more information, please contact your local bookseller or the Hachette Book Group Special Markets Department at special.markets@hbgusa.com.

The publisher is not responsible for websites (or their content) that are not owned by the publisher.

Print book interior design Sheryl Kober.

Library of Congress Cataloging-in-Publication Data

Names: Shoatz, Russell Maroon, 1943–2020, author. | D'Almeida, Kanya, 1986– author.
Title: I am Maroon: the true story of an American political prisoner / Russell Shoatz, with Kanya D'Almeida.
Description: First. edition. | New York : Bold Type Books, 2024. | Includes index.
Identifiers: LCCN 2023059359 | ISBN 9781645030492 (hardcover) | ISBN 9781645030515 (ebook)
Subjects: LCSH: African American political activists—Pennsylvania—Biography. | Prisoners—Pennsylvania—Biography. | Black Liberation Army—Biography. | Black power—United States—History—20th century. | Black nationalism—United States—History—20th century. | Black Panther Party—Biography. | Authors, American—20th century—Biography.
Classification: LCC E185.615 .S49183 2024 | DDC 323.1/1960730092 [B]—dc23/eng/20240228
LC record available at https://lccn.loc.gov/2023059359

ISBNs: 9781645030492 (hardcover), 9781645030515 (ebook)
LSC-C
Printing 1, 2024

CONTENTS

Contents

I met our chief, Maroon, in the Hole: in solitary confinement, in a state penitentiary, in the state of Pennsylvania. I said to myself: this is a Black man that wants to help the Black slave come out of bondage. We—me and my people—had not heard talk like this in our lifetime. We liked this rap. It was new, different, and we supported it.

—JOSEPH "JOE JOE" BOWEN,
FORTY YEARS IN SOLITARY CONFINEMENT

INTRODUCTION

Free Maroon

To visit a prisoner is to lose—just briefly—your own freedom.

The prison visiting room is no-man's-land, a midway point between liberty and incarceration, and it reminds prisoner and visitor alike of the arbitrariness, the insanity of the whole carceral system.

To reach this strange place, both parties must move through metal detectors and past guard stations with a ticket in their hand. For the visitor that slip of paper represents temporary confinement in the dungeon. For the prisoner it perhaps offers some respite, a short-lived release from the cage. At some point during the visit the tickets might be forgotten. There is much to discuss, after all, and never enough time. Sand falls softly inside the hourglass, unnoticed at first. But as it piles up around your torso, your shoulders, you are reminded with a suffocating urgency that the end is close. The prisoner feels the mouth of the prison opening behind him, sucking him back into a life sentence. The visitor eyes the guard, who in that moment is an ally, for it is up to

1

him—the keeper of keys—to honor the ticket, unlock the doors, and usher you back to your rightful place in the world of free people.

Here is where the gulf between prisoner and visitor is deepest. Your relief upon leaving is matched in intensity only by the prisoner's concrete misery.

To write a book with a prisoner is to confront, again and again, that distance between you. It is to surrender yourself repeatedly to the scrutiny of guards and censors, the invasive probing of their fingers, the cruelty of their rules, and the unyielding logic of their madness. Visits only on certain days, for certain approved visitors dressed in strict accordance with their Rules of Attire, for limited hours, which are sometimes canceled or cut short without warning. Letters destroyed, returned unopened, lost. Phone calls recorded, and interactions militantly monitored: No hugging. No handholding. Can we laugh? If you must but do it quietly. So we did. We laughed quietly. We devised our own language, a code to defy the sentinels, because the success of this whole operation rested on a long, hard, and slow reckoning with history and truth.

I first met Russell "Maroon" Shoatz in 2013 at the State Correctional Institution at Mahanoy, an all-male, one-thousand-cell penitentiary in rural Pennsylvania.

I sat in a plastic chair as the waiting room emptied around me. Eventually, hours after I'd arrived, a guard at the desk called out, "Shoatz? Russell Shoatz!" and I stood, realizing with a sense of unease that I was no longer Kanya D'Almeida. In here I was merely a visitor of Inmate #AF-3855, which is to say, Russell Shoatz, their highest-security prisoner. And as far as the staff were concerned, we were one unit.

I was led into the main visiting room and was momentarily cheered by the sunny, open space with its colorful cushioned armchairs occupied by families with children, couples in love (not hugging or kissing), fathers and sons. But the guard didn't stop there—he ushered me through that noisy, bustling room to a door at the far end, then down a flight of stairs, then through another door, and finally into a kind of cell, divided by a sheet of soundproof glass, with nothing on either side but two telephones attached to the wall.

Of course. Maroon was no ordinary prisoner. In the 1960s he'd been a member of an armed Black militant organization and stood accused of murdering a Philadelphia Park Guard at the height of the city's struggle for Black liberation. For two years he evaded arrest, living underground in New York City. Caught and captured following an armed robbery, he received a life sentence, and spent years in prisons across Pennsylvania. Twice he escaped from these facilities, which earned him the name of Maroon.

Throughout the vast archipelago of the Pennsylvania prison system, he is a legend. The state's department of corrections despises him. Old Timers and Lifers—men serving life sentences—revere him. And in the penitentiary, there is only one place for a man like him, a man capable of organizing the entire prison population: solitary confinement. For over two decades he lived in what was known as the Control Unit, an extreme form of solitary confinement at the State Correctional Institution at Greene, way down in the southwest corner of Pennsylvania.

Weeks before our visit Maroon had been transferred to the Restricted Housing Unit here at Mahanoy. I'd been told he hadn't had human contact in over twenty-two years.

I stared at the man on the other side of the glass. He was small, bespectacled, and seemed to shrink back against the wall behind him. Perhaps it was the result of having his hands cuffed to his waist and his ankles shackled, but he appeared meek and wary. Unimpressive to the point of being unremarkable.

I turned around, opened the door, and returned to the guard station, which was a glass box mounted on a platform. I showed my ticket.

"I'm here for Russell Shoatz."

The guard gestured to the room I'd just vacated. "That's him. Use the phone."

I went back in. The room seemed smaller, perhaps because the man had suddenly assumed a greater form—a giant looming large against the glass. With sweating palms and shaking fingers I pressed the receiver to my ear. He did the same, with some difficulty owing to his chains.

He spoke first, sternly. "Kanya? You were expecting someone different, weren't you? A big, impressive guy?"

I stammered out an apology, but he was relentless. "Yeah, you were. You were expecting some big tough Black Panther. They told you about Maroon this and Maroon that, and here you come and find me and thought you had the wrong guy."

We had been corresponding for months before this visit, long letters full of respectful salutations and anticipation of our first meeting. I knew his hand, the labored penmanship of an old man with a mind as sharp as an arrow. Already I had dedicated many hours to studying his political writings and personal essays and even a draft of his autobiography that had come to me in the form of a raw manuscript with instructions to turn it into a screenplay, the script for a biopic. This visit was my audition for the role of his biographer. I was mortified at having offended him and even more so by the tears gathering in my eyes—was I really going to break down crying in front of a man who had, among many other extraordinary feats, survived nearly twenty-three years of no-touch torture?

As though to spare me, he broke into a smile. "Well, well. Let's start again. Come on now. This is a historic moment, right? This is the day a Black Panther meets a Black Tiger."

I wasn't a Black Tiger, but I didn't dare contradict him. It was, after all, simply a nod to my country's history—a reference to the infamous cadre of female suicide bombers who'd operated as a special unit within the separatist Liberation Tigers of Tamil Eelam throughout a thirty-year civil war with the government of Sri Lanka. I was tempted to point out (if only to have it on record in the guard tower) that most Sri Lankans would be mortally offended at being labeled a Black Tiger. But I also knew instinctively that his greeting was a message, a way of speaking around our surveilled circumstances to say that although we stood worlds apart, we were bound by conflict, by the histories of our people, and therefore—perhaps—capable of hearing and seeing and understanding each other.

Over the next seven years, as I blundered and stumbled through Maroon's story, this assumption proved to be beautifully accurate but also dismally mistaken.

If the Black Panthers represented for Maroon a kind of life pulse—the nucleus around which all else revolved, allowing him to make sense of his past, organize his present, and lay plans for his future—then the Black Tigers were for me the opposite, a distant and abstract notion that touched only the far outer reaches of my existence. And so Maroon and I found ourselves, often, at loggerheads over the matter of what I called violence and what he referred to as armed struggle.

We had both been born into, and come of age in, times of war. For me, that meant Sri Lanka's double conflict: the thirty-year-long civil war that began in 1983, fought over land, liberation, and language between the government and a military force known as the Liberation Tigers of Tamil Eelam (LTTE) that claimed to represent the country's Tamil minority; and the insurgency-counterinsurgency of 1989 involving the People's Liberation Front (JVP), ostensibly to orchestrate a communist revolution to overturn what was then a neoliberal government. These two battles, which raged in the northeast and the deep south, spawned such horror, and spilled so much blood, that it seemed we would forever be a nation in mourning. No one was untouched. Ethnic pogroms sent members of my family fleeing to India, and my uncle, a journalist, was kidnapped from his home, and his bullet-riddled body dumped into the ocean amid a wave of disappearances and assassinations that ultimately claimed over sixty thousand lives. By the time I met Maroon in 2013, the civil war had ground to a grisly end, taking with it tens of thousands more people, most of them unarmed Tamil civilians. I was war-weary, sickened by violence.

Maroon identified as a POW, a prisoner of war, an enemy combatant against the government of the United States, but the contours of his war were less clearly defined. In Sri Lanka, the conflict had start and end dates, declarations of ceasefire mediated by international peacekeepers, and military campaigns that were confined to specific regions. Maroon's war, on the other hand, seemed to span centuries, beginning with conquest, genocide, and slavery, and extending forever into a future in which the prison system was the Final Solution. He was not a bystander to this history but an active participant in it, willingly conscripted.

For a while, our conversations went in circles. While I tried to draw Maroon out on his childhood, his gang affiliations, his decision as a young Panther to take up arms, he queried me about the LTTE with an interest bordering on reverence. For him, the Tigers were a success story, a group of civilians who had taken on and terrorized the state. They also enlisted child soldiers, I tried to argue; they also terrorized their own people. But look at their organizational structure, Maroon would push back. Their fighter planes, naval force, civil administration, their foreign diplomatic relations, their exchange of tactical training and weaponry with other militant groups, their recourse to international laws of war. And where did it get them, I wondered, strategically, politically, humanly? None of their aims realized, and their would-be homeland reduced to a tapestry of mass graves.

Theoretically, we could engage on these subjects: the legitimacy of Third-World liberation movements, the Palestine Liberation Organization, the Vietcong, the Young Lords, the American Indian Movement, the Panthers, the right to self-defense. But I needed more. I needed to know, intimately, from him, how it felt to pick up a gun. To beat, to be beaten. Why a person would choose what they chose. Maroon didn't appreciate this line of inquiry. At times he looked at me strangely, as though he couldn't fathom such naivete. *You grew up in Sri Lanka!* he'd say sometimes, in disbelief and frustration. *You told me there were bombs going off on buses and trains! What are you asking about gang conscription for?*

He dug in his heels, refused to engage further unless I read certain books, watched certain films, *Eyes on the Prize* and *Soul on Ice.*

In exchange, I gave him *The Cage*, an account of the final days of Sri Lanka's civil war. We chipped away at each other's illiteracy, tried to cross the channel of incomprehension. It was precisely at this moment, when we were looking askance at each other, that we were called upon to defend our unlikely collaboration.

Why him?

Why her?

What can she know about our struggle, this history, your life?

Think about your own country, your career, your people.

In answering these attacks from others, we grew closer, discovered that there was an implicit trust between us, and reached an unspoken truce to leave the sticking points aside and get down to work.

The original document—an unbound manuscript entitled "The Making of a Political Prisoner"—had already changed hands many times before arriving on my doorstep in a FedEx envelope. It was accompanied by a note from a man named Fred Ho, a Chinese American jazz musician and activist whose acquaintance I had recently made through artist channels in New York City.

"Russell 'Maroon' Shoatz is a brilliant and dynamic Black liberation fighter who has been incarcerated for three decades," Fred wrote, "but dig this—he escaped TWICE from prison."

He wanted me to fashion from Maroon's pages a screenplay along the lines of *The Hurricane*, the feature film based on the life of the wrongfully convicted African American boxer Rubin "Hurricane" Carter.

I had never even read a screenplay, much less written one. I had never heard of Maroon, or, for that matter, Rubin "Hurricane" Carter! I was largely ignorant of the scope of mass incarceration of Black people in America, the vast history of the Black Liberation Movement, and the potential complexities of a South Asian woman being enlisted to craft an intimate portrait of an American revolutionary. And yet I found myself agreeing to the assignment out of sheer intrigue and awe for what I vaguely understood to be a thrilling tale of jailbreaking.

I sat down with those 280 pages and read them over and over again. I tried to locate a digital version but was told by Maroon's children that such a thing no longer existed, and so, one summer back in Sri Lanka, I extracted the pages from my suitcase and enlisted the librarian at my old high school to transcribe them for me. The book was sprawling, unwieldy, chronologically jumbled. I kept losing track of people, places, dates. It dawned on me very quickly that before anyone undertook the task of a screenplay, the story itself needed to be filled in, tightened up, reconstructed.

I was a journalist at the time, based in Washington, DC, and in a year I would transition from the reporter's desk to the editorial desk. I was not a scholar of Black history, but I was trained in tracking down people and getting them to talk. In entering archives and finding my way out again. In listening, deeply, to oral histories. And so I suggested that we concentrate first on the autobiography. The hairbrained plan for a screenplay was laid aside, and it was understood that I would begin editing the book.

I later learned it was Maroon's second daughter, Sharon, who'd elicited the manuscript from her father by querying him incessantly about his life and the precise steps that had led him to where he was. He said he sat down one day at the steel desk in his cell and just started writing, anything and everything he remembered, details and timelines, omissions and inaccuracies, histories and memories. Initially I tried to work directly from the pages, letting Maroon's words guide me through the contours of his life. It was a little like following a river, exciting at first, but quickly impossible, as it disappeared into terrain I couldn't traverse, vanishing suddenly underground, then picking up speed and tumbling down cliffs at speeds I could never keep pace with.

And so, I laid the manuscript aside, opened a fresh document on my computer that I saved—somewhat naively—as "Maroon New," and began from scratch.

I met his family and hunted down his friends. I asked the wrong questions and received garbled, guarded answers. I threw myself into

a campaign to free Maroon from solitary confinement, thereby eras-
ing all boundaries between my roles as researcher, activist, writer, comrade, journalist, and spokesperson. I traveled to Philadelphia to gather
clues, exhume the remains of stories, and comb the archives, and in
the process I aroused the curiosity, support, resentment, and blessings
of many people who all wondered at our friendship, my motives, and
Maroon's judgment in agreeing to work with me.

When I spoke in public forums I was sometimes cheered, and other
times jeered at. I was warmly welcomed into strangers' homes, and
other times asked to leave. I was brought to the bedside of dying relatives to hear their final testimonies on Maroon, but I was too overcome
by my own notion of being an intruder to record what they had to say. I
lost my notes, and I was stripped of my research. People shared stories
they said they'd never shared before, and have vowed never to speak
of again.

More than once, I was approached by the women in his life, with
the suggestion that I ought to write their stories instead. By then I knew
some fragments of these stories, conveyed in Maroon's words, through
his eyes: stories of marital strife, domestic violence, stormy separations,
more than one broken heart. Perhaps I should have taken that fork in
the road. Perhaps I should have written a book about the women who
loved him, were abandoned by him, survived him, uplifted him, sacrificed for him, carried on for him. But I didn't.

I visited Maroon in one dreadful prison after another. I was never
allowed pencil or paper during these audiences with him. After the visits, while my husband drove us home, I sat in the passenger seat furiously scribbling notes before the details fled from my mind. I contacted
other imprisoned people, Maroon's comrades, and received an ava-
lanche of snail mail from lonely men on death row who just wanted
to be heard. Eventually I resorted to storing their unopened letters in
boxes under my bed, though I never threw them away. Friendships I
forged in the course of this project were crushed against prison walls
as we tried to keep afloat of Maroon's transfers, his ever-changing

prospects for release, his immensely complicated legal strategies, and his even more intricate family affairs. My husband, along with a very close comrade of ours from Pittsburgh, drove me all around rural Pennsylvania, and once we ate at a diner that sat across from the very intersection where, in 1977, Maroon was recaptured after evading the prison authorities for twenty-seven days.

I read and listened and watched and listened and read some more but could not commit a single worthwhile sentence to paper.

I remember the first time Maroon and I met without the glass separating us. Without his shackles, or a guard listening on the telephone, outside of that confined booth that had become a time capsule.

It was 2015. He'd just been released from solitary confinement and transferred to the State Correctional Institution at Graterford, an old, sprawling facility in Montgomery County where he'd once staged an unsuccessful escape attempt. When he entered the visiting room, I felt my body begin to fold, and I prepared to get down on my hands and knees to touch his feet in the mark of respect we're taught, in the East, to give our parents and teachers. Instead, I put my hands together, bowed respectfully, and embraced him.

We sat side by side on those awful prison benches—plastic bucket seats attached to a metal beam—and talked. But it was different. Maroon did not stare directly into my eyes as he'd done in previous visits or speak in his usual forthright manner. He'd become skittish, distracted, looking around at the other prisoners, sometimes lowering his voice or leaning in to remind me that here, out in the general population, he had to watch his step and mind his words. He wondered aloud, as he had many times before, whether publishing this book was a good idea after all.

The plan, from the very beginning, was to use Maroon's autobiography as a means to an end. It should be exciting, highly sellable, a blueprint for a screenplay that would catch the eye of some big Hollywood producer. While we were dreaming the impossible, we might as well go big—the film would ignite a national campaign for his release. He would move back to Philly and start a community garden, counsel the youth, work in the schools. He would live life again, as a free man, unlike so many of his comrades, who either perished behind bars or were escorted out of the prison gates in wheelchairs at the ends of long, painful clemency campaigns, hooked up to tubes or bags of fluid, just in time to die.

But a person's life story is a little bit like a war. When you study it closely the edges begin to blur, and you discover that it belongs to everyone who was touched by it. No one can own a war. Victors may claim a part of it, the victims might take another piece. The dead can have their own chapters, and the living will squabble over what remains. So, too, with a life. Especially for a man like Maroon, who long ago dedicated his life to a cause, it was difficult to hand it over and say: *Here it is, the heart of it, the soul of it, the truth of it. This is my story.*

We stopped editing chapters and began just to share words. When I no longer approached him as a journalist, extractive, digging, probing, he dropped his fighting stance. It freed us up to speak on matters other than war and politics—matters of the heart. How it feels to lose love in a dungeon. What it means to be sorry. How you respond when you reach out to someone across the bars and they say, *Too little, too late.* Slowly, over months, he answered all the questions I'd asked, and even the ones I'd never dared to ask, about the women in his life.

There was very little between us now. Only what I would call our original wound, the old rift, the question of violence. In the years I'd known him, I'd earned the equivalent of a graduate degree in American studies, with the members of the Maroon campaign acting as my academic supervisors and the prisons of Pennsylvania serving as my campus. To become a regular visitor to America's prisons is to wake up forever from the American dream. These are places you cannot unsee, cannot unknow. They underpin the empire. Everything—mass consumerism, mass shootings, mass military spending, mass surveillance, mass migration—is connected to the plague of mass incarceration. *Prisons are institutions of violence,* Maroon never tired of reminding me, *and the only thing more American than prisons is violence itself.*

Maroon was always best at espousing ideas. His flow was hip-hop—there was a rhythm and cadence to his oratory that was spellbinding to witness. The only times he tripped were when I tried to guide the ideas home, back to his origins, into the sacred spheres of family life or childhood memories. I didn't enjoy doing this. But I had no choice because still, still, there was a part of me that didn't fully understand: *I'm talking about you, Maroon. What did it mean for you? When your brother was punching you in the face? When you were attacking rival gang members? When you were being abused in juvenile detention centers? What does it feel like to be hurt? How does it feel to hurt another? Did you ever think another way was possible?*

The only time Maroon ever raised his voice at me was over this matter. We were in the visiting room, where he generally spoke quietly to avoid arousing the curiosity of the other inmates pressed close around us. But that day I must have said something that pulled a trigger in him because he said, *You still don't get it, do you? Violence wasn't a solution. No one said it was a SOLUTION. It was a language! It was THE language, the one America taught us to speak, the only language that America understands. We're not the victims of America's violence. We're her children.*

I was able to properly begin the book only after I'd said goodbye to Maroon.

I was two months pregnant when I visited him for the final time, at the State Correctional Institution at Dallas, in the middle of the winter, to say my husband and I were returning to Sri Lanka to have our baby. By now we'd abandoned and resumed and abandoned our project so many times that neither of us could remember the how or why of it anymore. There was no more disappointment or expectation. His legal team had big plans, high hopes, and the book, with all its admissions and remembrances, would only hinder their progress. I listened respectfully as he explained why it was best left alone. I took my leave of him fondly, affectionately, not knowing whether I would ever see him again. But as I left the prison, I made a promise to myself that before my baby was born, I would finish our project.

Among the belongings that I consigned to the pallets of an eastward-bound transatlantic container ship, and reclaimed months later from the port authority of Sri Lanka, were several boxes of material labeled *Maroon*. As the baby squirmed and grew in my body, I laid out everything—photographs, timelines, court documents, newspaper clippings, journals, bunches of letters held together with rubber bands—and began to write in the sweltering heat of the Colombo monsoon. I was in possession of binders that Maroon himself had assembled painstakingly over his years in prison, his version of family albums cobbled together from any pictures his relatives had been able to scan, print, and mail to him. I had my notes from the Schomburg Center for Research in Black Culture, in Harlem, where I'd hunted down and photocopied excerpts from the FBI files on the Black Panthers, everything from handmade posters to detailed military "training manuals" from the era when the Panthers adopted weapons training into their larger policy of community self-defense. I had the scans I'd taken from microfilms housed in the Philadelphia public library of local news reports surrounding Maroon's exploits. I had about half a dozen notebooks, many of them illegible, with haphazard notes from my prison visits, along with books—borrowed from friends, gifted from well-wishers, sourced from small, independent booksellers—about cops, solitary confinement, the Panthers, and Philadelphia; collections of the Black poets; and memoirs of political prisoners and their lawyers. Most importantly, I had the original manuscript, the same hard copy Fred Ho had sent to me back in 2012, annotated almost beyond recognition.

After seven years of research I had returned, full circle, to these pages. But it was different this time. I no longer felt I was studying a map of an unknown land. I had lived inside this world, learned the language. I had huge new stores of knowledge about Maroon's life and, perhaps more critically, I knew what had been left out. That there were things I would never know.

It was an eerie coincidence that in Sri Lanka a pregnancy is still referred to as a woman's "confinement," and so for six months I allowed myself to be there, to experience a kind of confinement, which was the only way to assemble the story. I gave birth just a few days after writing the final page.

To cowrite a man's autobiography is to lose—however briefly—your own voice. Just like in the prison visiting room, I had to accept that in this process I was no longer Kanya D'Almeida. I had to become interchangeable with Russell Shoatz. Each time I sat down to write I could feel the sand piling up around me inside the hourglass of his life, and I experienced again the old familiar panic that time was running out, or that I'd be trapped here forever because a man's life is like a war: it's impossible for just one person to decide they've had enough, to say, *The End.*

By the time I was able to ship the manuscript out to Maroon, cancer had come for him. He had started chemo; he was too sick to correspond. COVID hit and spread like wildfire through Pennsylvania's prisons. His health deteriorated rapidly. Through many channels I reached out to him, asked his lawyers and family to carry messages across that the book was finished, ready, needed only his approval, but always the same reply came: *Sorry. He's not up to this right now. It might jeopardize his chance of release. At this point, we just want to bring him home.* I appealed to Maroon directly through the terrible prison email system. This was a time of unrest, the George Floyd protests and the slogan *Black Lives Matter* reverberating around the world. The movement needs his story, I said. If not now, when?

And then, in September 2020, a letter from Maroon. Short, pithy, direct:

Let's do it.

Three months later, he was dead.

We failed. I failed. The movement failed to save Maroon from the fate of being wheeled out of the prison a sick man, just in time to die. He didn't get his hero's release, or the action-movie ending. The story tapered off into the terrible reality of a man who spent the majority of his life behind bars and was murdered by his captors. A slow execution;

an anticlimax. Ask anyone who has lived through a war how they felt at the close. Relieved. Battered. Grim. Devastated. Mostly, overcome with the waste, the waste of human life.

I was not able to attend Maroon's funeral. I sat with his death quietly for a long time. Long enough to realize that a man's life story is so much more than a war. And in the telling of it, a certain spell is cast, a particular kind of magic is made that has to do with freedom.

A prisoner's entire being is—must be—oriented toward freedom. For the less evolved, this might mean dwelling on a time before incarceration, or striving toward physical release. Maroon achieved something different: freedom inside the cage. So it became incumbent upon me, upon everyone committed to his struggle, to manifest that freedom beyond the bars of the prison.

Free Maroon!

For many years, this was our demand and our rallying cry. It was the name of our campaign, a slogan printed on T-shirts and banners. *Free Maroon NOW*, we said as we stepped up the campaign. Our tiny apartment in New York City was filled with flyers, brochures, stickers, and posters reminding me of the purpose of the mission, the impossible mission, which was to free Maroon.

But a maroon, by definition, is free. The more time I spent with him, the clearer it became to me that our slogan was less of a demand and more a reiteration of what already was, a kind of compound adjective for the man. A redundancy, even. Once I understood this, the autobiography assumed a different form, a different shape in my head. It ceased to be this ungainly, bulky thing that I had to maneuver through the corridors of the world and lug across the finish line, the whole of a man's life with all its attendant rages and sorrows and secrets. It became instead a collection of pieces, as of a jigsaw, individual parts small enough to be smuggled out and reassembled on the other side. Notes on freedom. A book on freedom, told in his own words to an unlikely collaborator, a life story transcribed on the other side of the world from where it was lived.

I don't know what he would make of all this now. He would probably cringe at the word *memoir*, and the thought of the events recounted here becoming a part of some distant past. He was never one for looking back. He didn't suffer from nostalgia, probably because it's a deadly condition for a prisoner. He had a different mantra: *Straight Ahead!* His signature tag that concluded every letter, every essay, every dispatch. I laughed to think what the prison authorities made of it, when their entire project was built upon trapping people in the past, pushing them down into the hole of history whenever they tried to raise their heads above it.

I believe Maroon would prefer to imagine this book as an arrow. Something sharp and streamlined, something in motion, heading for a target that the shooter can hardly see, but he knows its direction, his aim is sure: *Straight Ahead.*

I like to think of it that way, too.

Kanya D'Almeida, 2023

PROLOGUE

I am Maroon.

It's a title, an honorific awarded to those who fly the plantation. It's a stripe you earn when you go from being a prisoner to a fugitive.

Maroons are runaway slaves. In French *marron* means "feral." The Spanish *cimarron* means "wild." To Black people who were chained to the French and Spanish sugarcane fields across the Caribbean and the Americas, to those who tasted the misery of the cotton plantations in the southern United States, *maroon* means freedom.

I wasn't always Maroon.

I was named Russell Melvin Shoatz II, after my father. Years later, when I converted to Islam, I took the name Harun Abdul Ra'uf. I'm Russ to my sisters, Brother to my comrades, Old Head to my Corner boys, and Daddy to my children. To my captors I'm Inmate #AF-3855. During trials that lasted years I was referred to as the Defendant. White prosecutors told all-white juries I was a criminal. In prison I was nicknamed Little Dragon. I've been a milkman and a steelworker, a janitor and a general, an emir and a president and a prisoner of war.

I'm seventy-seven years old. I've been incarcerated for most of my life in penitentiaries across the state of Pennsylvania: Holmesburg, Graterford, Western, Huntingdon, Farview, Dallas, Rockview, Camp Hill, Greene, Mahanoy, Frackville, Coal Township.

I escaped from two of these institutions. On one occasion, I evaded capture for nearly a month. To be a maroon is to be forever on the run because the overseers never stop chasing them. But they also have to learn to be perfectly still, under a pile of leaves with the bloodhounds just inches away. When a helicopter's searchlights sweep over the mountains, maroons must be invisible. They must be able to fight, and they must know when to flee. A wall topped with barbed wire is not something to be feared but something to be scaled.

I paid for those twenty-seven days of freedom with twenty-two years of my life in the Hole—that's shorthand among prisoners for solitary confinement. For over two decades I was locked inside a tiny cell, a cage, with no human contact.

But even in a prison, a maroon is a free man. It infuriates his captors that no matter how fiercely they beat him, they cannot break him.

This is because maroons are revolutionaries. We are committed mind, body, and soul to the struggle against oppression. Maroons seldom act alone. We receive tremendous support from fellow fighters, sometimes from strangers. Safe houses provide food and shelter, and the very earth gives up its bounty to us in times of need. Yet our paths are often littered with loss, comrades who've fallen and family we've turned our backs on along the way. Ours is a hard road, full of stones and thorns. This cannot deter us from our mission. Those of us who've opened our eyes and seen it all, from the plantation to the penitentiary, we know that maroonage is not an option. It's the only way.

This is an account of how one man became Maroon. This is my story.

PART ONE

CHAPTER 1

DEAD, OR IN JAIL

I was born on August 23, 1943, in a hospital that no living person now remembers the name of.

My family—thirteen of us—lived in a three-story row house on Douglas Street in West Philadelphia. The street was so narrow that if one family parked their car out front, another wouldn't be able to get by. Our living room window was a front-row seat to anything and everything that happened on our block.

One of my earliest memories is a scene I witnessed through this very window: two white cops dragging one of my neighbors out of his home in broad daylight with everyone watching. He was an old dude, but the cops kicked him down his front steps, beating him all the time and yelling, "You black bastard, black son of a bitch, fucking nigger!"

I was six years old. I remember my father was standing beside me, and I kept looking up at him, waiting for the moment he would rush outside and put a stop to it. But he had gone all stiff and silent.

When the policemen finally forced the struggling man into their car, they turned around and faced the rest of us.

"Any of you other niggers want any of this?" one of them asked.

Most people drew down their window shades or shut their front doors. That was how it was. I don't even know what that old man did to provoke them—maybe nothing.

When it wasn't a neighborhood cop show, it was *I Love Lucy*.

Every evening at seven o'clock my mother would drag our bulky television set to the front door and a crowd of my neighbors, having lined up chairs on the sidewalk, would settle back to watch the popular shows of the day: *The Honeymooners* or *Amos and Andy*. It didn't strike me as odd. I had no idea that my family was relatively privileged compared to others on our block or that we were the only ones with a television. I didn't even know some folks in my neighborhood went hungry—until I visited the home of my buddy Tony Marshall. We were running through the kitchen and I must have been thirsty because I stopped to open the fridge and grab a cold soda, just as I would at home. But Tony pushed the door shut and stood in front of it. "We can't go in the icebox," he said. "We have to wait for dinner." He had a funny look on his face, like he was guarding something.

By contrast, my mother's kitchen resembled what I imagined a hotel's food preparation area to be, with two or three people cooking and three or four others in various stages of preparing or eating meals. My mother could almost always be found standing at the stove in her long, loose-fitting smock and flat shoes. She had a short temper in the kitchen and could holler when she wanted to, but this was always forgotten when we sat down to eat because she cooked up a *storm* every night. To add to this carnival-style atmosphere, my father liked to bring home gallon bricks of ice cream when he was away on his long-distance truck drives, and instead of dividing it up he would tell each of us to get a spoon. Then we would gather around the picnic table that he had built to accommodate us all, and everyone would just dig in and eat it as fast as they could. We were tight like that.

But my real world was out on the streets with my Corner boys from a gang called the Coast. They drafted me when I was eleven years old, on a hot summer afternoon in 1954.

I was messing around in the schoolyard with some of my buddies when the huge double-service gates swung open and a group of about twenty guys walked in. They were a little older than us, twelve or thirteen, but unlike us they were already gang members, so their presence was intimidating. They surrounded us in a loose circle and posed the question we'd been expecting:

"You box?"

My brother Arthur had been preparing me for this moment for years. For as long as I can remember he'd explained that boxing was a way of testing friends and foes alike. There was no getting around this—if you couldn't hold your own in the ring, you'd be beaten up. If you did well, you won the respect of your peers.

I had to fight three Coast members that day, a grueling test of endurance. For one full hour they went at me with punches and open-hand slapping on the head. When it was finally over, I was grinning through torn-up lips, my mouth warm with blood, my body swollen. Back then, this was the most important rite of passage for Black boys in Philadelphia.

From then on, I operated only according to the strict, unwritten codes that governed street life. Philly at the time was defined and dissected by gangs, each with its own customs, which it enforced on its own turf. Stumble into enemy territory and you were subjected to their rules. Step out of bounds in your Corner and you'd lose your place in the line. But play your cards right, show stamina and strength, and you graduated with honors: from "Peewee" status to Young 'Un to Regular and finally Old Head, the most senior rank, where your reputation was beyond reproach and your word was law. There was one final tier on the hierarchy, which Peewees like us viewed with a fascination bordering on reverence. It was a designation earned only by the most courageous, the most loyal, the most implacable gang members: Heart. To become a Heart on the streets of Philadelphia was to have achieved your life's purpose. You needed no further proof of your worth as a man.

Gangs were based on honor and principle. Nothing else in the city worked that way.

I learned early that schools were a waste of time. My first memories of a classroom involve being slapped by a female teacher at McMichael Elementary and then being forced to crouch under her desk for the remainder of the lesson. I remember some years later, at a different elementary school, being brought up to the front of an all-white classroom by the teacher, who led the rest of the students in this song:

You can get good milk from a brown-skinned cow
The color of the cow doesn't matter no-how!
Ho-ho-ho, can't you see?
The color of your skin doesn't matter to me!

Incidents like these left me so enraged that on one occasion, when I was about seven or eight years old, I lost my temper with a fellow classmate and repeatedly punched him in the face until he was a bloody mess. I had a broken wrist at the time and was wearing a plaster cast, but that didn't deter me—in fact, I used the cast to cause even more damage than I might have done with just my fists.

The funny part was I actually loved to read, and at home I devoured anything I could lay my hands on, from old paperbacks to encyclopedias. But any enthusiasm I had for learning drained out of me when I came in sight of those institutions where the white teachers behaved no differently in our classrooms than the white cops behaved out on the streets. If the cops were thugs, the teachers were bullies, with only a thin veneer of politeness masking deep racism. Either way, the lesson was the same: *You are powerless.*

When my family outgrew our house on Douglas Street, my parents moved us over to Fifty-Eighth, a white neighborhood full of what my father called "nice Jewish families." I don't remember a whole lot about Fifty-Eighth Street, with one exception: Mr. Adelman.

He owned a little corner store that sold five-cent ice cream cones. His customers were a mixed bunch of Orthodox Jews and Black families like mine. A few blocks away from Mr. Adelman's shop was a Black grocer who was struggling to stay afloat. I learned that the wholesalers who supplied small stores like Mr. Adelman's refused to sell in bulk to Black businesses. As a result, this Black grocer was forced to charge an extra two cents per ice cream. Back then two cents was the difference between a line of customers and an empty shop. I don't know what made me do it, but one day I decided to stage a one-person picket outside Adelman's Grocery. I made signs advertising *Negro Ice Cream Cones* and directed all the Black customers toward the grocer down the block, urging them to pay the extra two cents to keep that old man going. The boycott ended only when Mrs. Adelman came around to our house to complain to my mother. I don't remember my mother being angry at me—it was more like she was amused, maybe even a little proud. But she gently urged me to call off my protest.

A few months later, all you could see were *For Sale* signs up and down the block. I wondered what was so fascinating on the other side of town that made all those Nice Families pack up and leave, but soon there weren't more than a handful left. As fast as white folks moved out, Black families would replace them, until the neighborhood that began somewhere near Market Street, around the elevated train tracks, had transformed into a Black middle-class stronghold, stretching for miles before giving way to a lower-class colored community on the outskirts of Chestnut, Walnut, and Spruce Streets.

Not that it mattered where we went. To the cops, to the grocers, even to our white neighbors, we were just a pack of rats to be stamped on, locked up, or eventually wiped out. As kids we didn't need to be told any of this. We learned it and lived it every day. We listened silently to the taunts of our teachers and we bore the raw racism of the police.

Older dudes in the gangs told us what to expect when cops booked us: racial slurs, beatings. Rough rides in meat wagons. Fists, boots, and bruises. Our Old Heads gave us only one piece of advice: *Don't never let them pussies see that it hurts.*

When I went home every evening, I left my swagger at the door. It had no place inside a house that was ruled by a matriarch: my maternal grandmother, whom we all called the Big Cheese. She was a living relic from a different time and a different world—Jim Crow South Carolina, where she raised eight kids single-handedly after her husband was killed. She stood just five feet three inches off the ground, and I never heard her raise her voice. She didn't need to. If she bowed her head one way, you knew it meant one thing, and if she bowed it the other way, it meant something different. On Sundays she would simply say, "Time to go," and the whole family knew this meant they had to get themselves into their church clothes and walk the mile or so to the neighborhood chapel to listen to the mass.

I think my father was envious of her position, because whenever there was an important family decision to be made, he always said: "I know nothing is gonna be done until ya'll check with the Big Cheese."

She would not tolerate profanity, alcoholic beverages, or weapons at any family gathering. I learned this the day my cousin T-Rex was over at our place for one of the many birthday celebrations that went on at our residence, flashing his rifle around and generally talking big. Now T-Rex was no ordinary guy—he earned that name on the streets owing to his immense stature. But he was no match for the Big Cheese. When she saw the gun, she silently beckoned him into her bedroom. Never being one to miss out on an eventful confrontation, I barged in on them a minute later—just in time to see her placing a .45-caliber automatic rifle under her pillow. It was so big she had to use both hands to hold it. She had disarmed him. T-Rex returned to the party empty-handed.

When I think about it now, it was probably her presence that prevented outright war among us kids, because each member of the Shoatz clan had distinct, powerful personalities. Just stringing out my sisters' names was a mouthful: Grace, Yvette, Beatrice, Maria, Joanne, Lucille, Diane, and Rose. Threaded through this army of females was my older brother Arthur, myself, and Daniel, the baby of the family. I revered Arthur, disdained Daniel, and tried my best to ignore my sisters, but there was one I couldn't shake. Beatrice.

Now Beatrice was one of those girls you couldn't forget. She had a beautiful face and a strong personality that won her instant popularity wherever she went. It was her eyes that grabbed you. Huge, observant, deep eyes that missed nothing. She could scan a room and commit every detail to memory. And she had a way with words. She seldom raised her voice, yet she could slice you open with her tongue if she wanted to. But she could also make you laugh. Have you in stitches if she wanted to. She spoke in riddles, and respected most those people who could decipher them.

No matter what I did to stay out of her way, she and I would inevitably clash, and sparks would fly. I tried to offset her confidence by constantly approaching her with an attitude of tolerance toward a weaker party, but she wouldn't have that, and during one fierce altercation she pushed me through the dining room window. That won my respect! From then on, we were destined to be equals. She was always the one cutting me down to size, right when my gang status was on the rise!

I wasn't the only one who lived this kind of double life between the Corner and the kitchen table. One of my main road dogs, TZ Weston, had a brother named Danny who was in a rival gang, the Moon Gang. Out on the block the Coast and the Moon Gang were sworn enemies, but every night the Weston brothers sat down to dinner together.

Now, TZ was some kind of special cat, and he knew it. One thing was, he never left his house without his wide-brimmed hat that exactly matched his copper-colored skin. Every move he made was calculated for dramatic effect. It was hard to keep up with him because TZ was what the Old Heads called a war fanatic, a gang member who is super zealous about feuds with rival Corners that basically amounted to one continuous turf war.

TZ and I were tight as sardines. Every evening we met up at our designated spot, the sandwich shop on the corner of Sixtieth and Spruce Street. We'd gather our road dogs—or "walkies"—and go looking for trouble. With TZ, the first order of business was to get a "taste." We didn't mess with guns or drugs back then, but "getting a taste" was a beloved ritual among us all—especially the way the Old Heads conducted the ceremony. Before anyone was allowed to sip from a newly opened bottle of wine, they'd first spill a few drops onto the ground. They told us this was a centuries-old spiritual custom that originated in Africa. That made us feel some kind of way, especially when they said we were "pouring libations for those members who are dead, or in jail."

Dead, or in jail. Even as kids we knew those were our options.

Until then, it was war. Every day we were battling for recognition in our families, on the streets, in that miserable country that was the only one we knew. Gang life taught us about our world. Sure, we played stupid games after school with homemade wooden spears and swords with trash can lids as shields. But mostly we fought other Black boys from rival gangs, because these were the only people we could count on to give us a fair fight. This was before guns, when the call to brawl was "Put yo' fists up." It meant something. Winning a bout of hand-to-hand combat, what we called a "Fair One," earned you "stripes," and stripes bought you status, real estate on the streets—freedom to move without being jumped or set upon.

One great way to earn stripes was to get arrested. That particular initiation tested you against two serious adversaries: first, the cops in the police stations. Next, the sadistic supervisors in the juvenile detention centers.

One evening, TZ and I heard that some new boys on the fringe of our territory had organized a group on the corner of Catherine and Christian Streets that was not affiliated with the Coast. We immediately went on the prowl, advancing quietly into the formerly white neighborhood that had recently turned Black. We found two kids our age sitting on a stoop.

"Where you from?" I asked.

"Nowhere," the taller one said.

Wrong answer. The unwritten rule book of the streets stated that failing to declare your affiliation meant one of two things: You were hiding your membership to avoid a brawl. Or you didn't have the backing of a Corner. Either way, you were asking for it.

I punched one of them in the mouth as hard as I could with a blow that shattered his front teeth and spun him around. His friend cried out and leapt up from the stoop, but TZ immediately began to punch and beat him, while I rained blows on my victim. These boys didn't have any fight in them! They didn't even throw back a single punch before squirming out from under us and running away when our energy was spent.

We slapped each other high fives before checking out the damage.

"Man," I said, wrapping my T-shirt around my bleeding knuckles, "If this is the kind of Corner they got, then they *all* a bunch of pussies."

"Yeah, man!" TZ was grinning and I could tell he was real proud of my mangled fist.

We swaggered back onto our home turf, but before we could bask in our victory, two cops pulled up right alongside of us.

"Hey! Where do you niggers think you're going?"

Usually, I refrained from giving the cops any lip, because it was more trouble than it was worth. But I was all puffed up from the battle. Without breaking my stride, I said, "Home, officer. That's where we live and that's where we headed."

The cop said, "Pull over, Robbie," and his partner swung the car up onto the curb so fast we were nearly crushed.

One of them got right up in my face. "You're pretty smart for a nigger, aren't you?" He went to grab my arm but pulled back when he saw my battered fist.

"Would you look at that?" the one named Robbie said. "These must be them niggers who jumped those two kids back on Cedar Avenue."

"Naw, that wasn't us," TZ said promptly. "My buddy here hurt his hand when he fell off his bicycle."

The cop who had me cornered curled his fingers around the neck of my T-shirt and pulled me so close I could smell his salami breath.

Pig eating pig, I thought.

"Now listen to me, you lying son of a bitch. I know you didn't get that cut from a bicycle because nigger boys like you don't ride no bicycles. Your daddy's too broke to get you bicycles. Me and my partner here were just sitting down to our lunch when we get a call from some bitch screaming and hollering that her sons have been jumped on by two black sons of bitches, and she is going to take them to court. So, get your asses in that wagon, and shut the fuck up, and we'll see what she has to say."

They drove us to the Fifty-Fifth and Pine Street station, cuffed us, and marched us into a room that served as a combination court and assembly area. The magistrate's podium stood on a raised platform at one end of the room. On the outer perimeter were benches and desks piled high with paperwork, each manned by a policeman who was either scribbling on a piece of paper or questioning someone. As soon as we entered every single cop stopped what he was doing, almost as if a television had been tuned to their favorite show. Someone yelled, "You niggers better not try anything…You're on our turf now!" And the whole room burst out laughing.

Cuffed to either end of a wooden bench, TZ and I spent the next hour bracing against the blows. There was one cop in particular who produced a plethora of items that he brandished in our faces before giving us a little taste of how unpleasant they felt on our bodies: night stick, revolver butt, flashlight.

None of this was particularly impressive to us. The Old Heads on our Corner were constantly prepping us for these encounters with the cops by simulating this very scene. What we couldn't figure out was why we were being singled out for special treatment for doing something we did almost every single day—beating the teeth off other Black boys?

Turned out, one of those pussies' mothers had made a real stink about the brawl, putting on a big show for the magistrate about her son being injured and weren't we a menace to society and shouldn't we be put someplace where we wouldn't be a danger to good, law-abiding citizens?

So the magistrate, after a brief "hearing," gave his order and we were driven straight to the Youth Study Center: a high-rise facility right on the Benjamin Franklin Parkway that was most inaptly named, for studying was the very last thing anyone did in there. In fact, it could more accurately be described as a low-level prison.

A huge man named Mr. Nillson ruled this roost—six feet three and easily 270 pounds. His principal arena was called the Dayroom, a huge space paneled with floor to ceiling plexiglass windows that offered a fantastic view of Fairmount Park. On paper it was a place for approved activities like reading books or playing checkers. In reality it was a boxing ring, and our Old Heads had warned us that if we failed to perform here, we'd find ourselves at the bottom of the food chain: forced to give up our meals, pick up another boy's chores, or become someone's "girlfriend" and be subjected to rape after lights-out.

Right away I decided that I couldn't just wait around for an opportunity to prove myself. The level of danger facing me called for an immediate and preemptive act of aggression that bordered on recklessness. I had to size up and single out the toughest guy in the place and challenge him to a one-on-one brawl.

They called him Dagger. He wore the same clothes as the rest of us—dark pants, a powder-blue shirt, and work boots that had seen multiple prior owners—but he managed to stand out as if he had on military insignia. Shirt starched, pants pressed, boots brightly shined. When he walked the corridors, his minions ran ahead of him to clear the way. In the Dayroom he stood in a designated spot surrounded by bodyguards and received a stream of "visitors" who were either paying tribute or kissing ass.

I wasted no time in letting one of his boys know I sought a Fair One with Dagger.

But this wasn't a Philadelphia Corner. There was a different honor code here in the Study Center. Before facing off against Dagger, I was put through my paces in a boxing match with one of his people in an effort to weaken, exhaust, or subdue me. Not for nothing, though, had my older brother Arthur spent years training me for this very moment. I was no stranger to being pummeled by someone a lot bigger than I was. I could endure endless punches to the face and quite an assault on the rest of my body. So I stood my ground—for so long that some of the adult supervisors came in to watch the fight! I never did get to rumble with Dagger; the duel with his deputy went on until the bell rang for lights-out, by which time I had earned a decent rep and a strong foothold in the jungle.

Arthur was the first person I saw when I got out a few weeks later. Before we even greeted each other I could tell he was real proud. As soon as I walked in the door he was in my face, saying, "Put your hands up!" I dropped my bag and assumed the stance, the two of us going around in a circle feigning like we were gonna start throwing punches. I thought he'd let it go and give me a hug, but he said, "Didn't you learn nothin'? Come on, show me somethin'!" Without even thinking I threw two left jabs at his chest, followed by a quick left hook and a straight right hand to the chest, but he blocked me each time. Finally, he laughed. "Alright, alright," he said, and shoved me into the breakfast room, where the rest of the family was watching TV over their morning meal.

The next day I was sent off to school as usual but I felt something had changed. That was the thing about earning stripes: it put you on a one-way track to earning more.

All through middle school I acted up like crazy 24/7. Weekdays were for turf wars, and weekends were for crashing private parties in the mansions on Cobbs Creek Parkway where wealthy Black college kids lived. The cops dogged our steps—they knew our names and addresses and affiliations, they knew who was an Old Head and who was in line, they knew our meeting points and escape routes. So it was only a matter of time before I was sent back to the Youth Study Center and, following that, to a juvenile institution housed in an abandoned hospital on Second Avenue and Luzerne Street, where we spent most of our time renovating the sprawling complex in preparation for the next set of occupants.

I received every punishment the system could devise: school suspensions and police beatings, incarceration and humiliation. One of the worst incidents, which I still recall to this day, was being forced to see a psychiatrist at the Philadelphia General Hospital. During these sessions I sat in a white-walled office full of charts illustrating different parts of the human brain while the "doctor" asked a series of degrading questions like "Do you want to have sex with your mother?"—and if I didn't answer, I'd be sent right back into juvenile detention, which is to say, prison of one kind or another.

Somehow, despite my disciplinary record, I was admitted to John Bartram High School on Sixty-Seventh and Elmwood Avenue—an impoverished white neighborhood that was ruled by ragged white gangs who did not look kindly on Black students in their neck of the woods.

One gang, the Dirty Annies, made it their personal duty to rain hell down upon us every chance they got. The first time I encountered them, I was riding a bike home from school when a carload of white guys drove by yelling, "Hey nigger! We've been looking for you!" One leaned out the window and fired a number of shots from a sleek black pistol.

My road dogs and I weren't easily intimidated, but there was something terrifying about these dudes. They had none of the overstuffed laziness of the police nor the skittish fear of middle-class white communities. They were lean, mean white wolves, starved and serious. We were ignorant of their honor code and had no wish to test their limits. They weren't about hand-to-hand combat like we were. They carried sticks, chains, glass bottles, and weapons we would never be able to get our hands on. They couldn't get at us inside the high school building, but everything surrounding it, the school grounds, the school buses, even the bus depots, became the sites of a very dirty war.

All of the uncertainty surrounding this new territory of white gangs led to something I would never have believed possible—it united all the Black gangs in West Philadelphia.

My Corner, the Coast, formed the nucleus of a large confederation of semi-independent gangs that came to be known as the South Side. Typically, we stood in opposition to a similar constellation of Black gangs known as the Syndicate. Within these formations were dozens of gangs, each with their own wars and agendas—there was the Sixtieth Street Corner, of which my brother Arthur was an Old Head. Then there was Thirty-Sixth and Market Street, a Corner so deadly that it was alternately labeled the Black Bottom and Tombstone Territory. But when it came to confronting our new common enemy, we set aside old grudges and lingering feuds to reach an unspoken truce. The understanding was simply this: safety in numbers. Protecting Black high school students on the buses to and from John Bartram quickly became our main order of business. It gave us a purpose that we never seemed to get from our teachers or our studies. Often, we would cut class to debate and discuss our strategy—something we got down to a fine art. Once, when a white gang invaded a Black school bus through the windows and began assaulting every student on board, we were able to eject the whole posse, but held on to one "prisoner" as an example to the others that we were not to be messed with. It was a triumph, but not one the school administrators recognized.

I was expelled, and thrown into an all-boy's disciplinary institution called Newton, which sat right on the corner of Thirty-Seventh and Spruce Street. This one was run by what the principal called "anti-gang juvenile aid detectives," or JADs. Another day, another prison masquerading as a youth center. The only difference here was that in addition to fighting other students in the gymnasium, we were sometimes called on to do battle with the teachers as well!

Here, for the first time, I began to grow weary of spending my days in an arena. I found myself gravitating toward a range of workshops that, though conducted under intense supervision, were thoroughly enjoyable. I tried my hand at everything from tailoring and plumbing to carpentry and auto repair. I loved working with my hands, and with my father being a long-distance trucker, I guess I harbored an interest in engines, or anything that allowed me to get my hands dirty.

A lot of the time I ended up working alongside dudes from rival gangs, which enabled me to build a network of alliances that would serve me back on the streets. These were strategic friendships, forged in the fire of institutions that treated us no better than animals, that I could call upon in times of need.

Because no matter where I was, my mind was always on the streets where the gang battles raged. We might be locked up for long stretches, but when we were released, we returned to the work of divvying up the city. We mapped every alleyway and backyard, every stoop and short-cut. We performed this cartography with our bodies, drew the lines with our own blood. There was no such thing as neutral territory. Every scrap had to be either won and then defended or avoided. Ice-skating rinks. Movie theaters. Public athletic leagues.

Later, when I became involved in a much deadlier war—not against rival gangs but against the government of the United States of America—I realized that gang members are, in essence, urban guerrillas.

But before I became a soldier, I was a slave catcher. Before I became Maroon, it was once my job to chase runaways.

CHAPTER 2

THE MORGANZA SHAKES

It happened at Morganza, in the summer of 1960. At one point or another, every dude I knew did time there. It was a kind of halfway point between the Moyamensing County Jail, otherwise known as Moe Coe, and the string of state prisons we all expected to pass through some day.

Even among the most seasoned Corner boys Morganza had a rep. I still remember Pete, a big dude on our Corner who was known for being a Heart, meaning he'd shown exceptional courage in the face of great adversity on the streets. But after his stint at Morganza he was never the same again.

We were all hanging on the corner one day when suddenly he got this wild look in his eyes. His mouth drooped down and he just went rigid, and then his head started shaking like he was having a seizure or something and he was saying, "Nonononononono," getting louder and louder while we all stood there dumbfounded. One of the Old Heads tried to talk him down, gently saying, "Shut the fuck up, man." When that didn't work he grabbed Pete's shoulders, shook him, and slapped him so hard the sound of it echoed. Pete went limp. By this time I and some of the younger dudes were laughing like crazy, because we'd never seen anything like it before and we were scared as hell.

"Pipe the fuck down," the Old Head told us, "And get Pete a taste. He's got the Morganza shakes."

Still, none of that prepared me for my first glimpse of that Tudor-style prison in Canonsburg, which squatted right off Interstate 79 about forty miles south of Pittsburgh. It was a huge compound full of old brick buildings guarded by stone pillars and studded with oblong windows that watched like eyes from every wall. Even the trees that climbed up the sides of the buildings looked wasted, with their dead branches reaching like fingers into the rooms on the second and third floors. On any given day, there were six hundred juvenile "delinquents" locked up in what they called cottages for a variety of crimes, from gang activity or petty theft to rape and murder.

I was seventeen years old at the time, but I wasn't green. I'd been kicked in the ribs, in the groin, in the teeth more times than I could count. I'd done time at Moe Coe, where guards fed us rotten food, talked to us like dirt, and lazily oversaw fights between prisoners. I'd been part of a youth chain gang, an extension of the state's forestry service up in the Pocono Mountains near dilapidated coal towns like Wilkes-Barre and Scranton, what we called company towns. I'd learned the white ways of rural Pennsylvania. On the chain gang we cut trees from dawn to dusk, cleared brush from the roadside, trekked through snowstorms to repair broken power lines, and fought forest fires. When the sun went down, we descended from the mountains into the pitiful nightclubs to perform our hambone body-rhythm routine. One of the guys would sit on a chair slapping his thighs and fists at a staccato pace until the sound resembled a steady drumbeat, while the rest of us sang in three-part harmony: slaves by day, minstrels by night. Even when we managed to pocket a little money from these shows, most of it eventually went to our supervisors. Before I learned to despise it, I pretended to enjoy it. It was almost a game to us, dressing like lumberjacks, working our fingers raw in the freezing cold or coming face-to-face with massive wildfires, a new and exciting outlet for our energy. It was only at night, shut up in those miserable little cabins so far from home, that I experienced the cold terror of my confinement.

But even with all that experience under my belt, I have to say that Morganza beat all.

It was run by Whackers, and they were a law unto themselves. On paper they were just inmates like everyone else, but in our eyes, they ranked above the white supervisors and House Parents who made up Morganza's official staff. I guess the authorities figured out early on that the kinds of kids who wound up at Morganza came from the streets, where seniority was strictly observed. So they singled out the alpha males in each cottage and pressed them into service, creating an auxiliary supervisory staff who could be counted on to maintain order through varieties of terror. When a Whacker wanted to communicate something to you, it was done with blows and bellows. They had their own reserved seats in the lunchroom and the chapel, called Whackers' Row. They were exempt from backbreaking chores like buffing Morganza's old marble floors by shuffling rags from one end of a vast building to another on stockinged feet. They were gods, and before too long I was one of them.

Like everything else in life, I earned my place among the Whackers not through any underhand means or idle flattery, but after a test of endurance: two weeks in the Hole. At Morganza, this was a room furnished with just two items, a bed bolted to the floor and a ceramic chamber pot. At first, I was unimpressed. I'd been thrown in there for punching one of the white staff members in the face, and I kept expecting a whole posse of them to show up and finish the beating they'd started giving me down in the yard, a storm of kicks, punches, and slaps. I waited. Someone had nailed wooden boards sloppily across the two windows, allowing light to stream through a broad crack. I watched the light fade away. When it grew dark, I lay on the bare mattress, shut my eyes, and fell asleep.

I awoke the next morning to the scratch of metal against steel, the screech of the slot in the door sliding open. A tin cup and plate clattered to the floor. By the time I went over, whoever it was had slammed the window shut and I heard footsteps walking away. Two slices of stale bread would be my breakfast. What little milk the tin cup had once held was now a puddle on the floor.

All day I waited for the staff to show up and terrorize me. I used the chamber pot once. There was no water to drink, so I doubted I would need it a second time. I tried to go back to sleep. When I heard some of the guys out in the yard, I went over to the window and peered through the crack. I thought about calling down to them through the close-set iron bars, but something told me that would only delay my return to their ranks. I counted all my bruises, thirty, not including the ones on my face, which I couldn't see. I counted the number of steps it took to walk from one end of the room to the other, then across it. I guessed it was five by seven feet. I searched for something to read, turning up the mattress in the hope that the previous occupant had left something there for me. Nothing. Hours later, the slot slid back. Again, I was too slow to catch the cup and the milk spilled on the floor. I called out through the slot—only footsteps answered me.

I ate the bread as slowly as I could. In my mind I ran back over some of the fights I'd had with the dudes at Morganza, miming the punches I'd thrown, bobbing and weaving around as though ducking imaginary fists. I stopped after a couple of seconds, feeling suddenly embarrassed, as though I'd been caught acting crazy. For the first time in my life, I watched an entire sunset, from beginning to end, through the gap in the boarded-up window. Bathed in orange light, the cottages looked really impressive. Something cold welled up inside me, making me shiver even though the room was hot and stuffy.

When my dinner arrived, I was so hungry I almost ran across the room, but whatever it was that came through that slot was unrecognizable to me as food. I sat on the floor with that plate in my lap for what seemed like hours, but nothing could make me move the spoon to my lips. I fell asleep with my back against the door, and in the morning the "food" was a congealed lump.

I began to lose track of time. I crept around the room on my hands and knees, scanning every inch of the walls for some message that might have been scratched into the peeling paint. My shadow became my boxing partner; we'd go at it long and hard, stopping only when my knees trembled and then gave.

The chamber pot began to overflow. For a while I breathed only through my mouth, but gradually the smell faded into the walls like smoke.

When the door opened and a supervisor walked in, I was starting to lose track of how long I'd been in there.

"Get that pot and get your ass over here," he said.

It was heavy. Some of the contents slopped over the side. I emptied it in a bathroom down the hall, then took a shower while the supervisor stood outside. I kept looking down at my hands to see if I was real and moving. I commanded my body to do the simplest steps: Get the soap. Turn the faucet. Every time it obeyed, a puff of relief blew through me. When I was done, he led me back to my room and locked me in. The next time a plate of hot food slid in, I ate everything. I licked the spoon. Later, I vomited every last morsel into the chamber pot.

The room began to talk to me. The food slot hissed like a snake. The bed opened like a mouth every night and seemed to clamp around me when I climbed in. The chamber pot taunted me. I grew to hate these three objects with a passion. My eyes went over them, back and forth, back and forth. *Bed, slot, pot. Bed, slot, pot.* I started to eat like an animal. I used a fingernail to carve a message on the wall by the bed: *The Fair One Shall Prevail.* I believed, above all, in the integrity of a fair fight.

When I got out after fifteen days, an alpha inmate named Little D shook my hand. He said, "Alright, man, alright. You good, man? Doin' good?" and led me directly to a seat on Whackers' Row.

Of all the perks of being a Whacker, chasing runaways was my favorite. I loved being outside at night and the thrill of pursuit. The more I sensed my quarry's panic, the faster I moved across that desolate farmland into sleeping towns. Any kid who makes up their mind to flee Morganza has to be pretty damn determined, so it was never an easy chase. In the end, though, Whackers always prevailed. There was a reason we were considered an elite force. We had passed through fire and we were stronger and faster than just about all the other inmates at Morganza. We became so good at hunting that during my tenure at Morganza the stream of runaways slowed to a trickle. I was proud of this achievement—I always gave 100 percent to everything I did.

I didn't know then that one day I'd be on the other side of the hunt. I didn't know that one day I'd be the one racing across the cornfields, with only one thought in my head: *freedom*.

CHAPTER 3

SQUARING UP

At some point or another, everyone looks back on their life and sees a series of choices. For some, those choices are vast and varied. For Black men in Philadelphia in the 1960s, the menu was a little shorter.

I didn't know a single guy who decided to "go to college." It just wasn't something we entertained or aspired to. We drew tremendous strength and stability from our Corners, and never even considered peeling away from street life and everything that came with it. Like someone trapped inside a revolving door, I went into prison and came out, in and out, each time a little more hardened than before.

I no longer paid much heed to my parents. As far as I was concerned, they didn't know who I was, and their orders had very little impact on me. One day I even got into a physical fight with my father, and that might have been the end of it—if the old man hadn't outfought me! I'd never seen that side of him before. He was a long-distance truck driver who spent extended periods away from home, but when he was around he did all kinds of housework that I thought was beneath him. The few times he and my mother came to visit me while I was locked up, he wore his best suit, like he wanted to impress my jailers, and he used his White Voice and called people *Sir* in a manner that filled me with shame. But the day I raised my fists to him he called my bluff. Before I knew what was happening, he grabbed me and flipped me over backward, straddling my chest in such a way that I couldn't buck him off. He had me in a bind, his feet tucked under my hips, stopping me from launching myself off the ground or throwing him over to the side. I hurled my fist but he blocked it so forcefully that my knuckles stung. He slowly gathered up the front of my shirt, lifting my head and neck up off the floor and bringing my face an inch away from his. He didn't say a word, just searched my eyes for a long time before releasing me and heading off into the kitchen as though nothing had happened. I lay on the floor with a huge smile on my face and a feeling of relief that my father was more than the man I'd thought he was.

Back then, it was all about being a *man*—locating and exerting some sense of manhood in a world that barely acknowledged our humanity. A century after slavery not much had changed. My parents both came from the South and I spent summers down on my grand-parents' farm in Georgia. They had a sparse farmhouse and acres and acres of land. During the high season, white farmhands arrived and harvested their entire crop of bulging watermelons, hauling them off to market in the backs of their pickup trucks. When they paid up, my uncle always handed over the cash to my aunt saying, "Alright baby, that takes care of them hunkies for a while." It was clear to me that those white guys were not working for us—it was more like my family was trying to keep the peace in a place I didn't really under-stand. When I walked into the convenience store in town the owner would say to his friends, "Well lookie here, fellas, the cat dragged us in a nigger this morning!" If he was feeling generous, he'd serve me. Most days he just told me to "take my black ass back to where it belonged—out in the cotton fields."

Things were not much different in Philly, where open Southern bigotry wore a sly Northern mask of politeness. White grocers smiled at Black customers while charging them higher prices for substandard goods. Schools were segregated. And all those "youth facilities" my road boys and I were thrown into never had more than a handful of poor white kids sprinkled in amongst a sea of Black bodies. So I guess you could say we were always looking for ways to prove our humanity. To feel that our lives were really our own. Gang wars were one of the only sure ways to do this.

When I got out of Morganza, I discovered a big change on the chessboard. The Moon Gang had amassed an army. Their ranks had swelled to nearly five hundred, making them my number-one obsession in life. Everyone from the cops to my Old Heads to the storekeepers who operated within a two-mile radius of their base camp on Sixty-Second and Vine Street were making a point of studying the Moon's movements. These motherfuckers had taken to wearing matching white Jeff caps and chanting slogans like *When the sun goes down, what comes out? The Moon!* As far as I was concerned, that was a taunt, an invitation to subordinate them once and for all.

It all went down in the Battle for the Imperial—a popular skating rink and ballroom on South Sixtieth Street.

When dusk fell, the South Side assembled at the elementary school a block away from the battleground. I recognized faces from the Coast, Osage Avenue, the Sixtieth Street Corner, and the Gladiators, and dudes from Cedar Avenue and all of its subdivisions. This was the largest gathering of the South Side I'd ever been part of. When one of the Old Heads called for scouts, I volunteered along with a whole bunch of dudes who were new to our constellation. Scouting was a coveted assignment: If you were successful in your mission, you'd find yourself in extremely hostile territory and have to either run like a maniac or take a heavy beating. No matter the outcome, scouting earned you heart for taking one for the team, and I needed to regain some of the ground I'd lost while locked up at Morganza.

We split off and I, following my gut, headed straight for the White Castle on the corner of Sixtieth and Market. This was a popular restaurant, and I knew how to gain access to a back entrance that opened onto a warren of side streets, which I could traverse to take word back to my boys. The first thing I saw when I ducked into the restaurant was a sea of white Jeff caps stretched along Sixtieth making its way slowly toward the Imperial—just as I'd predicted, they were taking the easy route, the open road. Arrogance.

When I returned to the schoolyard, the Old Heads already had our troops in formation; they were just waiting for my signal to dispatch a rear guard to double back onto Fifty-Ninth Street and storm the Moon from behind while the rest of us, armed with as many rocks as we could carry, split into smaller battalions and concealed ourselves in close proximity to the site. Our front liners, meanwhile, had decided to fight only with fists, so they headed off to stand ground at the Sixtieth Street entrance to the ballroom.

It was a spectacular sight. The best that South Side had to offer stretched out on either side of the street, while the white-tipped orb of the Moon advanced from the north. When they got within ten feet of our front lines, they paused, and I knew then that Moon's military commanders, like our Old Heads, had a flair for drama. For a minute all was silent.

Suddenly, the Moon's ranks splintered. Guys stationed at the back came surging ahead, throwing the formation out of whack. Our rear guard had taken them by surprise, and before they could recover, we charged their already decimated front lines. For a while pandemonium reigned as weapons were discarded in favor of fists. I concentrated on dealing blows to anyone in a funky little white cap, all the while being slammed from every side.

I don't remember feeling any pain. What I do remember is the wine I had drunk earlier that evening making its way back up with each fist that collided with my gut. I shut my eyes to stop the reeling, punching blindly into the darkness. The next thing I knew I was hurling right into the face of a Moon Gang member who'd been about to knock my teeth out! That cracked me right up! Matter of fact, I was still laughing and hurling when the cops showed up.

We won the Imperial, but I lost twenty-three months of my life to Moe Coe.

When I got out the year was 1962 and there was a new, daunting task awaiting me.

By the age of eighteen those who hadn't earned Old Head status were banished to the sidelines. Those of us who'd secured our badges of honor were expected to Square Up. Roughly translated, this meant moving out of your folks' place, landing a job, and if you could swing it, acquiring a car. All of this was undertaken with one goal in mind: getting a girl.

For guys like me who'd grown up with sisters, this called for a major mental shift. I'd spent most of my life regarding females as secondary figures. My mother treated my father with a respect bordering on reverence: she never called him anything but Mr. Shoatz or Daddy. On the other end of the spectrum, my father treated my sisters like princesses, exempting them from what he called "heavy" household duties—which led to me ignoring them all as much as possible. While I was locked up, I had a couple of girlfriends from neighboring female detention facilities, including one crazy chick named Sugar who fought tougher than I did, but beyond that women didn't play a big part in life. However, when I came back from my final stint at Moe Coe, I was forced to recognize them as powerful new players on the block.

In my absence my sisters had grown into young women and even in my eyes they were stunning. My sister Beatrice was the undisputed leader of the pack. She had the shortest skirts and the sharpest tongue and most guys I knew were terrified to approach her. Because my brothers and I had carved out decent reps on the Corner, all my sisters were safe from heckling and harassment, and they took full advantage of the prestige by strutting around the hood fiercely. The refrain was "Man, those Shoatz girls are on *fire*." It wasn't just talk, either. Like us, girls had rites of passage of their own, and at that time it was pulling trains.

This was a sanitized phrase for the act, a euphemism for what—nowadays—might be better understood as group sex but in many cases might have been ritualized gang rape. Just like the Fair Ones tested a guy's stamina, Pulling a Train proved a girl's worth among her peers—how many guys in a row could she endure, or "pull"? It happened in strangers' houses and in parking lots, in playgrounds at night and in basements in the middle of the day. Guys were skipping school to ride on trains that lasted six, seven, eight hours. Turf wars were suspended as dudes from the Moon Gang pulled trains in the homes of South Side members. When you got out of jail, you could look forward to a train ride as a welcome home gift. It was Philly's latest craze, and every girl who wanted to earn stripes was expected to give herself up to it. One after another, dudes piled on, and I'm ashamed to admit I participated in it. In order to convince myself that my sisters were somehow exempt from this whole fad, I put up a wall between me and the women in my home, building it brick by brick with each train I pulled until I couldn't even see over the top anymore.

Of course, the cops came after us for pulling trains, acting like they cared about the girls involved. I don't know how they got wind of it, but they'd always crawl to a stop at the curb right when we were coming out of someone's basement, saying, "These must be the niggers who got that girl over on Walnut Street," and the games would begin. While driving us to the station, or beating us in the back seat of the car, the police always made speeches about what monsters we were for pulling trains, how much shit we deserved for inflicting such pain on "young girls." Somehow, their vigilance over train pulling never extended to the domestic violence that plagued all of West Philly as soon as the sun went down. As a kid I lost count of the number of times my neighbors' fights shook me awake: raised voices, cussing, a couple of short screams, and then the dull, constant throb of pummeling. I learned the sounds of every possible instrument striking flesh: open palms and fists, plates, TV antennas, baseball bats and walking sticks, toaster cables and dining room chairs. But whenever my mother called the cops, they'd say they couldn't interfere in domestic affairs. All of this led me to reason that there were no consequences for a man beating his own wife. I just figured the women tolerated that abuse the same way schoolgirls tolerated the trains.

That was the mindset I was in when I met my future wife. Her name was Rachel Freeman; we called her Betty.

I was nineteen years old when I first laid eyes on her on the corner of Pine Street. She was hanging with her sisters, all three of them leaning over the railing of their front porch watching a struggle between a Black guy and three white cops a couple doors down. These girls were a trio of ivory smiles and high cheekbones, and I decided right then and there that I was in love. I asked Betty out to a movie that night. When I arrived to pick her up, hours late and with a bloody nose from a brawl over on Market Street, she was sitting on the porch, furious.

I don't remember her showing any concern for my battered state. All I recall was her saying, "I don't like to be kept waiting."

That first date foreshadowed the sad tussle that was to become our marriage.

The relationship was doomed from the beginning. I knew next to nothing about how to share a life with a woman. Steeped in gang culture, I had spent most of my conscious years striving to be the ultimate macho man. To me, girls and women were at best possessions, ornaments, or playthings. To be owned and enjoyed, but never on the same footing with men. I had vague notions in my mind about how a man should treat his wife based on my father's attentiveness to my mother. But then, she returned his kindness with total obedience, which made me assume that it was the man's job to provide the cash and the woman's job to keep quiet.

But Betty was, in my mind, not that kind of woman. I believe she possessed a will almost as strong as mine.

The courtship phase of our relationship went smoothly enough. I knew how to wine and dine and dazzle her, so there were moments of great fun and affection between us. This phase, however, quickly dissolved into a battle of wills that brought out the worst in both of us.

A lot of girls back then were bent on getting between dudes and the Corner. I recall Betty constantly getting on me to cancel plans with my road dogs so she and I could have some "alone time," especially on Saturday nights. It straight up made me laugh. I never came right out and said anything, just listened and nodded while she was yapping and then went out and did whatever I damn well pleased.

On one occasion, a couple of my Corner boys crashed a party at Betty's family home. True to form, they started picking fights with the guests, including a cousin of hers who'd come up from Virginia. He was called Pooch and lived up to the name—not much of a street fighter! My main man, Ace, led the charge against Pooch, first challenging him politely then finally dragging him outside. Betty became hysterical. She demanded that I stop my boys from fighting him, and when I refused she attempted to intervene herself. This would have put most people on the horns of a dilemma, but I knew where my loyalties lay. I rejected her appeals and physically removed her from harm's way so the fight could proceed. Ace was a seasoned street fighter, someone I had grown very close to over the years. I don't remember the exact outcome of that brawl but it couldn't have gone too well for Pooch, because the next day Betty and I came very close to breaking up.

I had no script for this, no model to follow. My Corner boys and I were a world away from the courtship rituals and marital rites that governed our parents' generation. Our folks had been social climbers, coming up in droves from the South, buying "nice" homes, becoming middle class, turning the other cheek. We were a different breed, my boys and I, determined to fight back even if it meant the only ones we were fighting were one another. We were not content to sit and wait and see. We were searching, constantly on an undefined mission and a lot of the time making it up as we went along.

It didn't help that while we struggled to Square Up and Settle Down, everything around us was on fire. This was 1963. Cities were burning in

Alabama and Mississippi. The KKK was riding the night, laying waste to anything Black—Black children, Black churches. White hoods and white crosses and white terror. It was like we were being goaded into a brawl but our rivals were never within reach. They were too powerful, too prepared, too many. Bombs exploded on our television screens, but the pastors only told us to keep praying. Never mind that the pews themselves were being blown to dust. The flames of race riots licked at the edges of our consciousness but didn't do much other than add to our pent-up energy that could find no outlet except the streets.

Something was waking up in America but my road dogs and I were still sleepwalking. We were wracked with restlessness, poor choices, and wasted time. Only later would I realize that all of it stemmed from having an unfulfilled life mission. As the great Afro-Caribbean writer Frantz Fanon put it: "Each generation must, out of relative obscurity, discover its mission, fulfill it, or betray it."

For me, the life-altering event that would define my mission on earth happened the summer I first saw and heard Malcolm X.

CHAPTER 4

AN AWAKENING

It was the summer of 1963. Betty had dragged me to New York to turn over a new leaf. I was working daytime shifts at a garment factory in Midtown and night shifts at Macy's department store downtown, on Thirty-Fourth Street. Inside that huge Edwardian-style building I took inventory in massive storerooms, mopped down wooden floors, and shined the marble-sheathed octagonal pillars. When I was done with my sixteen-hour workday, I'd hit the streets of Harlem. It was there, on the corner of Lenox Avenue and 116th, that I witnessed the Nation of Islam rally that was attended by roughly sixteen thousand people.

The man on the raised platform was dressed in a suit and flanked by two huge security guards in black outfits and dark glasses. A clump of microphones crowded his podium, which was stamped with a logo of a white crescent moon and star against a red background. Over the speaker's head hung a huge banner bearing the faces of African men I didn't recognize above the names of their respective countries: *Egypt, Ghana, Algeria, Ethiopia.*

I stood in a soup of bodies that extended as far as I could see in every direction, filling the streets and sidewalks that had been cordoned off by police barricades. Women wore feathered hats and white gloves, men wore funky suits or gray overcoats. Every window of the brownstone buildings overlooking the rally was flung open, and heads and torsos hung out to catch the words that echoed from loudspeakers mounted beneath traffic lights at the intersection. Other onlookers clung to telephone poles to better see the speaker. Policemen lounged against the cattle pens, smoking and pretending to laugh—feigning indifference to the size of that crowd. But tension rose from their ranks, as palpable as the electric excitement among us spectators.

I wish I remembered every word Malcolm spoke that day, but I don't. What I do remember are three portraits he painted in my mind. The first was of what he called the "walking, talking blue-eyed devil," the White Man who had tricked us into believing that our freedom flowed from him alone. That we must live in accordance with his laws and scriptures, even though these very laws and scriptures had been used to enslave and impoverish us. The duplicity of that "blue-eye thing," with his clever words and ways, stopped being an abstraction to me that day and became instead a thing of great clarity. The second picture was that of the deceived Black man, lost in a den of vice, of whiskey and cards, so crippled by the hatred of the white devil that he was unable to love himself and his "brothers" as they deserved to be loved. And finally a portrait of America itself, the thing we all took for granted as an unmovable, fixed reality, a thing of such promise that we could not fathom abandoning it, or fighting it, but wanted only to be embraced deeper into it so that we could also share in its nectar. But Malcolm disabused me of that notion when he reminded us that Black people had never known American democracy, "only hypocrisy." That we had never dreamt the American dream, only woken up, day after day, into the "American nightmare."

He had to keep pausing because the crowd's response drowned him out. Kids sitting on their parents' shoulders hollered along with the women who were waving their arms and stamping their feet like they were in church. Each time he spoke about the police, he pointed at the cops stationed around us, and the crowd turned as one to look in their direction. Instinctively I got into my boxing stance, expecting them to lash out against this blatant mockery. When they didn't, my respect for the speaker took on astronomical proportions.

Later, after the crowd had thinned down to the last few stragglers, and a couple of dudes had started to dismantle the stage, I walked around like a zombie. I had learned to distrust men in suits—I associated them with school principals and prison wardens and my father when he was getting ready to do some bowing and scraping to the White Man. But this guy—this Mr. X or Brother Malcolm or whatever he was called—was something else. He made that suit walk the talk; he was the real deal. Until that moment, the desegregation movement had looked a whole lot like Black people turning the other cheek, something my Corner culture had taught me to abhor. In the university of the streets, we learned to confront our enemies. When you fight, you fight to win. So when I saw people hauled off stools at lunch counters down South, or hosed down with water cannons, or set upon by German shepherds, I was put right off the whole thing. I hated how they cowered and ducked and complied. How they allowed themselves to be handcuffed and led away. I didn't join the bus rides or the marches. What they called the movement was far away from what I knew, and I didn't think for a second it could wield the power necessary for a head-to-head battle with the while devils. But this dude had said something different. He was talking about respect. Winning it back the same way it had been taken from us, by sheer brute force. Telling us we could be men again. Something clicked—I'd been walking right when my path turned sharply left.

But gang culture is not easily abandoned, especially for Old Heads like me, who were revered by younger dudes on the Corner and expected to provide guidance and take an active role in the most dangerous wars. Guns had begun to leak into our neighborhoods, so battles were now swifter and deadlier than before. I was deep in this world, and not even my encounter with Malcolm X and the Nation of Islam could shake me loose completely. When Betty and I returned to

Philadelphia, I got right back on that hamster wheel, jumping from bar to brawl to bedroom.

Betty waited and nagged. I played deaf, blind, and dumb. The way I saw it, we were both stuck in our respective roles, she the hard-driving Black woman, me the gang-warring hustler. We did what we did because *that's what you did* back then: you met someone, got married, played house, and tried to convince yourself it was what you wanted.

When I asked her to marry me, I had no idea what I was proposing. I was twenty-one years old, and in my mind, I was offering her a life as my wife, which meant I would feed and clothe her, provide for my family, and continue on my path of rising through the ranks of my Corner. Beyond that, I couldn't envision a role for her in my life except as an appendage.

I remember only two things about our wedding day: repeating the priest's words like some parrot in a cage, and my Corner boys throwing fistfuls of rice at us outside the church. The way they pelted me with those grains felt like an attack. Later, at our wedding reception, my boys got drunk and threw some chairs around. I think I remember Betty crying, but I don't remember caring. I don't recall what kind of dress Betty wore, or the vows we took, or anything except the feeling that I'd betrayed my Corner.

I wish I could say things changed when our daughter Theresa was born in July of 1964.

My first glimpse of her was through the large windows of the maternity ward in the Philadelphia General Hospital, where I stood alongside a bunch of other fathers, who weren't allowed in the delivery rooms. The next day Betty brought Theresa home to the new pad I'd chosen on Fifty-Fifth Street, between Christian Street and Baltimore Avenue. I remember this little baby swaddled in blankets with a big smile on her face. But her smile must have faded pretty quickly, because less than a week later the house turned into my and Betty's own private battleground.

Looking back now, I think the only good thing about our marriage was that it served as a kind of birth canal into a different world. Our home environment was so unbearable that I found myself spending as much time as possible outside the house. And because I needed to provide for our new baby, I was forced into a series of jobs that not only pushed my body to its limits, but also gave me a solid foundation for the revolutionary work I would undertake in the years to come.

CHAPTER 5

SOFT SHEETS AND MOLTEN STEEL

Beckette's Dairies had a fleet of trucks two hundred strong. Between us milkmen, we served six thousand homes and businesses throughout the city. I rose at two thirty every morning, hauled myself down to a warehouse garage, and took off in one of Beckette's famous Stand-N-Drive Divco milk trucks.

As a kid I thought I'd probed every corner of Philly, but the milk round lifted the shutters on a whole new world of warehouses, distribution centers, loading docks, and wholesale parking garages. For ten hours a day, six days a week, all I'd see was people lifting up trapdoors and descending hidden flights of steps into underground storerooms, or disappearing inside massive floor-to-ceiling refrigerators, or signaling for me to use back entrances I'd never known existed. Before too long I had a second map etched in my mind, superimposed onto the one from my Corner days.

But it wasn't enough to know your way around. Beckette's trucks were beasts to drive. For one thing, the clutch and brake were in the same floor pedal, so when you needed to change gears, you could depress the pedal only so far before it engaged the breaks and brought everything—including hundreds of glass milk bottles in the rear—to a screeching standstill. Swinging this contraption through narrow streets called for great precision, and before long I was an expert. Maybe it doesn't sound glamorous, but I impressed a lot of my customers, which is to say the dozens of women I encountered on my rounds.

So many women. As many women as there were houses, opening their doors and welcoming me right on in. These were quick encounters because most of the women were married with kids. I didn't ask questions about their men, and they didn't seem to bother whether or not I had someone waiting on me at home. In and out. Every day. I became a bona fide philanderer and I had no qualms about it.

I also became a class A thief.

It was a pretty convoluted system of adding bits on the bottom and skimming a little off the top. Even the smallest adjustments to each customer's bill resulted in big payoffs at the end of the month for my buddy Mike and me. We were two of just three Black drivers in the whole Beckette operation, and here we were fattening our pockets at the expense of the hundreds of Black families we served, including those who were struggling to make ends meet.

We would have kept at it, too, if it hadn't been for the third Black dude on the fleet, a highly politicized man named Stanley Roberts.

Stanley was always giving us shit for stealing from "our people." He was also a dictionary for civil rights acronyms: he told us about the NAACP, the National Association for the Advancement of Colored People; SNCC, the Student Nonviolent Coordinating Committee; and RAM, the Revolutionary Action Movement. We sat at diners after our shift, and he held forth on when Temple University students were gearing up for big rallies and what their demands were: Swahili recognized as an official language, and the right to wear dashikis on campus. He quoted Cecil B. Moore and Malcolm X and seemed so sure of the change to come that he almost had me convinced.

But Mike was the devil to Stanley's advocate.

"Man," he'd say, pouring a whole jug of cream into his coffee, "sometimes hunkies is right, Black folks is fuckin' *crazy*! Tryn'ta walk around in some African getup, talkin' like a bunch of fuckin' monkeys, *shit* man. These kids gonna go up against Rizzo's boys and get their dicks handed to 'em. Pigs not going *no*where man, not for no AACP, not for you, not for nobody. So regular guys like me and Shoatz here is just gonna do what we can to get by."

"Shit man," Stanley would say. "It's no wonder Black folks is down with guys like you in the ranks."

For the most part, I had to agree with Mike. Everything I knew and everything I saw told me Black folks were down in the mud and nothing was going to change, so I saw no reason to alter my own lifestyle. The Philly gangster scene held me close and tight: fights on the Corner were followed by fights with Betty. My only distraction was the Strip.

During the day this was your average shopping district, a promenade of supermarkets and bakeries, a YMCA and movie theaters, fast-food outlets and clothing stores, stretching for over a mile from the intersection of Fifty-Second and Pine Street all the way to Lancaster Avenue. Pedestrians bled into a river of vehicles that flowed along the thoroughfare intersected by the elevated train tracks carrying the Market Street "El" train, Philly's most popular commuter line. But at night the Strip underwent a metamorphosis. Shopkeepers shuttered their windows and locked their doors. As the sun went down, gaudy lights flickered to life, drawing nocturnal creatures from their homes and into throbbing bars and pulsing nightclubs. The sidewalk became a kind of fashion runway, a parade of men and women dressed to kill. Traffic slowed to a crawl as drivers showcased their flashy rides, hoping some chick would take them up on the unspoken offer. No one stayed in the same spot for long. The goal was to see and be seen.

By this time, I was recognized as an Old Head on my Corner. My crew had its headquarters on the Strip, in a bar and grill on Fifty-Sixth and Walnut Street, which was where I spent all of my free time. Since I had to be at the dairy by three in the morning, I never had to face Betty after these excursions: I went straight from the club to the loading dock for a ten-hour shift. I was usually home around two o'clock in the afternoon. Ideally, I would have avoided Betty and gone right upstairs to bed in the hopes of catching a few hours' sleep before hitting the streets with my boys. But Betty refused to allow me any rest. She insisted that the hours between my shift and the Strip belonged to her, and she would drag me out on all kinds of errands and outings that left me wrecked with sleeplessness.

One night she'd arranged for us to see Ike and Tina at the Imperial Ballroom, one of the hottest cabaret venues in West Philly, located on Sixtieth and Walnut. A big-ticket act like Ike and Tina drew huge crowds of people dressed to kill—the men in mohair or sharkskin suits, the women in iridescent dresses and lizard shoes. We had a table directly in front of the stage. This was before the musical duo had burst into international fame, when they were still doing the Black circuit, and they had the whole house rocking. Right in the middle of the show I fell asleep. All I remember is Betty shaking me roughly awake, hissing at me in her embarrassment that I'd passed out in full view of the performers! It would have been funny if Betty hadn't railed at me for months afterward—she never let me forget it.

Her nagging fired me up. Mostly we went at it in verbal sparring matches, but at some point I started physically manhandling her, and once or twice I slammed her against a wall. Her response was always to pack a bag and go to stay with her sister who lived a couple of blocks away with her husband and children.

Betty shared a closeness with her mother and sisters that I couldn't understand. They had a way of closing ranks around her that both intimidated and infuriated me. In some ways they resembled my Corner, except that they rolled even deeper because they were blood and that made me feel some kind of way. I was always looking for ways to lash out at these women, but they never gave me an opportunity. Even though Betty's sister was constantly over at our place with her kids, she didn't try to meddle in our affairs other than on the rare occasions when I became physically violent. Mostly Betty's mother and sisters provided a kind of safe haven for her that I couldn't touch—they were always there on the other end of the phone or providing an escape route from our cracked and wounded marriage. It seemed as though all of her emotional needs were met by this posse of deeply loving and loyal women, and I hated it. I hated that she shared a bond with them that she didn't share with me. I hated that she didn't actually need me. But I would be damned before I said any of this aloud or changed my behavior toward her. The most I was prepared to concede was to go over to her mother's or her sister's place, apologize, and bring Betty back home with me.

Betty gave birth to our second daughter, Sharon, in the summer of 1965, and I'm ashamed to admit that her arrival into our world did not prompt me to change my ways. Once a week I threw money at Betty for groceries and baby supplies. If I was feeling guilty about my philandering, I brought home bigger offerings: furniture and electronic items, which I paid for with the money I'd pinched from my customers that week. None of my efforts seemed to appease her, just as none of her castigating had any impact on me. As far as I was concerned, I was doing my duty, providing material comforts for my family.

The only thing that gave me pause was seeing the impact of our domestic strife on our daughters. Our first-born, Theresa, assigned herself the role of Sharon's guardian. Still a toddler herself, she held her little sister close while the tempest raged through the house. Somehow, through it all, she retained that radiant smile of hers, the same one she'd shown me the day she came home from the hospital. Sharon, on the other hand, grew wide-eyed and solemn as she observed the ugly scenes that had become part of our daily life as I recall it: name calling, throwing and breaking things, Betty's family tearing into our home to protect her, and me storming out when I just couldn't bear it anymore. Once, our daughters even witnessed me striking Betty. The worst part was, I never really knew how Betty perceived our relationship, or how she experienced this time. I knew she was unhappy, but because we seldom talked—in ways that weren't arguments or all-out fights—it's possible that, to this day, she holds an entirely different set of memories than I do.

I felt something tearing inside me. On the one hand I was enjoying my hard-earned status as an Old Head turned hustler. My Corner boys doted on me and the Young 'Uns outright worshipped me. In this world, I had done my time and was reaping the benefits. I was flush with the cash Mike and I were systematically pilfering from Beckette's Dairies, which allowed me the trappings of the hustler: Flashy clothes. Dropping dough all over the Strip. When I entered a bar people turned their heads. But when I walked into my own home I received nothing but a long list of demands and accusations from Betty. Not once did I feel it necessary to give her an explanation of my motives or an honest answer regarding my actions. I did not feel I owed her anything beyond sharing a home and, occasionally, a bed. Truth to be told I much preferred the beds of my customers: soft sheets and no expectations.

Eventually, I was fired from my job for falling asleep at the wheel. I had been expecting this. I'd started drinking on the job, and once or twice got into accidents with the Divco that I couldn't simply explain away. It was time to move on. I turned my back on Beckette's and drove five miles out of Philly to answer a call for laborers at the Conshohocken steel mill.

It turned out to be the hottest, hardest, dirtiest job I'd ever worked, and it unleashed a physical strength that I never knew I possessed. It made all my years of rumbling and Corner brawling look like kid's play. Every time I thought my body had reached its limit, I found I had a little more in the tank, and a little more after that. Even on days I thought I wouldn't be able to return, I got my ass down to that steel mill and got to work.

To survive the fires that raged in furnaces from dawn to dusk, we had to wear a flame-retardant hot suit, gloves, steel-toed boots, a safety hat, and glasses that were so dark it took my eyes a while to adjust to them. You didn't need to exert yourself in order to work up a sweat. You just stepped onto the main floor and the beads started to roll down your back, down the sides of your forehead. Floor managers instructed us to use the salt-tablet dispensers that stood at hundred-yard intervals throughout the building to replenish the minerals that poured out of us in waves. Stretchers and first aid kits lay concealed at strategic points around the floor waiting for collapses and casualties. Cranes, trains, and trucks rumbled throughout the plant. Our supervisors told us to keep our ears tuned to their horns and whistles, but after a few days on the job I found myself drifting into a kind of daze as a I worked. None of the tasks I was assigned required anything more than the bare minimum of brainpower. This was straight manual labor, and by the end of my first month on the job my body was stronger than it had ever been, every muscle bulging as I lugged, dragged, and shoveled my way through the day. I emptied coke cars. I poured molted steel—what we called "the heats"—into molds on open hearths, which were long, split-level structures that formed the nucleus of this entire operation.

Our designations were meaningless: second helper, third helper. They didn't come close to capturing what we did. Third helpers were really shovel gangs, eight or nine to a team, responsible for cleaning out the furnaces once they'd been emptied. We had to advance on the huge doors and brace against the flames and sparks in order to shovel a dolomite solution along the walls. Our flesh became mangled and mottled from the steel that splashed around as the cranes moved huge ladles from one mold to another. Each ladle was the size of a two-story building, solid and deep enough to catch and hold molten steel. Second helpers were beasts of burden. We worked on teams shoveling mineral additives from storage bins into wheelbarrows, then pushing them across the floor, which ran the length of several city blocks, before emptying their contents into the furnace or into waiting ladles. Our supervisors made damn sure that each barrow we transported was laden with its allotted cargo: five hundred pounds. Anything less on the scale and he'd send us right back to the bins to load up until we hit the mark. The barrow itself weighed sixty-five pounds. To lift, balance, and push this container was a feat in and of itself. Making it all the way to the furnace was another story altogether. The first time I made the trek, I was almost certain my body would buckle. Each step seemed to add more weight to my load. After one round, I swallowed a couple of salt tablets, then went back. I lost all sense of time. All I could do was put one foot in front of the other, again and again and again, until the last storage bin was empty. Later, limp, I asked my supervisor how much weight I'd transferred. He never lifted his eyes from his clipboard.

"That one there was five thousand pounds," he said, nodding toward the empty bin. "Highest grade of steel we make."

I was exhilarated. This was the job for me, one that took everything but my last breath, then asked for more. It was a test and I wanted it every day. I didn't care about the monotony of it. I managed to block out the fact that this was just another chain gang, that no matter what I did, I always ended up in a long line of Black laborers, in burning heat or biting cold, while above us white men shouted down instructions, ate sandwiches, and counted out the money.

All this would sink in much later, as I sat in a cell recalling how, no matter how grueling my shifts at the mill, I never dreaded them as much as I did going home to Betty. Whenever I arrived at the house, I remember, I was greeted either with rancor or with the heavy silence that told me she'd packed her bags and taken the children to her sister's. At the time, I swallowed all this like the cold beers I drank at the end of my shift. I was only vaguely aware that beyond the factory walls everything was aflame. Even my Corner boys grew hazy behind the curtain of smoke that rose from the furnaces. I was so exhausted every night that I couldn't do much but collapse.

They say every revolutionary must pass through fire. If the Hole at Morganza had been a kind of baptism of my will and a strengthening of my mind, then the mill at Conshohocken initiated my body into a world of pain and steel that would define the greater part of my life.

CHAPTER 6

THE SCORCHING SUMMER OF '67

Philadelphia in the 1960s belonged to Frank Rizzo, the police commissioner, and his soldiers. They weren't your average pigs scooting around in wagons and beating on kids. They were a military force in training and the city was their lab. Rizzo pioneered a new kind of urban warfare that America hadn't seen before. He didn't rely on the National Guard or state troopers. He was more interested in turning his own city cops into GI Joes—armored and tanked and always ready to rumble. He wanted a war, and like most army generals he got what he wanted, plus a little more than he bargained for.

Before my life took a political turn, Frank Rizzo's plans didn't affect me one bit. While the Philadelphia police force got in formation, I took yet another job, this time as a cabdriver. This gave me a bona fide excuse to be out all night crawling around the Strip. But I never really picked up many passengers. I didn't need the money. What I wanted was a few hours of solitude. I told myself it was to get away from Betty, but when I was in my car, surrounded by the lights and buzz of a Friday night, I realized I wanted a break from all of it. There was always something or someone tugging at me. My Corner boys summoning me to a brawl. One of the many nameless women I associated with trying to get

a little more action. Betty wanting a husband and my children need-
ing their father. There were times when I simply parked and watched
the comings and goings of people as if I were watching a movie about
someone else's life. Or I'd drive slowly along, watching the gas gauge
drop notch by notch until it was time to go to work.

In 1967, I turned twenty-four, and Betty gave birth to our third
child, and first son. Russell III was born in May, right on the cusp of
a scorching summer. Tensions between Betty and me reached a boiling point and bubbled over: we got into a terrible confrontation that,
as I recall, resulted in her calling the cops on me. And not just any
cops—Frank Rizzo's cops. Animals in uniform who liked to make an
example of Black men who mistreated their wives. They broke down
my door and dragged me upstairs, where they discovered a shotgun in
my bedroom. I was arrested on the charge of unlawful possession of a
weapon. I spent a night in jail, and the next few months seething with
rage at Betty. I don't recall ever feeling so hateful toward another person. In those moments, and in that state of mind, I could have actually
killed her.

I don't remember who bailed me out of jail, but as soon as I got
onto the streets I rented a U-Haul truck, tracked down my buddy Ace,
and enlisted his help in cleaning out my and Betty's apartment—she'd
taken the kids to her sister's place as usual. I sold everything I could and
stored the rest. I wanted to punish Betty. I wanted to strip her of everything she owned. She had thrown me down before the dogs of war, and
I was determined to get even—not with them, but with her.

One night, bored out of my mind with the routine, I drove one of
my Corner boys and two young women we were acquainted with out to
Lawnside, a popular club spot in New Jersey. On the way home I pulled
over on the side of the highway and asked one of the girls if she wanted
to "take a walk" with me, leaving the car to my Corner boy and his
date. We found a secluded spot behind some bushes and started kissing
and undressing. We were in the middle of having sex when a pair of
police headlights swept over the area. They literally caught me with my

pants down! In the ensuing chaos I was separated from the girl—I ran toward the car and she must have gone in the opposite direction—and when I got to the vehicle it was surrounded by police cruisers. I wasn't worried about my Corner boy—our honor codes dictated that if either one of us was caught we would cover for the other party. All I could think about was avoiding arrest so that news of this dismal affair didn't reach my wife.

Crouching behind some foliage on the roadside, I crept away from that scene. I discovered I was in a rural community, and as I jogged along I eventually came upon a used car lot. I tried a couple of doors before finding one unlocked. I was in the process of hotwiring the ignition when a whole pileup of police cars descended on the lot, sirens blaring and lights blinding. It didn't take them long to find me.

I was charged with car theft—and with rape. This second charge shocked me deeply because as far as I was concerned, the woman had joined our joy ride of her own accord. Later, as the case went through the court, I learned that she was married, lived a few blocks from my parents' house, and that her husband frequented Champs Gym, a popular boxing spot of which I was also a member. I guess she was so terrified about being caught with another man that she made up a whole rigmarole about me. Fortunately, her girlfriend who was also there that night refused to go along with her story, and the charge was dropped. However, I was thrown in jail for attempting to steal the car.

Stanley Roberts bailed me out. As I collected my watch and wallet from the front desk at the police station he said, "Man, when you gonna pull your act together?"

We drove home on the Benjamin Franklin Parkway and as we came in sight of Twenty-First Street we saw the mob. There must have been two thousand students in the crowd, probably more, none of them older than fifteen or sixteen. When they passed our car—their fists raised in the air, others pumping placards—Stanley honked his support. At first I couldn't make out what they were chanting—there were too many voices, all muddled together like a deep hum coming up from inside the earth. Gradually two words took shape: "Black Power. Black Power."

They surged toward the twenty-story limestone building that housed the city's Board of Education, but Rizzo's storm troopers stood between them and the huge double doors. The cops had dressed to confront an army: every man wore combat boots, a bulletproof jacket, and a helmet with the face mask lowered. They slapped clubs in their palms as they lined the sidewalks, penning the demonstrators into their corral. They jabbed with their batons. From behind the safety of their riot gear they taunted and jibed. The students pressed on, still chanting. *Black Power. Black Power.* Suddenly a megaphone screeched to life. The voices coming through were muffled, ripped with static. Then Rizzo's words came loud and clear: "Get their black asses."

He'd trained his pigs well. They didn't even hesitate before setting upon a bunch of unarmed kids. All around us drivers and passengers were abandoning their cars, sprinting across the parkway, ducking into restaurants. Police clubs crushed anything that moved. Girls were screaming, trying to take cover, but every way they turned they met a wall of riot shields. One girl tried to push through the police barricade. They fought her down to her knees, then one of the pigs grabbed her hair and dragged her across the street so viciously I thought her scalp would come away. I don't know why Stanley and I stayed where we were. Maybe we were stunned. Maybe it was something I needed to see. Right in front of us a cop was beating on a Black boy so hard he'd stopped moving. I wondered if he was dead. The cop kept going, bringing his club down again and again on the boy's back. When he finally stopped I thought he had tired himself out, but when he straightened up I saw the baton was broken. He tossed the two pieces in a nearby trash can and walked on.

When I got home, Betty was on the phone with her sister like she always was. I slammed the door and stood there waiting to be noticed. I was all shook up and I wanted her to see my face, to ask me what I'd seen. But she just huddled over the receiver.

"Quit your yakking and get me some food," I said.

She spoke louder into the receiver, something about who the hell did I think I was, staying out all night, making her and the kids worry, and now trying to act like some big man around the house.

I don't remember her exact words. What I do remember is snatching the phone out of her hand and yelling something like, "Damn right I think I'm the man around this house, cuz *I am* the goddamn man around here. You see another one? You got one upstairs?"

I think Betty became hysterical then. We wrestled over the phone, and I remember her screaming, "I want my sister! I want my sister!" She hammered her fists on every inch of my body she could reach. I fended her off, then hit back, while Theresa stood at the top of the stairs, watching closely, not making a sound.

CHAPTER 7

HISTORY, PRIDE, POWER

I suppose you could say two things saved me: a person, and a place.

The place was the Muntu Cultural Center, which opened on the Strip sometime in the early sixties. This was where I was first introduced to African art, music, dance, clothing, history, food, and all the cultural rituals of my ancestors that I'd never cared to know about. I had always harbored a deep shame whenever the connections between the African continent and Black people in the United States were brought forth. I now know that came from one primary source: watching too many *Tarzan, Lord of the Jungle* movies. But at the Muntu Cultural Center the men who taught the classes and gave the presentations were the most knowledgeable people I had ever known, with the exception of Malcolm X. There were also some learned women there, but the thing that impressed me most about them was how good they looked in their African dresses, sporting large natural hairstyles. This was an entirely different kind of experience from anything I had ever known. I always learned something of value there, and being in the company of those beautifully attired men and women—and even children—gave me a sense of pride in just *being Black*. It was also strangely peaceful and serene in this setting. No alcohol or drugs were permitted, and everyone was so courteous and considerate toward one another that it became a welcome respite from my daily world. Never before had I felt such a sense of renewal in the company of my own people.

Regulars at the Muntu Cultural Center were deeply engaged in the Black revolutionary spirit of the sixties, which was largely being shaped by the Nation of Islam and the Revolutionary Action Movement, or RAM. One of RAM's founders, Max Stanford, was from Philadelphia, so the group's ideas filtered down to guys like me through discussions at the Muntu Cultural Center. RAM believed that the only way to end centuries of oppression, violence, and segregation was to create a revolutionary Black nationalist mass movement in America. To do so Black people would need to unite across various class and political interests into a Black liberation front: a community-based formation that would be led by Black youth. But the masses of Black people in America, me included, were so confused and misdirected that we first needed to be awakened from our stupor. This would be achieved only by creating a Black cultural revolution, whose purpose would be to destroy centuries of conditioning that had bound us to the attitudes, philosophies, habits, customs, and mores of the White Man: in other words we had to "lose our Negro minds." In its place, the cultural revolution would have to instill four things in the consciousness of Black people: an awareness of Black History; a sense of Black Pride; Black Power, with the goal of achieving self-determination for Black people in America; and finally Black Unity.

RAM identified four primary obstacles to the awakening of a new Black national consciousness: the Black church; Black colleges; Black barbershops and beauty parlors; and finally Black politicians. They referred to these groups as "reactionary institutions" that would always oppose self-determination in favor of integration into White America. The work of revolutionary nationalists would be to expose "bourgeois reformism" and replace it with "revolutionary nationalism"—on the economic front this meant boycotting white businesses and starting Buy Black campaigns. On the social front it involved reclaiming our African heritage and redefining Black beauty. And on the political front it entailed massive antidraft campaigns, a constant struggle to convince Black people that they should not fight and die in White America's imperialist wars.

Back then I wasn't open to a lot of talk and theorizing. I was always on the move, working or gang warring or hustling. Long before I ingested all these lessons, I was drawn to RAM's beret-wearing Black Guard. This was the organization's most militant unit, with members as young as fourteen years old, who were being trained in self-defense. At the Muntu Cultural Center members of the Black Guard were constantly either conducting or participating in karate classes. Watching them practice martial arts with military precision told me that the Muntu crowd meant business!

My old skin was loosening, becoming an ill-fitting garment on my body that I would soon have to shed. And it was at this precise moment that I met her. That person. The woman who turned it all around.

One night, after my shift at the steel mill, I decided to head down to the Strip for old time's sake. I went straight into a bar called Jackson, where I found one of my road dogs holding court at a booth in the far back.

"My man!" He practically shoved away the girl who was sitting in his lap in his eagerness to greet me. "Where the fuck you been? We thought you'd Squared Up something *real!*"

"Yeah, man, I been busy…working over at Conshohocken, ya'know? The usual, just trying to get by."

"Well, there's someone here I've been meanin' to introduce you to for a long time, man. Shit, she was just tryin' to tell me you were some kind of figment of my imagination, damn. And now you walk in the fuckin' door!"

My road dog hollered out a name I didn't hear. The woman had her back to us, and when she turned around the first thing I noticed was a cigarette holder perfectly positioned between two fingers, a curl of smoke snaking up around her face and coiling around her long, red-painted nails.

She said: "Yeah?"

"This is Shoatz, this is my man! Russ, this chick likes to say her name's 'Michelle Adams,' but whatever, man. We call her Lisa."

Right off the bat she told me that she and her husband, Eddie, had recently separated after having a kid together. I immediately let her know I was also married, with children of my own. That was the first thing that differentiated Lisa from all the other women in my life: I was honest with her.

The second thing was friendship. We actually got to know each other before we even went out on our first date, which was orchestrated by her cousin. He and I had tickets to the cabaret, and he casually suggested I take her instead. That night I learned she was the kind of person I felt 110 percent comfortable with. We could talk, really talk. We started spending a lot of time together. Whenever I came to her after being with someone else, I told her, just like that. And she listened! Without ever making me feel any kind of way about it. We kept telling each other we were "just hanging out"—coded language at the time for no-strings-attached kinds of relationships—but I was starting to feel something I had never experienced before. I found myself canceling plans with other women to be with her. I caught myself thinking I wanted nothing and no one *but* her.

Lisa had her own style and her own vibe. I wouldn't say she was immune to all the cultural changes happening around us, but I always got the feeling that whatever she did—what she wore, the opinions she held, the way she moved—came from a place deep within. She didn't believe in doing what was expected, and certainly never what was instructed! She was the kind of woman who could weigh things up like a calculator. She had this kind of cool, calm logic to her that was utterly alluring, not just to me but to a lot of men and women around her.

One evening we were sitting on her father's couch, holding each other, when Jerry Butler and Betty Everett's "Let It Be Me" came on the radio. Simultaneously we both said how we much we loved that song, which made us crack up. From then on, that was "our song." It never occurred to me to listen to it with Betty, or anyone else.

That year I got into a huge brawl on Christmas Eve with the manager of the clothing store where I'd taken a part-time job for the holidays. I'd had too much to drink at the office party, and somehow he and I ended up going at it like wild animals on the floor of the warehouse. Someone called the cops, and since this dude was in a senior position over me, I was the only one taken in to the station at Eighth and Race Street. Since the manager never bothered to come in and press charges, the judge told me I was free to go. I could have walked right out, except there was something troubling me. There was an older dude being arraigned alongside of me. He'd been picked up for vagrancy and looked pretty down on his luck. The judge had just assigned him to the Philadelphia House of Correction. For some reason I really felt for this man, so I requested a hearing with the judge and offered to take the man home with me, if it was simply a matter of getting him off the streets. Amazingly, the judge agreed.

The two of us walked out into heavy snowfall. I'd abandoned my car in a snowdrift in the store's parking lot, so the only option available to us was the subway. As we trudged through that freezing night, it began to dawn on me that I was in for the fight of my life with Betty if I brought this homeless man into our house. All the way to the subway station I battled with myself, insisting that I was a man and could do as I pleased. But the more I thought about it, the more I realized how much hell I'd have to pay with Betty. I stopped in the middle of the street and said, "Look, man, this isn't going to work." He just kind of half smiled, like he'd been expecting this. I felt like shit. As we huddled together in the doorway of a shop or someone's stoop, I hit on the idea of finding a cheap hotel right there on Race Street. I got him a room, gave him whatever cash I had on me, and we parted ways.

I don't know if it was the guilt of letting this brother down, or my swollen black eye, or the fact that I was on foot without a car that made me feel like such a loser in that moment. All I knew was I needed some loving. I could have knocked on a dozen doors—any of the women I was hooking up with would gladly have taken me in that cold winter night. Better yet, I could have gone home to my wife and kids, who were expecting me back at a reasonable hour so we could open presents together on Christmas morning. But I went to Lisa. Not because of convenience or obligation, but pure desire to find comfort in the arms of someone I trusted.

No matter how bad things got I could always go to Lisa. The best thing about her was that whenever I showed up, she always greeted me with a kiss. No questions, just the joy of being together. I melted in her presence and her embrace.

But I also feared her—she was so sure of herself. She had her own apartment and couldn't have cared less about material possessions like the ones I'd always been compelled to offer Betty to win a bit of affection. That was what it came down to—the fact that Lisa didn't need me or anything from me made me want her all the more! And pretty soon, my attachment to her sought an outlet in the only way I knew: a showdown.

It happened the day her ex-husband, Eddie, came to visit her. I had never paid him much heed; they had a kid together and I figured they had shit they needed to square. On one occasion I witnessed him chasing her into her father's house and I walked away from that scene feeling like it was none of my business. But something stuck in the back of my mind, the knowledge that this guy was capable of acting crazy toward Lisa. So when he came over that day and told Lisa, "Let's go out on the porch," I walked out to my car, loaded up my shotgun, and crept down to the landing, where I could monitor their exchange. I was actually hoping he would do something besides talk—something that would give me an excuse to shoot him. I had my finger on the trigger. Fortunately, something shook me loose. I looked down at the gun in my hands and told myself to get a grip. No woman was worth this aggravation.

Between Betty and Lisa, I was all kinds of messed up. There was a court hearing related to the incident of the cops kicking in my door, for which I obtained the services of a state senator. He argued that the cops used excessive force to enter my home, which prompted the judge to drop the weapons possession charges against me. Fresh from that little victory, I walked out of the courthouse and traded my car in for the latest model of an Oldsmobile Toronado: a sleek golden-winged beauty.

I apprenticed myself to a couple of hustlers on the Strip. This meant partying with them every night and learning their ways. I started driving up to New York City to purchase marijuana by the pound. Back in Philly I made up five- and ten-dollar bags and slung them on the streets along with locally produced meth. Eventually I recruited one of my Corner boys, a nineteen-year-old who called himself the Bandit, to handle my sales, allowing him to hang on to 40 percent of the profits. A few months later I was dabbling in insurance fraud. I obtained the services of a crooked doctor and solicited select Corner boys to stage accidents with. I raked in the insurance earnings and added them to my kitty, which I was constantly depleting. My old walkie, Ace, rechristened me "Dutch," after the Prohibition-era gangster Dutch Schultz. I walked around with a fedora hat on my head, the crown pinched into a sharp, diamond crease. Part of the game involved throwing parties for the other hustlers, hosting crap games at my apartment and generally expending a huge amount of money and energy on a lifestyle that left me cold and empty inside. Everything about my life felt like one big overblown movie, and it made me act crazy.

One Saturday night I drove over to Lisa's house as usual. Finding she wasn't home, I stopped off at her sister Florence's place in search of her. Florence hopped into my Toronado and we set off on our usual Saturday-night partying rounds, expecting to link up with Lisa at some point during the evening. Along the way we picked up Ace. He was my main man and I was closer to him than I had ever been with any of my other Corner boys. The three of us went to several parties in different sections of the city before heading back to West Philly. Ace had gotten pretty intoxicated, and while I drove he began to first hug and then paw Florence, who sat between us.

Now, this was nothing out of the ordinary for Ace and me. We had been enjoying nights like this since we were young boys. Plus, to my knowledge Florence wasn't involved with anyone and she was a good-looking, self-sufficient female that any guy would make a pass at. She rejected his advances once or twice, and I thought it would end there. But Ace wouldn't let her be, and after a minute or two I did something I'd never done before: I commanded him to leave her alone. This was a violation of a cornerstone of road dog culture. We had strict codes never to put anyone, let alone a woman, between ourselves and our walkies. Ace must have read my words as a challenge, because he made a renewed, aggressive attempt to kiss Florence. I slammed on the brakes, leapt out of the car, ran around to the passenger side, and yanked Ace out by his shirt. Before he could even register what was happening, I struck him hard across the face with a small pistol. This sobered him up and he attempted to lunge back at me, but I just stepped back and took careful aim of the pistol with both hands, right at his forehead.

He froze. And in a tone of great disappointment said, "What's wrong with you, Dutch?"

The whole time Florence was leaning out the passenger-side window, pleading with me not to hurt him. I wanted to. I wanted to shoot him right there. But something made me lower the pistol. We climbed back into the car and drove back to West Philly in silence.

I was furious but I didn't know at what, or who. Betty bore the brunt of my madness. In one instance that is branded in my mind, but that she may remember entirely differently, she fell to her knees and wrapped her arms around my legs in an effort to prevent me from hitting her. Lisa experienced it in more subtle ways, like having to watch me parade around with other girls on my arm in an effort to prove that she and I were nothing more than casual lovers.

I grew irritable and jumpy from a lot of pent-up frustration. I couldn't have it out with the other hustlers, so I looked for places to vent my venom. I had heard from one of my younger crew members that the Bandit hadn't been paying for his consignments of dope and meth. I'd also got wind of him bragging that his weed dealing was part of some mafia-style organization. I didn't respond right away. Partly I knew he was trying to goad me into a dramatic confrontation in the hopes of building up his reputation. But I was in a tough spot because I couldn't afford the rumor that people could just take my drugs or money and get away with it. He was playing the whole thing up with a lot of flair, avoiding places he knew I hung out or slipping away if he knew I was approaching. He wanted me to come after him.

One evening I was hanging with some of my crew on Sixty-Third Street when one of the younger dudes came running to tell me the Bandit was right around the corner. I grabbed a baseball bat from my car, checked that I had my knife in my pocket, and went hunting. He saw me approaching and adopted an attitude of nonchalance verging on defiance. It made something go *snap* in my brain, and before he or I knew what was happening I'd slammed him over the head with the bat. It happened so suddenly that he lost his balance and couldn't regain it. I beat him until the bat broke, at which point he squirmed away and took off down the street. I chased him into the rear of a hotel on Sixty-Third and Walnut, a dead end. Nowhere to run or hide. I wrestled him to the ground. Pinned him down with the full strength of my body, and used my free arm to extract my knife and deftly depress the catch that released the blade. I had it poised above his face and neck when, out of nowhere, I heard a voice in my ear shouting, "Don't kill him! Don't kill him!" It was another Old Head from my Corner, a dude I'd been rolling tight with for some years. I didn't realize I'd been followed. I didn't even realize I'd been about to stab this kid to death. I went cold all over, but the adrenaline was still pumping fast so it took the Old Head a few more seconds to convince me to lower my knife and tell the Bandit in no uncertain terms who he was working for.

I never did get that money back. But I didn't care. Because something happened a few months later that turned my life around.

Lisa gave birth to our son.

When I saw that baby boy lying in his tiny bed in the hospital nursery, I gave up all pretense and abandoned myself to the rush of adoration I felt for him. This was a first for me—maybe because, unlike with my other kids, Lisa's and my son was a true love child.

Even more than that, he was a child with a purpose, because shortly after he was born, Lisa and I went from being a couple to being comrades in the struggle for Black power.

CHAPTER 8

THE BLACK UNITY COUNCIL

It all started with an organization called the Black Unity Council, or BUC. It was established to serve the needs of the community bordered roughly by Market Street on the north, Baltimore Avenue on the south, Fifty-Sixth Street on the east, and Sixty-Third on the west—the neighborhood I'd called "home" for the greater part of my life.

I was trying to turn my life around. In a sobering move, Betty had moved to Virginia, taking our kids with her. I knew I needed to make some big changes, so I quit my job at the steel mill, dumped my gold Oldsmobile, and enrolled at the John F. Kennedy Training School in South Philly, an institution that paid me a stipend to take a course of my choosing. I opted for tool and die making. I also ditched cab driving in favor of being a janitor at my family's church, on Fiftieth and Spruce Street, which effectively brought my hustling and drug peddling to an end.

I was still hanging out at the Muntu Cultural Center, where I'd reconnected with my old Corner boy Victor "Sharp" Davis. Like me, he'd become interested in a world beyond the streets, and had been studying the movements for Black power, or Black liberation, that were unfolding across the country. We talked at length about how we might contribute to the struggle and decided that our best option was to keep it small, and local. We brought a couple of trusted people into our circle—Sharp's brother Wes, a dude named Lewis Young, and my sister Beatrice.

I'd always known that Beatrice and I were two sides of the same coin. As kids we'd clashed, but now we saw qualities in each other that we admired. Both of us were feisty, fearless, and downright determined; when we set our minds to a task or a project, we would lay down everything we had to see it through. Beatrice was, by then, a highly respected and influential woman in our community. I think it was partly due to the fact that damn near anyone who had a secret to tell, or was in possession of a delicate piece of information, or had a confession bottled up inside them, went to her. She had a reputation for being a very discreet and tight-lipped individual, so she became a kind of living archive. I would go so far as to say she was viewed as something of a deity for her ability to allow people to lay their burdens down at her feet and send them on their way with her blessings.

So, the five of us, sitting together in the church, drafted up a statement of principles and got to work.

In the beginning the Black Unity Council had clear, straightforward goals: we needed to start a food-collection drive for families in need; we wanted to acquire a building in which to host cultural events; a daycare center would be crucial to our activities, along with a liberation school for teenagers and preteens; and of course, with two of our founding members being Old Heads, we would have to initiate some kind of gang-intervention program to deal with the violence that had become rampant in our corner of Philly.

Witnessing our efforts, the pastor pretty much turned the entire church facility over to us, and it was there that we held meetings or drew up posters announcing community events or assemblies.

Our work coincided with an explosion in Black community-based organizations, political formations, and paramilitary groups around the city and the country. RAM by now was a well-established force to be reckoned with. They would go door to door in the roughest parts of the hood recruiting young men and women into their ranks—I once witnessed two of their members deliver a child on the kitchen floor of a house on Diamond Street, which was a very gritty, glass-strewn neighborhood full of boarded-up homes whose front porches were crumbling from rot. There was also the Republic of New Afrika, or RNA, which had purchased land in Mississippi and was looking for homesteaders to join them in a migration back to the South. There was the Black Guard, which formed in response to attacks against Black demonstrators by the National Guard. There was Herman Rice and his Young Great Society, and an extraordinary brother who called himself Mau Mau, after the anti-colonial Kenyan liberation army that fought a war against the British. Mau Mau was well-versed in African history and spoke fluent Swahili. His attire marked him out as a true soldier, every day of the week. We never knew what organization he represented but he was a force to be reckoned with, even by himself.

The BUC teamed up with one group—Ron Karenga and his United Slaves (US) Organization—for an educational event in our neighborhood. We charged an entrance "fee" of one can of food and were able to stockpile hundreds of cans to distribute to families in need. Ron Karenga had lined up some powerful speakers for the evening. One of them, a man named Playthell Benjamin, impressed me so much with his broad and detailed grasp of history that I fell in love with the discipline. I felt like a young priest, or missionary, who had just found his calling. Hungrily, I began not only to read but also to amass a small library of my own. I discovered the works of the revolutionary Algerian writer and thinker Frantz Fanon, and his words soon became a kind of guiding principle in my life: "Each generation must, out of relative obscurity, discover its mission, fulfill it, or betray it."

Studded through my political awakening was an obsession with self-defense. This came partly from years of being steeped in Corner culture, where the prevailing philosophy was one of preparation and retaliation: you were always ready, either to launch an attack of your own or to retaliate against an attack on your people. But there was now a second, far more pressing influence on my desire to be better armed. It was the growing belief among many Black revolutionary groups that community service alone would get us only so far. Some formations of Black militants, for instance, were all trained martial artists and carried crossbows, the only weapon that could legally and openly be used in Philly without a license. That made us male members of the BUC sit up and pay a little more attention to the group.

From then on, all we could see was our own weakness in comparison to the white establishment. For instance, when Martin Luther King was assassinated, those of us who had become politically inclined, including Sharp and me, went on the rampage. We tried to burn down a number of large furniture and clothing stores in our neighborhood, places we had come to view as alien establishments because of their white ownership. In fact, there were just three Black-owned stores or businesses in the entire neighborhood in which the Black Unity Council operated! As a kid I'd been aware of this imbalance but never really grasped the totality of the underlying system of oppression, in which a white minority lorded over Black people in their own communities. Our attempts to vandalize these businesses failed—the white owners had elaborate security systems in place and relationships with the police, whose arsenal of weapons far outstripped anything we could muster. Incidents like this stung, almost mocking our ability to act out in ways that captured the magnitude of our rage.

For a time, this boiling frustration was kept at bay by the women in the Black Unity Council. They were true community leaders and managed to bring whole families into the heart of our operation. My sister Beatrice was so zealous about her efforts that at some point or another, every member of the Shoatz clan contributed in some way to the cause. When my brother Daniel came home from a tour of duty with the US Air Force in the Far East, he teamed up with our paramilitary instructor to teach us a lethal style of karate he'd learned overseas. My mother, who'd been active in the PTA for years, brought in a number of concerned white individuals to a series of meetings engineered to address the critical state of the relationship between Black and white communities within the education system. My sister Yvette, a Peace Corps member recently returned from a foreign tour of duty to set up an alternative school under the auspices of the Philadelphia Board of Education, became instrumental in our plans to secure a space for our combination daycare–liberation school on Fifty-Sixth and Locust Street. We called it the Black House and acquired the necessary hardware—children's desks, chairs, and school supplies—through a process we called "expropriation."

Our ongoing self-education about the history of Black people in America had brought us to the conclusion that we were owed reparations. We'd been kidnapped from our native lands, gagged and bound and shackled on slave ships, and brought to a country that had treated us like animals, robbed us of our languages and cultures, and amassed unimaginable wealth on our backs by stealing the fruits of our labor. Seeing that the government would never admit to this reality or agree to pay back what had been stolen, revolutionary groups in the sixties were committed to acquiring resources and materials through any means necessary. Generations of slavery had impoverished our people. Now we would simply take what was needed. I had spent many years stealing from my own people, a hustle I'd pretended to enjoy but that had, over the years, coated my heart with something slimy and foul. To now experience the rush of expropriating resources from the White Man was like waking up from the dead.

Lisa had, by this time, become deeply involved in the BUC's work, and we raised our son in the heart of it. At one point, Betty even agreed to send Theresa and Sharon to join Lisa and me in our house on Reno Street. I set up a blackboard and chairs in the middle of the main front room and got excited teaching them about Black history. I had never realized a home could be a place to be jazzed about. As a kid I'd always treated my house as a kind of temporary rest stop, a place to eat or sleep before getting back to my real life on the streets. With Betty I'd gone a step further and filled the house with material comforts that I wrongly believed would compensate for the emptiness between us. But that shared space with Lisa was like a safe house, the place where we discussed all matters related to the movement and to our lives. Lisa tolerated nothing but my best self. The one time I raised my hand to her she simply said: "I'm a sista and you're a brotha, and brothas don't hit sistas." Shortly after that confrontation, she dropped the name Lisa and adopted the name Asani, based on the Swahili word meaning *rebel*. We weren't married; we both agreed that we didn't need the United States government to sanction our union. But that nom de guerre bound us to each other and to the struggle for Black liberation in America.

In 1968, I graduated from my training school and obtained a job as a machinist, first at General Electric and then at Westinghouse. They were both busy turning out war-related products for the ongoing conflict in Vietnam. I was spared from enlistment because I was still legally married to Betty and had three kids dependent on me. But there was another war that I was reluctantly embroiled in and equally disgusted by: the never-ending gang battles on the streets of Philadelphia.

That year, one of my Corner boys was shot and killed, allegedly by members of the Moon Gang. Arriving on the scene clad in my African dashiki caused a stir. I was a highly respected Old Head, which meant my moves and my words carried a lot of weight. But a lot of our members, particularly the young bloods, were unsure of how to relate to a gang-war fanatic turned revolutionary "brother." They expected me to lead them in a retaliatory attack. They were not prepared for my speech about Black-on-Black fratricide.

I found myself up against a boy named Dan Warlord who'd become the undisputed leader of the area and was already preparing his counterattack. I had personally driven this kid on lightning raids into the Moon Gang's territory just a few years ago, and he knew damn well that until very recently I'd been the foremost champion of "an eye for an eye, a life for a life." There on the street we clashed in an ideological battle for the minds of the other young men. Dan questioned my loyalty to the gang, my integrity, and my courage and insinuated that I had become "timid" with age. I was struck to the quick by his words, so much that I briefly considered participating in this "last" gang war—just to tide me over until the BUC could come up with some more powerful method of resolving such disputes. Instead, I fell back on pleading with my members to end the blood feud that was causing the wasteful loss of Black life.

I lost. I had to stand and watch as my Corner piled into their cars and headed for Moon territory. Two of them were shot that night by a skilled Moon fighter named David Richards, himself a respected Old Head, who had long since made a name for himself on the streets of Philadelphia. A lot of people told me that David Richards bore a strong resemblance to me. That in a different life, in different circumstances, we might have been brothers-in-arms rather than rivals. They said we thought alike, acted alike, in our dedication to whatever we perceived our life purpose to be. The difference was, I had turned that energy toward the movement, but it appeared this David Richards—who I learned was three years my junior—still had his gun trained on other young Black men.

In that moment I knew that interrupting this cycle of bloodshed called for a lot more than rhetoric. One evening the BUC was invited to address a huge gathering of rival gang members in the auditorium of the West Philadelphia High School. Sitting on the stage looking out at hundreds of antagonistic, energetic young men was exhilarating but intimidating. Less than five years ago, I'd have been among them, probably instigating some kind of disruption that would bring the whole thing to a halt, out of bravado or boredom. Fortunately, a highly capable community organizer had secured job opportunities and funding for various activities ahead of the meeting, and he handed these out to various gang leaders in exchange for them taking the stage and publicly advocating for an end to warfare in the community. It was one of the BUC's earliest successes.

But by far our most successful campaign was the picketing of a major national telephone company.

Two of our members, John King and his wife, Alice, both of whom worked for the company, brought our attention to the poor working conditions of the predominantly Black female switchboard operators. This fit right in with our understanding that in addition to facing daily physical assaults from a highly militarized police force, Black people were also victims of an economic warfare that had begun after the Civil War. On paper we'd been granted equal status to whites, but in reality we'd been forced into a second kind of slavery: wage slavery at the hands of businesses that refused to fairly compensate us for our labor. Everywhere we looked, Black workers put in longer hours for less pay than whites, worked menial jobs, and never dreamed of being promoted or appointed to any kind of senior or management position.

The Black Unity Council lost no time in joining the telephone workers' struggle to form a union, a move that brought us into direct conflict with a pack of white middle-aged union reps. These were old-school dudes, tough as nails, who had no doubt seen some battles and bloodshed in their times. They showed up to a meeting on Fifty-Second Street, smack in the middle of the hood, but were unfazed by our paramilitary formation and held their own until the Black women workers eventually voted them down.

We launched the picketing of the telephone company with a good deal of drama and media coverage. Our side of the picket line was a mix of men and women in African garb and combat clothing. On the other side were uniformed armed guards hired by the company, which was now facing a public relations disaster. They were forced to create a Black caucus and even appoint a Black public relations expert to oversee negotiations. This dude lived in a nice home in a trendy part of the city. He would invite us to formal cocktail parties where he attempted to get us to sell out other caucus members. One night he even asked me to join his PR company, promising I could "do more from the inside than from the streets." I literally laughed out loud in his face—he had no idea he was dealing with an ex-hustler who had zero interest in the kind of lifestyle he was dangling before me. Eventually, after holding out for several months, the workers won the right to better pay and promotions.

All the time, a shadow was creeping up behind us. If there is a calm before the storm, this was it, the era when the Black Liberation Movement celebrated some of its biggest victories. Thousands of people were putting their shoulders to the wheel, bending the great arc toward justice. But a war is a war. It rushes forward to its bloody end. A deeply militant strain was emerging in the BUC and it would not be contained. For too long Black people had been made to walk in chains under terror of the whip and the lash and the gun. America had feasted on us, set its dogs on us, built its prisons for us. Finally, we were starting to defend ourselves against the attacks. Those who'd taken it all on the chin were beginning to sit up and stand their ground.

So once the weapons started filtering into our ranks, we could not conceive of laying them down.

CHAPTER 9

A PEOPLE'S ARMY

Armed struggle is never undertaken lightly. It is always the final straw, a decision made by a man with his back up against the wall, when all other means have been tried and have failed. Everyone comes to it differently, some with conviction, some with doubts, in desperation or in anticipation of something—anything—that can change their circumstances. I am not talking about kids wielding guns in gang warfare or a soldier enlisting in the military. I am talking about revolutionaries, those who have rejected once and for all the oppressor's monopoly over violence, those of us who have rejected the state as the only legitimate purveyor of death.

For many members in the BUC, that decisive moment occurred the night a Black boy was gunned down in his own home by one of Rizzo's cops. It started with a routine traffic stop and ended with the cop chasing the boy on foot into his mother's house where, after a desperate struggle, he shot the kid to death. The cop himself received some minor knife wounds when the boy's mother, after witnessing her own son's murder, attacked the killer cop. I remember standing outside that house, across from the state liquor store on Sixtieth and Spruce Streets, watching the medics attend to the policeman's injuries while the body of the dead child lay on the sidewalk. I was overcome with a feeling that was completely alien to me. Until that night, I'd feared the police. For all my bravado, I'd been too intimidated to ever even think about talking back to or confronting those devils in blue. But as a large crowd gathered around me I was seized with a desire to jump one of the cops who was milling around, commandeer his weapon, and shoot him with it. It was the first time my instinct for retaliation had been directed toward a target other than a rival gang member. I struggled to contain what was boiling inside me. I reasoned that if I acted rashly I would endanger a lot of innocent bystanders. I told myself I was a respected community organizer now and must behave accordingly. With a huge effort I pulled myself together and headed for my sister Beatrice's house, where we began to draw up posters graphically laying out what had occurred and inviting the community to a meeting to discuss this latest senseless tragedy.

The following evening scores of people poured into the church—mothers and their kids, old couples and adolescents, even representatives from local gangs who came to pledge their support as organized units. The Black Unity Council was thrilled with this turnout but unfortunately we weren't prepared to offer concrete solutions, or even guide the discussion in a clear direction. We were unable to channel the energy of this mass gathering, and as a result a few opportunists in the crowd tried to usurp us.

One of them was a preacher at a different neighborhood church. On the heels of the BUC's meeting, he set up a kind of town hall in which he invited community members to express their grievances directly to representatives from the police department. When we arrived, we found this Black preacher standing at a podium right alongside a white cop! This infuriated us, but we tried our best to assault him with a battery of questions that wouldn't allow him to rationalize the murder of that young boy. There were a couple of fired-up people in the room, including Mau Mau and an old buddy of mine, a Vietnam War combat veteran who had been wounded and decorated for uncommon bravery under fire. This position gave him license to demolish the police supervisor's assertions that his officer had "no choice but to use deadly force." But we quickly realized that most of the people in the room were older community members, affiliated with that particular church and too trusting of their pastor, who was essentially acting as a buffer for the cop—shielding him from blame and deflecting some of the more damning comments and questions. It was clear that he was attempting to curry favor with the police department to advance some agenda of his own.

That was when Mau Mau staged a walkout of a large crowd of angry young men. Out on the street, my old Corner boy Dan Warlord volunteered his house for an impromptu meeting. I couldn't believe this was the same guy who just a year ago had openly accused me and the entire Black Unity Council of being too soft because we turned our backs on gang wars! We all piled into his living room, where Mau Mau led us all in a heated debate about our need to form Black community militias. Every person in the room had been sickened by the preacher's bootlicking of the cops, so it didn't take him long to convince the rest of us.

That very evening, a youth-oriented paramilitary formation called the Liberators was born. Mau Mau wanted us to immediately dissolve the BUC and come on board as senior members of this new group, but we were reluctant to simply give up on our non-military plans to build a school and cultural center. So we agreed to a close alliance for the time being.

But something inside me had changed. I knew I would no longer be content to attend assemblies or sit in discussions or even further my self-education without a corresponding commitment to self-defense, meaning armed struggle.

Gradually, the male members of the Black Unity Council began to stockpile weapons. At first we limited ourselves to what could be acquired legally, but when word spread that we were slowly transforming from a purely community-driven organization into a paramilitary formation, we discovered a black market for heavier-duty arms and ammunition. Guys with contacts came out of the woodwork with offers, leads, smuggled goods. On one occasion we secured a large box of US-military hand grenades, which we divided amongst our members. We had been in possession of them for barely twenty-four hours when I heard on the news that someone had lobbed a grenade into the police substation on Twenty-Fourth and Market Street. This sparked a citywide police search including raids on our members' homes, where cops tore up floorboards in a desperate attempt to locate our stockpiles. We had to act fast, but cautiously. Rizzo's pigs were hot for us and it was nearly impossible for a Black man to move freely carrying such an incendiary load. So some of the female members of the group stepped up and volunteered to transport the grenades to safe houses or nondescript locations where they could be stashed until the coast was clear. Thanks to their courageous actions, we managed to avoid a full-on crackdown, but the whole incident shook us up because it made one thing very clear: the state had tolerated our community service work, but it would not tolerate any of our attempts to embark on a serious self-defense strategy. While they might turn a blind eye to food drives and gang-intervention programs, they would not sit back while we accumulated firepower. It was around this time that the FBI opened a file on the BUC, a fact we wouldn't discover until many years later.

Almost immediately following the grenade attack and subsequent raid, a split occurred within the BUC, a huge crack in our foundation that could not be ignored, patched up, or stepped over. On one side of the line were the more militant members of the group, who felt completely validated by the police's panicked response to our guerrilla tactics. But all the women lined up on the opposite side. They were vocally opposed to the new direction we were taking and wanted to continue on the same track as before—strengthening our local base, building our school. It brought our membership into the heart of a highly explosive debate within the Black community, which centered around the myth that, historically, Black women had been so overbearing that their behavior tended to stunt the social growth of the Black man. This was said to have begun during slavery, instituted and perpetuated by the slave owners as a way of keeping the Black man and woman forever divided. I've since educated myself on the deep flaws inherent in this argument, all of which stem from men's failure to understand patriarchy as the dominant oppressive system in our society. Unfortunately at the time, this myth of the domineering Black woman and the emasculated Black man had gained wide acceptance in the struggle, and women were always admonished to curb their harsh tongues and forceful personalities in order to "help" the Black man become more assertive in his efforts to uplift the race. So though Asani and the other women made a spirited defense of their positions, they were outflanked when the male members accused them of "stifling" the men. In the many intervening years between then and now, I have revisited this moment: the moment when the BUC officially became a paramilitary organization. Nothing, not even the gift of hindsight, can tell me whether or not we made the right move. All I can say is that it was a decision taken exclusively by the men, and any women who remained in our ranks did so purely out of loyalty to their male partners.

Back then, we didn't have a lot of time for analysis, or introspection. Shortly after the police raid, I found myself in a chair at a local barbershop listening to some older Black patrons discussing a hunting expedition they'd been on. It turned out they were members of a group of Black hunters who had their own lodge and firing range in south New Jersey. A yearly membership fee entitled you to frequent both establishments, and even bring along guests. Within a week I had signed up and carted a handful of BUC members out into the Jersey wilderness, along with our high-powered hunting rifles and shotguns. Of all of us, Asani displayed the best marksmanship, shouldering that rifle like she'd been born with it and demonstrating almost deadly precision, even though it was her first time on a range. I was thrilled by her performance.

But that first trip out into hunters' territory showed us how woefully unprepared we were to withstand any kind of serious armed attack, what with our rudimentary knowledge of weapons and, with the exception of Asani, our amateurish shooting skills.

Still, we developed a taste for the outdoors. Sharp's relatives had a farm in southern Virginia, near the place where Nat Turner carried out his slave revolt in 1831. We camped out there and taught ourselves to shoot. On weekends when we couldn't get out of the city, we disappeared deep into Fairmount Park, a massive reserve of thousands of acres of forest right in the heart of Philadelphia, which resembled the terrain and vegetation of much of rural Pennsylvania. We ran ourselves ragged in that park, learning to navigate trails and traverse through dense foliage and undergrowth, and generally toughening up our bodies in preparation for whatever lay ahead. We didn't know what that would be, only that in order to face it we would need to be completely self-sufficient, able to live on next to nothing, to travel light, to endure great hardships, and to possess a range of skills that would allow us to outlast our adversary. This was urban guerrilla warfare training 101, and in the absence of an official manual we created our own.

But this new direction we were going in was not without its risks. White America has a deep and lingering fear of armed and organized Black people, and we had to exercise constant vigilance not to arouse unnecessary suspicion, rancor, or aggression. This was especially true of our training sessions out in Virginia, where we were surrounded and outnumbered by rural white communities.

On one such occasion, Lewis, Sharp, and I had made the trip out to the farm to work on our sidearms training. We had brought along a revolver and an automatic pistol. Lewis, being the best shot among us, had become the de facto trainer. Both he and Sharp were making tremendous progress in handling the sidearms, but despite my best efforts, my marksmanship was not improving. It seemed like a lost cause, so I attempted to offset that disadvantage by becoming very proficient in altering, concealing, and rapidly firing a shotgun.

After hours of weapons training, we strapped on our combat boots, canteens, and knives and did a four-mile military run before calling it a night. When we got back to the farm, Sharp's relatives were looking a little shifty. They wouldn't come right out and say it, but they let us know that a couple of their neighbors—who were openly racist—were aware of our presence and had made remarks that amounted to thinly veiled threats that they would not tolerate Black radicals with loaded weapons running amok on their territory.

After that we kept a pretty low profile, but on our way back to Philly, just outside of town, my car broke down! On any other occasion this wouldn't have been a big deal, but after the warning from Sharp's family, none of us really wanted to hang around on a roadside of a hostile town in our military garb with bags full of guns. We decided that Sharp and Lewis would hop on a bus with our supplies and I would call my father—the best mechanic I knew.

He showed up, no questions asked, and got right to work. It had been a while since we'd hung out one-on-one. While tinkering with the engine he commented a little sadly that I now spent all my time with the brothers in the movement and only called on him to get out of a scrape. That really got us talking—about all kinds of stuff we'd never addressed. He told me how much he and my mother had just wanted to give us kids a "better life," and how disillusioned they were with the state of things. He'd always been a man to keep his head down or look away. But now he kept a loaded shotgun in the front room and every evening he kept watch through the window—if he saw white policemen manhandling someone in the street, he intervened. I couldn't believe it! As kids we'd sometimes spend hours looking for the old man's revolver and could never lay our hands on it because he had it tucked away between the ceiling and the roof rafters. Now here he was with a weapon locked and loaded and within arm's reach at all times! It made me look at him a whole new way.

It also made me realize that we were now a true guerrilla army, with the complete backing of our community. The lines between trained paramilitaries like me and ordinary "respectable" folks like my dad had become so blurred that it would frustrate any efforts the cops made to single us out.

We started using this to our advantage. Instead of hiring storage units or warehouses for our supplies, we concealed them in our own homes. I kept at least one semiautomatic carbine with thirty-shot magazines, a shotgun or two loaded with double odd buckshot, and an automatic pistol and revolver as well as several hand grenades in the bedroom. I always had at least one of these weapons close at hand whenever I was on the second floor of our house, and a high-powered rifle lived in our downstairs closet. I used lumber to reinforce our front door: after witnessing and hearing about numerous police shootings in the neighborhood, we had learned that if you could prevent the police from kicking in your door, and if you could withstand a few salvos of intense gunfire, you stood a much better chance of talking your way out of an otherwise potentially lethal situation. In the event that our fortress was breached, we had a drill that required Asani to gather up the children and place them in our old cast-iron bathtub, which would offer them some minimal protection from flying bullets.

Every day was studded with reminders of how perilous the situation was for our children. One afternoon I was drilling a fellow BUC member on the proper cleaning and handling of a rifle in our dining room when I accidentally fired a bullet through the ceiling. In a panic I rushed upstairs to the kids' bedroom, which was located directly above the dining table, but fortunately the bullet had lodged itself somewhere between the two floors. On another occasion I was practicing the rapid loading, unloading, and simulated firing of a rifle when it went off, shooting a bullet through the blackboard on the wall in our middle room. But the most troubling situation Asani and I faced was the day our son got hold of a revolver. I wasn't home but Asani told me that he removed the gun from a drawer in our bedroom and was standing at the head of the stairs brandishing it in a threatening manner as she came toward him. He was holding it with both hands, aiming it right at her, just like he'd seen us doing in our drills. Asani was deadly afraid it would go off, but she knew she had to disarm him before he turned and ran, possibly injuring himself or one of the other children in the process. She patiently eased her way up the stairs while gently coaxing him to hand over the weapon. He held his ground the whole time, making shooting gestures and laughing like it was a game. When she finally managed to wrestle it out of his hands, she cuffed him out of frustration and sheer relief. Shortly after that scene, Asani became pregnant with our second child. And almost simultaneously, Betty demanded the return of our two daughters, Theresa and Sharon. I was loathe to give them up. I was thrilled to be raising them in the thick of the movement, teaching them Black history and even training them in martial arts like karate! But after a few furious phone calls from Betty, I relented. I would never live under the same roof as either one of them again.

I never had time to dwell on any of this because life was happening faster than I could live it! If we had any doubts about the road we had chosen, they were always quieted by the Black Power conferences we attended regularly. These were large gatherings where activists from all over the country came together to discuss what could be done to transfer some of the country's political, economic, and social power into Black communities' hands. These assemblies sharpened and clarified our basic position, which was that capable and committed Black revolutionaries should be organized into militia-style armed units. We arrived at this conclusion after careful study of the prevailing conditions of Black people in America and of white society's response to the Civil Rights Movement since the Birmingham bus boycott of 1955. We were living and witnessing the emptiness of the phrase "nonviolence." Wherever the movement raised its head, it was violently attacked by the racist elements in society and their servants and lackeys within the police forces and the National Guard. This would in turn provoke Black people to embark on reckless rampages of counterproductive rioting, burning, and looting, which would trigger further attacks, repression, and violence from the state. We saw this cycle as a tremendous waste of life and resources, and believed firmly that militias that were set up, organized, trained, educated, and controlled by the Black community would go a long way in correcting the problem. We were fed up with lawlessness and rogue banditry—especially those of us who came from the streets and had known nothing but turf wars, hustling, and incarceration. What we wanted now was discipline in our ranks, formations of culturally and politically educated Black men and women capable of leading us out of the plantation.

Unlike in the early BUC days, when I'd had to fight for respect among gangbangers who saw me as some kind of sellout, we discovered a newfound reverence for our political activities among the local community. I remember nights when a bunch of us from the BUC would be walking down the streets in our military fatigues and combat boots and gang members would approach us in the dark with their old challenge: "Where ya'll from?" Instead of calling out our gang affiliations, we'd simply answer, "We're from the Black Liberation Army!" It was enough to immediately make them apologetic. They'd say, "Sorry, man, we didn't know ya'll were *brothers*." There was a profound shift in the very culture of the city. The heart that beat in Philadelphia's chest now pumped fresh blood to a fresh beat: a politically awoken rhythm that found its echo throughout the country. We were on the lip of a bigger, national movement, which initially reached us only through news bulletins about iconic Black freedom fighters: Max Stanford, a leading figure in RAM whom the authorities were trying their best to destroy. Herman Ferguson, who was playing a prominent part in the gargantuan struggle to bring New York City's school system under community control. H. Rap Brown, chairman of SNCC, who had earned the accolade of public enemy number one. Stokely Carmichael, who was widely considered the only person capable of unifying and leading the many emerging Black revolutionary formations around the country.

For several years the BUC had been a kind of island, aware that we were connected through our roots to a vast mycelial network of revolutionaries, but otherwise acting independently at a highly localized level.

This changed in the summer of 1969, when we sought out and began to build an alliance with the local chapter of the Black Panther Party for Self-Defense.

PART TWO

CHAPTER 10

WHEN WE WERE FREE

B efore he was assassinated in the Audubon Ballroom in Harlem in 1965, Malcolm X warned of a global race war. He did not hesitate to name the cause of the prevailing situation: a long history of white racism, colonialism, and empire, against which the colored minorities of the world were now rising. He described America as a powder keg, and her Black population as the fuse capable of lighting the explosive substance within and pretty much setting the whole damn world on fire. He prophesied a total revolution—not a polite tussle over "civil rights" but a full-blown battle for the basis of emancipation, which is to say, for land.

Long before most Black people got on board with his message, the federal government took Malcolm X's words to heart. Under the leadership of J. Edgar Hoover, the FBI began to systematically search for and catalog the most capable individuals and organizations dedicated to Black liberation in America. Not for a minute did the agency underestimate the threat posed by dedicated and disciplined groups of Black freedom fighters and their white comrades. The bureau's archives, which have now largely been made public, include everything from training manuals to correspondence to propaganda materials created by these groups.

The Black Panthers accounted for the FBI's largest file and was the target of the bulk of the agency's efforts and resources, including informants, detectives, spies, and a range of other undercover agents and operatives. To this day I believe this was due to the party's clarity of vision. They had a thorough grasp of capitalism and fascism that came from a lived experience of Blackness, and that enabled them to reach and unify masses of people who had previously been lost, apathetic, or afraid.

When I and other BUC members first visited the Panther offices located on Nineteenth and Columbia Avenue in North Philadelphia, we were largely ignorant of the level of government surveillance of their activities. It was only gradually, as our link with the party deepened, that we would come to understand the lengths to which the state was prepared to go to not only eviscerate the Panthers, but bury all trace of them forever. It was only after we had joined forces with the BPP that we came to fully comprehend what it meant to be blacklisted by the United States government, and to feel the deadly weight of its so-called national security apparatus.

Our first point of contact, in the year 1969, was a dude named Mitch Edwards, a defense captain of the party's chapter in Philly. He must have been close to my age, midtwenties, and he was responsible for training and leading a platoon of teenaged Panthers stationed at several offices throughout the city. Given the Black Unity Council's status as a prominent and respected local group, that initial meeting was one of equals. However, it quickly became clear that the Panthers had a whole lot going for them that was beyond our scope or ability.

For a start, they were a national organization. They had a newspaper, a tool the BUC had never even considered, which allowed them to educate a much wider audience on their programs and ideas. Most crucially they had a fully functional free breakfast program for kids, which earned them tremendous goodwill in the neighborhoods and also served as a model for a community-based form of independent government.

As far as we were concerned, the Panthers had one weakness: they had not dedicated sufficient time and resources to developing a comprehensive military strategy, which forced them to suffer humiliating defeats and unnecessary casualties at the hands of the police. In December 1969, Chicago police officers staged a raid on the party's headquarters, killing Fred Hampton, the twenty-one-year-old chairman of the Illinois chapter of the BPP, and twenty-two-year-old Mark Clark, an active party member. Police also severely wounded several others, including a female Panther who was in the advanced stages of a pregnancy. We watched this news with growing frustration that the party's top leadership wasn't willing to take the steps necessary to protect their own cadres from death and incarceration.

Then, in a sudden but welcome change of direction, Huey P. Newton issued the following directive: "Our organization has received serious threats...We draw the line at the threshold of our doors. It is therefore mandated as a general order to all members of the Black Panther Party for Self-Defense that all members must acquire the technical equipment to defend their homes...Any member of the Party having such technical equipment who fails to defend his threshold shall be expelled from the Party for Life."

Now we were on the same page! This newly stated position, combined with the dissemination of official Panther pamphlets entitled "Forming Self-Defense Groups," was the green light for many members of the BUC to give themselves wholly to the Panthers' cause. These pamphlets served as a set of uniform guidelines for rank-and-file Panthers to recruit, organize, and train thousands of grassroots community volunteers into militias that would serve the Black community. It was exactly the kind of program the BUC had undertaken a couple of years earlier, but on a massive, nationwide scale. This change of direction was sufficient to put us completely in the service of the Black Panther Party.

We began to sell the Panther newspapers and help out with their breakfast program. We flocked to their political education, or PE, classes. It was expected that BUC members would not only attend all Panther rallies, but in many cases provide the necessary security during these functions, a task we were only too happy to fulfill despite the repeated objections of our female members. What we saw as the party's genuine concern over police repression and surveillance, Asani and the other women in the BUC called "Panther Paranoia." They believed many of the male leaders and activists were prone to hysteria, often jumping to conclusions or overreacting to perceived security threats.

One evening I was on duty at a political discussion when a couple of unidentified vehicles began circling the neighborhood. When we decided we needed some heavier artillery, I was sent home to pick up shotguns, rifles, and one of my metal ammunition carriers. It was dark when I got to our place, and Asani was alone with the kids. She tried to stop me from leaving, first with verbal pleas and finally by physically blocking my path. When I went to get around her, she grabbed a hold of the shotgun I had in one hand. She had fire in her eyes! She told me to stop acting crazy, to call off the discussion for the time being and reconvene when things had cooled down. It was a struggle to wrench the gun away from her, and as I turned my back on her and the kids, I realized that the question of armed struggle was becoming more than a disagreement—it was widening into a gulf, eating away at the complete trust and honesty that had once existed between us.

But there was no stopping the train. The city had caught the revolution virus and it was spreading to the most unlikely people and places. Up in North Philly, a priest named Father Paul Washington opened the doors of his Church of the Advocate for various Panther activities, and we packed the pews with local supporters whenever a Panther Central Committee member was in town to give a talk. Panther offices had sprung up all over: on Nineteenth and Columbia, Twenty-Ninth and Susquehanna Avenue; at Thirty-Sixth and Wallace Street; at Forty-Seventh and Walnut. There was also a facility in Germantown, and others would eventually find spaces in West and South Philly. A handful of loyal party members ran these operations, capable and dedicated men and women who, it seemed, worked round the clock in the service of the movement.

The first Panther activity that I participated in was a mass rally in front of the State Office Building on North Broad Street in support of a nationwide effort to win the release of Huey P. Newton. He had been arrested in 1967 in connection with the murder of an Oakland police officer named John Frey, and a huge coalition of Black and white liberation groups had been demanding his freedom. The words "Free Huey!" had become a kind of rallying cry for the whole movement, and these protests generally drew hundreds or even thousands of people. Mitch Edwards led the Philadelphia rally—we marched around the building, listened to speeches, and sang liberation songs.

Shortly after that, I drove a bunch of Panthers and Black Unity Council members to New York City to attend a similar rally demanding the release of the Panther 21—the largest single group of Black Panthers imprisoned anywhere in the country. These New York–based Panthers stood accused of coordinating a major attack on two police stations in New York City. Their arrest represented just the tip of the iceberg of the government's attempts to neutralize Black revolutionaries. The Panther Party leadership at the time devised the ingenious tactic of turning their members' legal trials into high-profile media spectacles. This effectively transformed any arrested or detained Panthers into living martyrs, people who had sacrificed their freedom for the cause. It put the authorities in a terrible dilemma because it turned their own weapon—the courts and the courthouses—against them! They were trapped between the options of releasing revolutionaries back into the community or dealing with a torrent of negative publicity around these controversial trials, including in the international press.

When we arrived in the city for the Panther 21 trial, we assembled at the courthouse in downtown Manhattan alongside hundreds of protesters. As we marched we sang, and the song went something like this:

Free the twenty-one! Free the twenty-one, you fascist pigs!
Free the twenty-one, we need our warriors beside us!

Uniformed New York City policemen, mounted on horseback, followed us around the block. We listened to a speech by Don Cox, the West Coast field marshal for the Black Panthers, who was at that time probably the third or fourth in command of the entire party.

But rallies were just one square on the chessboard. Before too long, the local Panther cadre in Philadelphia had informed their West Coast leadership about the Black Unity Council's hardcore training in self-defense. Shortly thereafter, we received a request to share our military hardware with the top brass of the Panther Party.

Until then, we had been laboring under the impression that the Panthers, being a coordinated national movement, possessed their own arsenal. To learn that a small local outfit like the BUC could be called upon to beef up their supplies was a serious wake-up call to guys like me and Sharp. But we quickly shook off our disappointment and put out a call among our female membership for a volunteer to transport a number of hand grenades in her personal luggage on a flight to California—a task she undertook despite the women's opposition to our armed activities, and with hardly any fanfare for her courage.

Because that's how it was back then. It was a time of doing, a time of sacrifice. It was, in a way, a time before fear. We were audacious. We did not ask if something *could* be done; we asked only what *needed* to be done. There were no limits to our demands because we were demanding things first and foremost from ourselves. No more holding a begging bowl out to our oppressors. Instead, we had identified the needs of our people and drafted the terms and conditions under which we would struggle for them. The Panther Party's training manuals included strict instructions on how to transform from civilians into soldiers: rise early, develop physical strength, discipline our minds and bodies. Every day was boot camp, right there in the heart of the city, in broad daylight. It was a time of regimented militancy, but you could also say it was the time when we were most free.

Panthers were hijacking planes to foreign countries where they could seek asylum, mainly Cuba but also a few with sympathetic governments in Africa, including Algeria and Tanzania. By this time Eldridge Cleaver had established a kind of Black Panther government-in-exile in Algiers, and he personally received those who managed to escape death and incarceration on American shores.

As for the authorities, the only thing worse in their minds than the flight of wanted Panthers was the exodus of white people into the arms of revolutionary formations.

Groups like the Weather Underground, whose membership was entirely white, became a thorn in the side of the establishment, undertaking some of the most daring attacks on the state and even breaking their members out of jail. On college and university campuses things were reaching a fevered pitch, spurred on by students who were opposed to the outmoded, authoritarian, and racist school administrators. This, coupled with vehement anti–Vietnam War sentiment among the student body, brought white, Black, Latino, and Asian students together in huge numbers to demand sweeping changes in the education system. They clamored for a dismantling of the old colonial curriculum, to be replaced with programs that taught them the true histories of their own people: Black studies, Latino studies, Native American studies, Asian studies. In all of these movements, it was Black students who led their peers into the most militant forms of protest, occupying buildings or organizing sit-ins until their demands were met. Sometimes these actions turned violent, with students taking up arms in self-defense, and that was big news because people felt that if privileged college and university students were resorting to such extreme measures, it meant unrest had reached new heights. Panicked authorities called in the pigs and turned their campuses into active shooting galleries, riot police versus unarmed students. But of course it was the massacre of four white students by the National Guard at Kent State University in Ohio that stole most of the headlines.

By now the notion that we were embroiled in a full-scale conflict was no longer in dispute. This awakening, the awareness of ourselves as combatants against a hostile government, connected us to much larger, and much deadlier, armed uprisings around the world. For some years Huey P. Newton and Bobby Seale had been reproducing and distributing the writings of the Chinese revolutionary Mao Tse-tung, who taught us that "political power grows from the barrel of a gun." For many of us it was a new sensation to learn that Black people's quest for emancipation in the United States bore such a strong resemblance to the plight of brown and yellow people around the world, many of whom believed that the oppressed must turn to guerrilla warfare to win their freedom. We familiarized ourselves with the works of the Afro-Caribbean revolutionary Frantz Fanon and the Argentine-Cuban guerrilla leader Che Guevara. We read Marcus Garvey and Ho Chi Minh.

In 1967, Muhammad Ali famously answered a young white reporter's questions on his draft refusal by saying: "If I'm going to die, I'll die right here fighting *you*. *You* my enemy, not Viet Congs or Chinese or Japanese. *You* my opposer when I want freedom, *you* my opposer when I want justice, *you* my opposer when I want equality. Want me to go somewhere and fight for you? You won't even stand up for me right here in America."

A couple of years later another Black man made headlines for taking an equally bold stand. But he would pay for it with his life.

Jonathan Jackson was only seventeen years old when he stormed the Marin County Courthouse in California with several semiautomatic weapons. He proceeded to free three Black prisoners from San Quentin prison, one of whom was standing trial while the two others had been brought as witnesses. Together, the four young men took a white judge, prosecutor, and three jurors hostage, demanding, in exchange for their release, freedom for the famous Soledad Brothers. This was a group of Black prisoners including Jonathan's brother, George Jackson, who would soon be facing trial for the killing of a white guard at San Quentin prison—a charge that all three accused denied. During the courthouse raid, neither Jonathan nor any of his accomplices fired a single shot from any of their weapons. They used piano wire to bind their hostages, and verbal commands to usher them from the courtroom. When they were accosted by a bevy of newspaper reporters and cameramen on the courthouse steps, Jackson and the three men he'd liberated allowed themselves to be photographed, while reiterating their demand for freedom for the Soledad Brothers. Finally they bundled their hostages into an escape van destined for a nearby radio station, where they intended to transmit their message to a national audience. The whole thing was a brilliantly maneuvered, bloodless operation—until local police fired on the van, killing Jackson, two of the prisoners he had liberated from the courthouse, and the white judge.

When I walked into a friend's house that evening and saw the pictures from that courthouse splashed across the front page of the newspapers, I froze. I couldn't take my eyes off the image of Jonathan Jackson, assault rifle in one hand, disarming cowing sheriffs, while in the background the three liberated Black prisoners stood guard over their bewildered-looking captives. Before I could even pick up the paper to read the whole story, I began to cry. I had seen Jonathan's face in the papers many times before, always in connection with his brother George and their revolutionary ideas, but seeing him now as a martyr was a new sensation. It made me feel that we had a true leader, someone who was urging us through his own actions to intensify our struggle for liberation. It was not a feeling of sorrow—more of a renewed conviction that all three young men had died a glorious death, one that their oppressed kinfolk could not only understand, but actually envy.

I took the newspaper out to my car and sat alone for a while, trying to collect myself. But only one thought was flashing through my mind: *The shit was on.* All doubts, restraints, and equivocations were things of the past. Those of us who had committed to this fight were going all in to either win our freedom or perish in the attempt.

I wasn't alone. In the coming days just about everyone I encountered seemed to be in a state of delirium, enthused, energized, and just plain *ready.* It felt like a huge wheel had been shifted from a rut, pushed with great difficulty to the edge of a slope, and was about to be sent rolling. Once it got going it would gather too much speed to stop, so we either had to keep up or get crushed beneath it. Pictures of Jonathan Jackson and the Marin County hostage crisis circulated far and wide: they were reproduced in the Panther papers, and penetrated every home in America through television screens.

They also set in motion a train of events that would culminate in the August 29, 1970, attack on the Philadelphia Fairmount Park Guard Station.

I will not jeopardize any party's freedom or safety by revealing what I know about that attack, but I must state for the record that it was carried out in accord with, and at the behest of, the leadership of the Black Panther Party. It was an attack that would cost me everything but my life; since that fateful summer day, I have been a fugitive and a prisoner for forty-seven years and counting.

CHAPTER 11

THE ATTACK ON FAIRMOUNT PARK

I won't say we were naïve. At no point in our lives had any of us enjoyed the luxury of innocence. We had come up rough, in a tough world. And the less you have to begin with, the less "sacrifice" plays a part in your life. We knew what was coming: the underground phase. Something every revolutionary movement must at some point encounter. We knew also what we'd be giving up: our families. Life among our community, faces unhidden. Our names, our identities. Freedom to move or even exist in the daylight. All of that sat heavily on our shoulders, but it wasn't enough to deter us. The honor codes we'd acquired during our gang days, the lives already lost in service of the movement, the unspoken pacts and promises we'd made, all this loomed larger than any personal motive or desire, so that when the call came, we answered.

The Panthers were ambitious. The party was led by young people, full of fire, who were not content with sporadic actions. They had a political vision for America that would have to be organized and orchestrated on a national scale. So it came as no surprise to any of us when the Central Committee announced in early 1970 that they intended to host a Revolutionary People's Constitutional Convention, where Black nationalists and representatives of all the various liberation organizations inside the country would be called together to rewrite the United States Constitution. Because of Philadelphia's historic significance as the site of the Declaration of Independence in 1776, the city quickly became the center of gravity for this event.

By this point, owing largely to the actions of the BUC, Philly had earned a reputation as a revolutionary stronghold, a reputation that ran parallel to Frank Rizzo's status as a man who believed not in the divine right of kings, but in the divine right of cops: the only man capable of containing and possibly even neutralizing the power of our people.

Up until now, we had managed to avoid open confrontations with Rizzo's army, carrying out clandestine activities or burying ourselves within the community as a shield against a full-scale attack from the police. But this had resulted in a perception within the movement that us local cadres were not willing to step to Rizzo. There was a refrain that *stung*: Why had no one in Philly "corrected" (meaning "offed") one of his pigs? A rumor began to circulate that Huey P. Newton actually feared assassination at the hands of one of Rizzo's henchmen, which might even deter him from attending the plenary session of the Constitutional Convention. So from various quarters the die was being cast for some kind of confrontation that would prove our commitment to the cause.

Asani and the other women members of the Black Unity Council hated this mindset. Many of these women were mothers, including my sister Beatrice—she and Sharp had become a couple and had a son. So the female members were perpetually fighting our efforts to move ahead with military plans. I had come a long way in my notions about women. Since my failed marriage with Betty and subsequent partnership with Asani, my perceptions had broadened to find a place for "sisters" in the struggle right alongside the men. But I guess I still didn't truly view them as equals since I was able to brush off most of their concerns, objections, and oppositions about the direction the movement was taking and what it would mean for the mothers who were left behind. Sometimes when you're the one controlling the kite you don't think about how fast the string can unravel. You're too busy flying.

In any case, the male BUC members reached a consensus that in the event of the men being forced to go on the run, the women would remain aboveground in order to take care of the kids. To do this, they would need three things: Food for their families if the breadwinners had to disappear for a while. Money for the BUC's activities, which would have to continue with or without us. And a warren of safe houses that could conceal us, and eventually deliver us to more secure locations after we launched our attack. This last one was the easiest. A huge support network radiated outward around us, starting with our families and extending to neighbors, community members, churchgoers, shopkeepers, schoolteachers, bus drivers. The rest of it would need to be acquired the old-fashioned way: through expropriation.

In the early hours of August 28, we assembled at one of the safe houses. Two rented vehicles waited outside: a large truck for the food haul and a small van for the bank raid. Every man in the group had his instructions: someone would watch the bank all day, keeping track of the employees' movements and keeping an eye out for suspicious individuals who might be undercover cops. That person would also join the actual raid later that afternoon, so they had a vested interest in making sure no detail went unnoticed. Two teams were dispatched to different parts of the city where they would wait with our rented vehicles for a signal from the expropriators. Meanwhile, Wes Davis and I went "grocery shopping."

For hours we followed a couple of haulers around on their delivery routes to various supermarkets. There were a few false starts and one aborted attempt, but by ten o'clock in the morning Wes had managed to commandeer a fifteen-ton refrigerated truck packed with frozen food. This entailed stopping the vehicle, subduing and restraining the driver, donning his white clothes, and getting the booty to a safe location, all without harming any innocent parties and without arousing suspicion from any authorities.

Not for nothing had we spent years preparing for this moment. As soon as we had the driver safely on the floor, Wes made a call to our two standby teams. In a loose caravan we made our way to a predetermined spot right outside of Philadelphia, where we backed the rear end of the meat hauler directly into the back of our rented truck and got busy transferring huge amounts of food into our possession. Then, as one of the teams drove our loot back to a Panther facility in the community, Wes Davis and I took the meat hauler deep into the suburbs, followed by two of our comrades in an escort car. I don't even remember the name of the nondescript town where we finally abandoned the truck and its driver, leapt into the escort car, and drove back to execute part two of the plan. Sometimes adrenaline makes you forget everything but the most critical details. Plus, the hard part was only just beginning.

Once back in Philly, we switched vehicles again. This constant turn-over, the constant change of guard, was built into all our plans. Nothing predictable. Stay one step ahead of our adversary, keep ourselves and them on their toes. Our bench was deep, adaptable, flexible. Half the team took up positions outside the bank—they would be tasked with engaging the police or any hostile force that might attempt to sabotage our escape. Lewis, Sharp, and I would do the heavy lifting.

Lewis was driving the small van. Sharp, who had been watching the bank all day, joined me in the rear, where we donned coveralls over our regular clothes, our weapons hidden from sight—he was armed with a handgun; I carried a sawed-off shotgun in a gym bag. Since I had never managed to master sidearms, a shotgun remained my weapon of choice!

Lewis circled the block once, then let us out around the corner from the bank. We approached on foot, hyping ourselves by repeating Panther slogans and the words of revolutionary leaders. We could not afford to think, or slow our pace. We paused only once, in the foyer to don our masks. And then it was just happening.

We had allocated only three minutes for the entire raid and it went something like this: Weapons out, order everyone down on the floor. I kept everyone lying flat while Sharp vaulted the tellers' counter and collected the money. You'd be surprised at how much cash you can gather in three minutes. It feels like a lot longer when you have a roomful of hostages. Countdown, one hundred and eighty seconds. *Time.* Sharp leapfrogging back over the counter, both of us backing out of the bank, guns trained on the workers and customers still sprawled on the carpet. Our masks coming off, guns sliding back into bags, the two of us jogging across the street and past a fire station, where two dudes sitting outside had clearly become suspicious of what was going on inside the bank.

Faster. Halfway down the block we opened a gate between two houses, raced down an alleyway, across the street, into another alley, down an embankment, across some train tracks, up a different embankment, steep, panting but not stopping, up and up to the place where Lewis was waiting. Into the rear of the van, but not for long. He slowed down close to the house where we had launched that morning's activities, let us out, drove on while we disappeared.

By now, the police were on the loose, saturating the neighborhood, sniffing, stopping, searching, seizing. They made the mistake of busting through front doors, leaving the back alleys clear for us to scale fences and backyard gates all the way to safety. Guerrillas in their urban jungle habitat always make it back home.

But that was our last big stand. The following day, the day of the Fairmount Park attack, was the day everything changed.

There are various accounts of the evening a guard was shot to death in the Cobbs Creek outpost of Fairmount Park. There is the official story, peddled by the authorities and picked up by reporters, that lives on in microfilm in the archives of the Philadelphia public library. The families of the slain guards have their own tales of grief, as do the families of the men who were arrested in connection with the killings. My comrades, no doubt, will all remember things differently, diverging in the details. Court transcripts preserved the "legal" version of what happened. Lawyers and judges may retain one set of facts, while the cops retain another—and cops have long, stubborn memories.

Only five people admit to bearing witness to the events of August 29, 1970: a group of young boys, between the ages of eleven and sixteen, who happened to be walking home after basketball practice just after

8:30 p.m. that Saturday night. They said they were heading down the driveway toward the guardhouse on Sixty-Third and Catherine Street when they noticed a man on the path up ahead. They described him thus: "20 to 25, a Negro, five feet ten inches tall, weighing 170 with a bush haircut, small trim mustache, dark zipper jacket, dark pants and almond-shaped spectacles with gold frames." Just then an emergency patrol wagon pulled onto the driveway carrying two patrolmen, Henry Kenner and Joseph Harrington. The man flagged this vehicle down. It was dark—they couldn't make out much else of what happened. They heard gunshots. In a panic they entered the guardhouse, which was manned by Sergeant Frank Von Collins, a seventeen-year veteran of the Fairmount Park Guards. There with him were two park policemen, Anthony Massimo and Lawrence Bradley. When they heard the boys' account, the two policemen took off in their patrol car in search of the "Negro man." They found Harrington in his vehicle—he'd been shot in the mouth and was rushed to the Misericordia Division of Mercy Catholic Medical Center. Kenner managed to get one shot at the suspect as he fled on foot, but missed his mark.

With the five boys beside him, Von Collins made a call to a sergeant at League Island Guard House, at Sixteenth and Pattison Street in South Philadelphia, who supposedly said to him: "Frank, get your gun before you head out." Moments later, an unidentified man strode into the guardhouse. Drawing a pistol from his pocket, he is supposed to have said, "What's happening boys?" while advancing on Von Collins's desk. Von Collins ordered the boys to take cover in a side room. From behind the door, they heard several shots. They were found, sobbing, in that room twenty minutes later. Outside, Von Collins was dead at his desk.

Before the Fairmount Park guard's body was cold, Rizzo had decided that the men behind the attack were "Black nationalists," part of a "racist, revolutionary group called the Black Unity Council." He was beyond livid. Never before in the history of the city's oppressed Black populace had anyone dared to so frontally attack its racist and brutal police, and Rizzo unleashed a wave of repression, violence, and surveillance upon the Black community that none of us had witnessed before.

Barely an hour after the attack he had dispatched five hundred policemen into 787-acre Cobbs Creek Park with instructions to comb it through "inch by inch," setting in motion the biggest manhunt in the city's history. Soon the peripheries of South Philly's Tasker area and the Fairmount region of North Philadelphia were teaming with cops decked out in riot gear and strapped with shotguns. K-9 police units picked their way through embankments on either side of Cobbs Creek with massive, thousand-dollar German Shepherds straining at their leashes. Other squads descended on every neighborhood where Black people lived, and these search parties unearthed a strange and unlikely arsenal: a loaded six-shot .22-caliber revolver concealed in a brown paper bag; a foreign-made 7.65-mm automatic revolver wrapped in a pair of trousers tossed by the side of Cobbs Creek Parkway. In a respectable home on Fifty-Sixth Street and Osage Avenue, a loaded .30-30 rifle, boxes of ammunition, and three hand grenades; a fourth grenade, identical to the others, lying in a car parked on Market Street. On their hands and knees underneath another parked car a few streets down, police found a plastic bag holding a .32-caliber automatic pistol, a cartridge belt full of bullets, and yet another live fragmentation hand grenade. Upturning a large shaving kit on his desk, an unsuspecting officer was confronted with a loaded .38-caliber revolver and a live grenade with a string attached to the pin. As the police fanned out across Philadelphia, they came upon suitcases containing a pound of C-4 and an M-16 army rifle, and other suitcases holding a .45-caliber Colt, a .36-caliber cap and ball, a .38-caliber revolver, and a .38-caliber Brazilian pistol.

All these weapons were proof of an insurgency, but where were the insurgents? It confounded the pigs, made them rampage worse than ever: a confused animal is an angry one. Gun battles broke out in the community between police and residents, but the residents always seemed to have the upper hand. Two highway patrol officers were gunned down after they stopped members of an underground activist cell who were driving around in the vicinity of the Fairmount Park attack. Before dawn the following day, three men posing as trash collectors attempted to smash their way into the Panther office in West Philly. Later, helicopters and a mini-tank carrying hundreds of cops descended on other Panther Party offices in Germantown and North Philadelphia. All these measures were part of a massive, coordinated raid ordered by Rizzo with a single goal in mind, to arrest the five primary suspects in the Von Collins murder: Lewis Young; the brothers Wes and Victor "Sharp" Davis; twenty-three-year-old John King; and me.

But every way they turned, the cops either came up empty or found themselves fighting a losing battle. The Panther cadre had anticipated Rizzo's response, so when the axes and sledgehammers hit their doors, they answered with a hail of bullets from the upper floors behind sandbagged windows. Suffering casualties, the police were forced to withdraw to a point from which they could safely level a steady stream of gunfire on the Panther facilities for hours. They had the advantage of endless ammunition, and may have planned to simply outlast the Panther's supply of bullets before launching fresh attacks. But even this move was thwarted by the courageous and spontaneous actions of the surrounding community, who came out into the streets en masse in defense of the Panther offices and the frontline cadres. Confronted by scores of unarmed residents including women and children, the police were forced to enter into negotiations that allowed the Panthers to lay down their arms and surrender without fear of being murdered in broad daylight. Frustrated and humiliated at having to bow to this kind of community pressure from a group of people they barely considered human, the cops lashed out in other ways: on Columbia Avenue, on Wallace Street, on Queen Lane, Black men and even young boys were torn from their beds in the middle of the night, lined up against brick walls, forced to strip, beaten, cuffed, and marched off to police stations where they would spend several days in outdoor enclosures being brutalized and terrorized. Rizzo gave press conferences warning white residents to stay in their homes. "We are not dealing with men," he said. "We are dealing with criminals, barbarians. You'd be safer out in the jungle. Animals don't attack you for no reason." Photographs of us five suspects were circulated widely. Rizzo demanded—and received—federal arrest warrants for the fugitives. Pigs hammered on our families' front doors at night, sent in detectives and the FBI, brought out the big guns, then even bigger guns. They cast the net so wide they did manage to entrap a couple of my comrades, but I made it out of Philadelphia.

I didn't do it alone. Like so many revolutionaries before me I hitched a ride on the Underground Railroad, that old train that's carried so many slaves away from the plantation to freedom.

CHAPTER 12

FLIGHT

Shortly after Von Collins was shot, I stopped a motorist outside Fairmount Park and forced him to drive me to the home of the only person I knew in that neighborhood—my Aunt Vera. She was deep in the underworld of gambling, numbers playing, and gun running, and I knew she would have resources I could use. When I arrived she was standing behind the cash register of her little convenience store, ringing up a ham sandwich, a soda, and a pack of cigarettes for a customer. She didn't ask any questions or even say a word to me, just eyed me from behind her thick glasses. When the man left she walked across the store and flipped the sign in the window so that it read *Closed*. Then she shoved me through a door behind the counter that opened onto a staircase leading up to her living room, and drew all the curtains. For hours the drapes reflected a neon pattern of red, white, and blue—searchlights from cop cars pouring over every crack and crevice in the city.

We sat together all night long. At 11 p.m., she turned on the news. At that moment the television was my only connection to the rest of the BUC. I had no way of knowing who had been picked up, or what information they had been forced to divulge, and we were under strict orders to assume that in the event of a major police crackdown like the one that was underway, all previous plans should be discarded and fresh ones laid.

I had Aunt Vera make a call to Asani, instructing her to bring over a suitcase of essentials as soon as movement was possible. She arrived the next morning with the weapons and with news, but without our kids, whom she'd left with her sister. She said the cops were still swarming all over the streets. They had picked up Lewis Young and Wes Davis and were on a determined hunt for John King, Victor "Sharp" Davis, and me. I needed out, fast, but I couldn't show my face—already it had been plastered all over the newspapers, posters were up in police stations, and every television owner in Philadelphia knew what I looked like.

So while Aunt Vera got busy finding me a ride, Asani took me into the bathroom and shaved all the hair from my face and upper body, shaped my eyebrows, and teased out my Afro until it was almost as big as Angela Davis's. She dressed me in blue jeans, suede boots, and a shiny imitation leather jacket that I left open to show off my newly smooth chest and stomach. She had me put on sunglasses and practice using feminine gestures accompanied by an exaggerated high-pitched voice. The city's most-wanted guerrilla would blow town disguised as a flamboyant homosexual, carrying a suitcase full of guns and grenades, riding passenger in a nice car belonging to a nice couple just taking a little weekend vacation outside the city.

And though we hadn't planned it this way, Asani climbed into the back seat with me, and sat with her shoulder pressed to mine all the way to New York.

CHAPTER 13

SOLDIERS IN THE STRUGGLE AND ENEMIES OF THE PEOPLE

This was the war of the flea. Our goal was to drive the dog of empire to madness with our incessant, invisible presence. Soon it wouldn't even know where we were biting, it would just burn all over with itching. If we had started out as a nuisance, a swarm of mites, then the 1970s marked our advancement into the plague that would pester, torment, frustrate, and eventually infect the oppressor's social, political, and economic system with a deadly disease called revolution. We would make America froth at the mouth before keeling over.

In Philadelphia I was wanted for murder in the first degree, assault and battery, unlawful weapons possessions, and conspiracy. But when we reached New York City, Asani and I were received like royalty.

In Harlem, a leading Panther named Rishad told us that the central party headquarters in Oakland, California, had praised our attack on the Fairmount Park station as a "right-on move," which in Panther parlance was one of the highest laudatory statements. Rishad had been instructed to give me all the assistance I needed, including enabling me to lie low until things cooled off. To that end, he'd arranged for us to stay with his own relatives in upstate New York, and pretty soon we were on a train heading for Peekskill, a small city sitting on a bay on the east side of the Hudson River.

From the train station we caught a cab to the address we'd been given, but asked the driver to drop us off a few streets over so we could approach the residence on foot—I was still cautious and jumpy and felt that pulling up in a taxi might draw too much attention. As we were walking toward the house we noticed a number of Black women, of various ages, standing on the street and peering in the direction of the train station. They looked like some kind of welcoming committee who were expecting their out-of-town relatives! That put us at ease. We walked right up to them and they greeted us like long-lost friends. These women were Rishad's relatives. They had made a home in a former pool hall that had adjoining living quarters, which I later learned had once served as the local Black Panther Party office. We were offered one of the main bedrooms in this house, all the while being taken care of like family. All the women were warm, welcoming—and extremely security conscious. As we were getting settled we discovered that they had rifles placed all over the house.

But there was a lapse. These women talked. As that first day and evening wore on, a number of their associates began to stop by the house, apparently to "get a look" at us. That made me extremely nervous because I didn't want anyone but the immediate family to know our whereabouts. To their credit they responded to my concerns immediately, and a male member of the family quickly came up with an offer to have us moved to Tennessee, where we could conceal ourselves until Rishad and the New York Panthers could hook us up with the underground movement.

We drove down South with a white college student, Asani sitting up front beside the driver and me in the back seat, almost hidden by our luggage. He dropped us off at a safe house in eastern Tennessee belonging to a young Black couple and their newborn baby. But I wasn't happy to spend more than one night there; there were too many people, still, who had knowledge of our location. First thing in the morning I hit the streets in search of an alternative. I found an advertisement in a store window targeting college students in search of a bedroom in someone's home. It turned out to be a huge four-bedroom colonial-style residence owned by a middle-aged Black woman sitting right on the edge of Knoxville College, a predominantly Black school. We passed ourselves off as newlyweds, adding that I was a "returned army veteran," wanting to enroll in the nearby college. A satisfactory story for the proprietor, who ushered us right into our own little bedroom and thereafter left us alone.

For the first time since leaving Philly we took a deep breath and set about making inquiries about our children and comrades back home.

We learned that the dust was slowly settling in Philadelphia. A couple of days after the Fairmount attack, six policemen had been hospitalized with gunshot wounds and another was in the morgue. Not one Panther or BUC member had suffered a single injury. Our homes had been raided and our offices ransacked, but within a matter of days all the Panther facilities were back up and running. Those who were on the run were being successfully concealed by the underground network, and even those who'd been jailed witnessed a massive outpouring of support as hundreds of community members came together to raise funds for bail, pack the courtrooms during hearings, and generally apply an unprecedented amount of pressure on the city to release them. It bears mention that all of these efforts were led by women, who remained stalwart in the face of continued harassment, threats, and intimidation from various quarters, including the police and the FBI.

It was also thanks to their steadfast commitment to our cause that the Revolutionary People's Constitutional Convention took place as scheduled, in September of 1970. The local Panthers who had been bailed out were feted as heroes by fifteen thousand participants who descended on Philadelphia to draft a new constitution. The rallying cry behind every single workshop and session was: "Seize the Time. All Power to the People!" Huey P. Newton himself showed up to address the gathering—and Frank Rizzo left town, announcing that he had an urgent police conference to attend out of state!

If there was a moment, a time, to be seized, it was then. We had demonstrated a brilliant lesson in armed self-defense that had shaken up the whole system, and it should have been built upon by the entire movement against oppression in the United States.

At that time the Panthers had a presence in over forty cities across America, from Boston to Los Angeles. Strung between the East and West Coasts were Panther strongholds in Washington, DC, New Orleans, Chicago, Detroit, Des Moines, Kansas City, Omaha, Denver, San Diego, and Seattle. We witnessed a fraction of it as we traveled the Underground Railroad, and it lit our hearts on fire.

Our decision to leave Tennessee was twofold. For weeks I had been trying to make inroads into the politically conscious elements of the Knoxville College student body. My objective was to find some young people that I could possibly recruit, organize, and train into an underground guerrilla cell. But after chasing a few leads I understood that none of the students were serious enough for what I had planned. In the meantime, I was keeping up with my weapons training as best I could. This mostly consisted of improving my speed at dismantling and loading firearms and working on my quick draw with the automatic pistol. One morning I was going through this practice routine, but because I'd been drinking I was not in complete control of my faculties. So in the course of one draw, once I had spun around after getting the gun out and aiming it, I mistakenly pulled the trigger and fired a shot through the front door of the house. It busted through the glass and the adjoining storm door and may even have struck a neighbor's front door across the street! Obviously I couldn't walk out in broad daylight to assess the damage, but I was petrified that I'd given my game away.

Asani was furious. She'd already been incensed by my drinking, which had become more regular the longer I was forced to keep a low profile. But mostly she feared our separation. We had made contingency plans in the event that we had to go back on the run, and these plans entailed us going in different directions so as to make it harder for whoever was on our trail to follow.

While she railed and steamed, I found the address of a repair shop in the phone book, procured the necessary materials, fixed the glass and painted the door, and made arrangements to immediately leave Tennessee.

We traveled by bus through the Carolinas until we got to the city of Winston-Salem, home to an active and highly militant chapter of the Panther Party. Their city office was constantly being spotlighted in the Panther paper for its tight formation and steady leadership in a state with a strong Ku Klux Klan presence. Before we made it to their headquarters, however, we spent one night on red alert in a hotel that a Black taxi driver had recommended, which turned out to have an exclusively white clientele! From the moment we stepped into the lobby it became clear that we were nothing but guinea pigs to test the newly won civil rights of Black people in that state. The other guests stared in open hostility, and the hotel staff quickly bundled us away into our room. But there was no way Asani and I were falling asleep. We sat up all night prepared to roll hand grenades down the corridors if it came down to it!

The next morning we located the Panther's office and discovered that everything we'd read about in the party's paper was true. It was a wild scene! The office itself and all of its surroundings were charged with excitement. It's hard to describe how fired up Black people were over political and social issues back then. There was no fervor over music, drugs, religion, or "job opportunities"—all that energy was being channeled into community awareness, agitation, and action. It was clear the party had won the admiration and allegiance of legions of urban youth, who had proved themselves ready and willing to carry out any instructions that trickled down from the leadership. Although the movement was steeped in the tactics of guerrilla warfare, we did not resort to "terrorist" measures by striking civilian targets or carrying out random acts of violence. Everything in our arsenal was directed toward hitting the armed apparatus of the state, usually local police or other symbolic targets. This made it a little harder for the authorities to paint us as purely dangerous fanatics—since there was a consistent pattern and logic to our actions.

On top of this there was a growing army of white radical activists, most of whom belonged to what they called the Catholic Left: a nationwide group of highly committed priests, nuns, and Catholic laypeople who were terrific allies and spokespeople for our cause. Their titular heads were the brothers Phil and Daniel Berrigan, Catholic priests and World War II veterans who had been inspired by the Civil Rights Movement and were leading a spirited attack against the United States' involvement in the war in Vietnam. They were also at the forefront of efforts to make Martin Luther King's brand of nonviolent direct action acceptable to the white middle classes by consistently provoking and succumbing to arrests around anti-war issues, often going so far as to refuse on moral and religious grounds to recognize the authority of the courts to take them to trial. They also preached that young Americans should refuse to be drafted into the armed forces, and urged those already conscripted to desert and leave the country. A couple of years before I arrived in New York City, Daniel Berrigan had disappeared underground after he and several other Catholic activists allegedly used homemade napalm to destroy hundreds of draft board records at the barracks in Catonsville, Maryland. Despite being sought by the authorities, he managed to resurface from time to time, often to address huge gatherings of activists by delivering powerful speeches that left the government utterly humiliated. These dedicated white activists were closely linked to the Panthers' underground network, an alliance that represented the movement's potential to unite diverse sectors of American society.

To top it all off, exiled members of the leadership claimed to have established a fully operational international bureau with government-provided properties, budgets, and diplomatic status in the then-revolutionary nation of Algeria, where fugitive Panthers could seek political asylum.

Just as we had begun to celebrate some of our biggest victories, the Federal Bureau of Investigation unleashed a massive and costly counterintelligence operation on the Black Panther Party. It proved highly effective at seeping into our tight ranks and sowing deep mistrust among our members. We had been preparing to confront violence and military crackdowns; we were not prepared for the intrigue and subterfuge that flooded the movement as the FBI recruited informants and released spies and snitches into the heart of our operation. They knew we were a poor army, limited in all but one resource: people. Our community was our greatest weapon both above- and underground. Once infected with paranoia, it became increasingly difficult for the Panthers to sustain their work on a national scale.

I witnessed this firsthand because, as a fugitive, if you can't trust your people, you might as well be out on the ocean without a life raft.

It was September of 1970. At my insistence, Asani had returned to Philadelphia and I had made a base in New York City where I could scope out potential new recruits. I got a day job loading and unloading trucks, since I needed to supplement the cash stash I'd brought with me, but my nights were spent getting a decent lay of the land. As I moved from the apartments of radical hippie couples to the basements of sympathetic churches in Washington Square Park to illegally occupied buildings on the Lower East Side, I encountered the full spectrum of individuals committed to the cause of Black liberation: women like Safiya Bukhari and the novelist Grace Paley; radical white priests who were preaching revolution from the pulpit; a brother named Aaron Reed Myers who I would roll with for a couple of years before he was riddled with bullets from an NYPD–FBI task force.

These meetings would take place at night, in rundown buildings, with everyone sharing whatever food or wine could be procured with our limited resources and sitting around on the floor talking late into the night. I seldom offered my opinion or weighed in on these explosive debates—since I was trying to assess the trustworthiness of every person I met, it was more important for me to listen silently.

I realized pretty quickly that there was growing disappointment with leadership figures like Huey P. Newton. The Free Huey movement had run for the duration of his trial in California in 1968 and throughout his two years of incarceration in that state, with activists at home and abroad heaping pressure on the authorities to release him. When Huey finally walked free in 1970, expectations were running sky-high that this dynamic "super revolutionary" would consolidate the party's message and mission, lead us on our next aggressive charge, and raise the struggle to a higher level. It was a critical time, with converging forces within the white Anti-war Movement, the nonviolent Civil Rights Movement, and the armed Black Liberation Movement all reaching their climax.

But Huey fell short. For one thing, he no longer possessed the stage presence that most people had come to associate with the Panthers; when he spoke he lacked the rousing, militant rhetoric of a great orator and wound up sounding more like a college professor who bored his students to sleep with a whole lot of fancy words that only he could understand. There were whispers that something was really wrong—was Huey selling out? Had he been "gotten to" by the authorities while in prison? Then came the death rattle: Huey announced that the Panther Party was preparing to send volunteers to Vietnam to assist the National Liberation Front, or NLF, in their fight against the US-backed South Vietnamese government.

Everyone I talked to in the underground circuit was equally outraged by this news. Here we had put our lives on the line at the recommendation of the party leadership—given ourselves up to martyrdom, jail time, or life on the run—and rather than bring the struggle to a head, the top brass was planning to weaken our chances by sending our own cadres to the other side of the world instead of dealing with those in need right here at home. I personally had expected top East Coast Panthers to make contact with me when they heard I had settled in New York, but instead it seemed like they were avoiding me, leaving me to fend for myself. Maybe this was because Richard Nixon had recently singled me out on national television as one of the country's most-wanted fugitives. I accepted the label proudly, but obviously it had put the Panther leadership on their guard.

To make matters worse, the Central Committee had begun a purge of loyal and hardworking Panthers based on suspicions and rumors that they were informing on the Panthers' activities to the FBI. Expelled members—including, eventually, most of the Philadelphia Panthers—had their names and sometimes their pictures placed in the Panther paper under the banner *Enemies of the People*. Such preposterous actions were all but ignored by the communities these individuals had been working with for years. Often the dismissed members continued their activities in the same facilities as if nothing had occurred, indicating the extent of the rift between the Central Committee and the rank and file of the party. Things got so bad that Panthers on the East Coast stopped reading and circulating the *Black Panther*—the party's official newspaper and one of its oldest recruitment and organizing tools. They began their own publication called *Right On*. Speculation of deep government infiltration into the top ranks of the party worsened after a confrontation between Huey and Eldridge Cleaver, the party's minister of information, was broadcast live on national television, threatening to plunge the Panthers deeper into a fratricidal war. Already, clashes between the Panthers and Ron Karenga's United Slaves Organization had led to multiple deaths of Black men.

As for me, I had vowed long ago to stop warring with fellow Black people. I had no time for the spectacles and skullduggery that was taking place at the top. I was still living on the run—bedding down in a different spot every couple of days, keeping abreast of the news, trying to secure passage out of the country. One plan involved me traveling through Montreal, but this was thwarted by the actions of Quebec separatists who had kidnapped a number of high-level government officials, resulting in the entire province being placed under martial law. I was frustrated by the inability to move, by the growing ranks of fugitive revolutionaries who were being ignored or isolated by the Panther leadership, and by the paranoia in the underground network that prevented me from forming an effective cell capable of carrying out tactical actions.

So one fall afternoon in 1971 I walked into the underground parking lot of a hotel and, when the attendant left his office to park one of the guest's cars, selected a set of keys, climbed into the corresponding vehicle, and drove away. Within ten minutes, I was in the Lincoln Tunnel headed for New Jersey.

From the long rides I'd taken with my father throughout my childhood, I knew that Routes 1 and 130 were trucker territory, mostly free from the type of patrols that peppered the New Jersey Turnpike. I avoided the Benjamin Franklin Bridge, which would have taken me straight through the center of the city, where I risked too much exposure; instead, I took the Tacony Palmyra Bridge, timing my movements so that I entered Philadelphia during rush hour. I crawled into West Philly, confident that the heavy traffic would deter any routine stops by local police. I drove to the home of my sister Beatrice and circled her block twice searching for signs of surveillance before parking the car. I used back alleys to get to her back door. It was late fall, and by the time I knocked on the kitchen door the sun was down, concealing me in darkness.

She pulled back the curtain. I think it took her a couple of seconds to recognize me, or maybe she just had a hard time believing I was really out there. She flung the door open, dragged me inside, and slammed it shut, all without saying a word. But the minute I was safely in her kitchen, she started hollering. One by one all of my sisters came running, shouting and screaming like they were at a funeral. I guess that was when it really hit us all what momentous events we'd lived through. These women had borne the brunt of the authorities' fury. Every day had been a learning experience, they told me, in what it took to go against the most organized, oppressive power in the world and emerge in one piece. Every day they had to reinvent the wheel by overcoming their fears and doubts anew. Ignorance was a thing of the past. Independence was all they knew now. They had survived and were still standing, and that evening with all of us in the kitchen was a celebration. For a little while all we could do was hug one another. I had my sister Maria on one knee and Rose on the other. Everyone was talking at once, laughing. It seemed like the kitchen kept expanding as more and more people poured in.

At some point Asani arrived and dropped our youngest daughter in my lap. Now that was a real shock—when I last saw her she could barely hold her head up, but in just a couple of months she'd grown into a frisky little girl with a big mop of hair. Holding her, I was overcome with some kind of feeling, but before I could put my finger on it, Beatrice was telling me I needed to conceal myself in the next room because my father was on his way to her place. She said both my parents were under tremendous pressure to divulge my whereabouts to the police. Cops were doggedly visiting their home, and the FBI was intimidating them to the point that my traumatized mother was on prescription medication for anxiety. Beatrice was afraid my father wouldn't be strong enough to keep the news of my visit from the police. But I didn't agree. When he came in I revealed myself gently, greeted him calmly. I don't remember if he embraced me, or whether we just exchanged a few words at Beatrice's kitchen table, but after a few minutes he got up and walked outside. I followed him, only to find him sobbing in the next room, and I knew then that I had been right to let him see me.

For those of us in the struggle, these were rare moments and encounters. There simply wasn't time to put ourselves or our families, much less our feelings, ahead of the task we had embarked on. That very evening, Beatrice helped me procure some weapons and later drove me to the head Panther office in North Philly. I made contact with a couple of my former cell members who'd been released from jail following the shootout. They were already back to work in the community, and one of their biggest concerns was how to liberate our brothers who were still behind bars. There was a limit to how much pressure the women could exert as a civilian force on the outside, particularly when it came to those who'd been locked up for blatant attacks on the police. Rizzo's pigs were deeply loyal to their own kind. People they had labeled "cop killers" would walk free only over their dead bodies. Clearly there was a need for a second prong, a simultaneous but separate approach that was more in line with our revolutionary ideals: jailbreaks.

Just as with all of our other armed activities, we took a straightforward approach to this task. They were necessary actions, obligations that we owed to ourselves and our comrades. The authorities had proved highly skilled at identifying, isolating, and eradicating the best of us. On one end of the spectrum were the fugitives, escaping with their lives but forced to remain at large—either overseas or underground—and thus rendered relatively impotent. On the other end were the corpses and the martyrs who lived on in spirit as inspirations, but whose genius or courage could never be truly replaced. Prisoners lived somewhere in the middle. Fighting for their release and finding substitutes for them on the streets was a huge drain on people's energy and our limited resources. Thus it became incumbent upon inmates and their supporters on the outside to do whatever needed to be done to remove them from the custody of the state and return them to their rightful place in the movement.

If the 1960s marked a period of open armed hostilities between the United States government and the Black Liberation Movement, then the 1970s was the decade of jailbreaking.

CHAPTER 14

WANTED

I don't know a whole lot about regret. I had wasted so many years hustling and gang warring that by the time I joined the movement I pretty much acted in exact accordance with my principles, which meant I had a clear conscience about everything I did. Back then every day involved some kind of life-or-death decision and I never really had the time to stop and ask if it was the right one; I did what I thought was best, at any given moment in time, for me and the movement. Even now when I look back I can only try to assess how close those decisions brought me to my goal of dismantling a system of white oppression and winning freedom for Black people in America. Everything else—the failures, disappointments, or unexpected twists that brought about outcomes I could never even imagine—is secondary.

I spent two years underground. Two years of caution, silence, crouching. Two years of living out of a shoulder bag, crashing in a different squatter settlement on the Lower East Side every night, using Laundromats, and eating communal meals on the floors of strangers' apartments, rice and beans, bread and wine. There was plenty of hospitality and generosity among like-minded people, but no discernible organization or leadership. In the evenings there was jazz, and African drum circles, along with spirited conversations, but in the daytime everyone seemed to be sleeping history away.

The Panthers were disintegrating before my eyes, plagued by infiltration and infighting. Every effort I made to get out of the country was thwarted by broken links in the network. I had no money, no contact with my family, and hardly any trusted comrades. The people I'd built a movement with, the leaders and the foot soldiers, had been killed or incarcerated. Each day brought back the words of my Old Heads from our Corner days: *We pour libations for those members who are dead, or in jail.*

Dead. Or in jail.

The worst part was, as far as the movement went, being imprisoned was as good as being dead. Everyone I encountered in New York City was lamenting the incarceration of leaders like Angela Davis, but no one seemed to be seriously planning any prison breaks. It was like they'd accepted the situation for what it was.

Frustrated, I tried to build a small New York cell comprising a couple of dudes who were down to get serious with me: there was a young brother named Lock, who told me he'd been raised around the migrant labor camps in the South and had become very active in the workers' struggle there during the first wave of the Civil Rights Movement. He was in his early twenties, and full of misdirected energy. I also pulled in his cousin Freddie, about a decade older than Lock and with a clearer head for revolutionary theory. In time, I managed to draw a couple of others into my loose formation: Randy, Red, and a guy named Aaron Reed.

Unlike with the BUC members whom I'd come up with since childhood and had trusted with my life, I wasn't too sure about these guys. I was never 100 percent confident in their ability, commitment, or trustworthiness, but I didn't have a lot of options. So I did the only thing I knew how to do: work my body to the bone. Under my guidance we undertook daily calisthenics in public spaces around the city: Tompkins Square Park or the East River, Washington Square Park or Central Park or Riverside. We did military and weapons drills at a shooting range, and finally began a painstaking accumulation of stolen vehicles, or "hot wheels," as we called them. This entailed hitting up warehouses or the underground parking garages of big hotels and watching like a hawk until one of the guards or parking attendants left the keys unattended. We grabbed a set of keys, matched it to the vehicle, and drove right out of the garage, then stashed the hot wheels in some nondescript corner of the city for future use.

We also began a thorough study of revolutionary theory and praxis. My main education tool with these guys was the *Minimanual of the Urban Guerrilla*, written by the brilliant Carlos Marighella, a Brazilian revolutionary who theorized ways to overthrow that country's brutal military dictatorship and replace it with a Marxist system of government. He was assassinated in 1969, shortly after the book's publication, but that didn't stop his manual from traveling around the world via Cuba. In 1970 the Panthers acquired a copy and distributed it to certain key activist cells, including the BUC. While underground I adapted it for my own circumstances, and it proved very useful in holding the attention of guys like Lock and Freddie. They were blown away by the clarity of vision laid out in the book.

It was long, slow work. I kept running up against the shadow of the FBI's Counter Intelligence Program: Every direction I turned, there were people with fake names and bad vibes. There was suspicion and second-guessing. Plans were swiftly made and abandoned equally quick; or else they slowly curdled in the soup of secrecy that the movement was swimming in.

From time to time I'd meet up with New York Panthers who gave me a lot of mixed messages. Rishad, the party member we'd first met in New York City, who continued to be active in the movement, told me Kathleen Cleaver, who was Eldridge Cleaver's wife and a major leader in her own right, wanted to organize a summit of the representatives of the various Black guerrilla cells, a very risky and complicated undertaking. He said that the international bureau had received money and weapons from the Algerian government and was promised more, as well as training facilities, if the underground movement could send a cadre to Algeria. He wanted me to help provide shadow security for the detail that would escort Kathleen around. That was the last I heard of that plan!

I was introduced to Zayd Malik Shakur, a highly capable member of the Black Liberation Army who was operating aboveground at the time. I remember urging him to go underground like me to avoid detection by the authorities—two years after that encounter, he was shot dead on the New Jersey Turnpike in the company of his comrades, Sundiata Acoli and Assata Shakur, who would go on to become one of the FBI's most-wanted female "criminals" in the years to come.

I also encountered several of the Panther 21, including Ali Bey Hassan and Fred "Badru" Dalton, who'd been released on bail following our nationwide protests during their trial. Shortly after meeting Badru, I learned he'd been arrested on weapons possession charges and flung into the Bronx House of Detention. A couple of sisters in the movement approached me about helping to liberate him from this institution, a request I was ready to immediately honor, though I was unsure whether or not Badru was aware of the plan. But after several weeks of careful reconnaissance of the detention center—and with the breakout planned down to the very finest details including sniper positions, the acquisition of multiple getaway cars, and securing weapons and escape routes—an unknown entity called off the whole operation.

By now I was growing weary of the doubts and paranoia. I've never been very good at glancing over my shoulder—my instinct has always been to look straight ahead. I'd entered New York City on the run and underground, a subway rat. Now I needed fresh air. Some creatures aren't built to cower or hide. Sooner or later they have to stand up tall, even if it means exposing themselves to the hunter's rifle.

Through a Herculean effort I managed to make contact with my sister Beatrice. She informed me about a Philly-based revolutionary named Hamilton who was the driving force behind an underground cell that was single-mindedly dedicated to liberating revolutionaries from penitentiaries across the state of Pennsylvania. A few years earlier,

Hamilton's younger brother had been captured in connection with the shooting of the highway patrolman shortly after the Fairmount Park attack. Hamilton was fixated on liberating his brother along with a couple of my former cell members. I'd heard about his efforts for a long time—he had actually been going around to the homes of those arrested or dispersed in the Fairmount attack to ensure our families were being well taken care of. But it took me a while to make contact. As my sister Beatrice pointed out, you couldn't just walk up to Hamilton. With the authorities hot on his trail he was about as elusive as I was.

So I risked another trip to Philly. Before letting anyone else know I was in town, I found Asani. We spent one night in a cheap hotel, an encounter which did wonders for my emotional equilibrium and morale. The following morning, I began to circle the Black Panther office in North Philly until I could attract someone's attention. On my third pass Mitch Edwards's partner, Nefertiti, came out and I slowed until we made eye contact. I then swung around the corner and parked a block away. I made my way back through a side street on foot. Nefertiti had obviously got the message because she was still standing on the step looking all around. When I got close enough, I motioned for her to follow me. Concealed in my car, Nefertiti gave me what information she could, including the name of the sister of an imprisoned revolutionary. I drove to this woman's house, and she helped me make a series of phone calls that enabled me to track down the man I was looking for: Hamilton.

Face-to-face in a room together, we silently summed each other up. Almost immediately both of our walls came down. We didn't need to exchange a single word to know that we were both for real. We calmly congratulated each other on our ability to survive the chase of the oppressive forces with our fighting spirits intact. Then we got right down to strategizing.

Hamilton had a leg up on me in the jailbreaking department. A few years earlier his cell had succeeded in liberating a brother who was being transported from a state penitentiary to the Philadelphia General Hospital. This brother was David Richards—the Moon Gang member I'd once viewed as my staunch rival on the streets. In the intervening years he had transformed into a committed revolutionary and taken the name Mustafa. I was unaware that we'd been on parallel tracks for years, and now here we were, smack in the same movement, battling on the same side.

According to Hamilton, a successful liberation attempt depended heavily on what he called dry runs—test drives to familiarize ourselves with routes, layouts, and blueprints so that when it came time to act there would be no surprises. With this in mind we decided to kill two birds with one stone: we'd perform a dry run on the Philadelphia House of Correction, a large prison located in the Holmesburg area of Northeast Philly; and under cover of the ensuing chaos, we would raid a bank to procure some much-needed resources for the movement. Nothing about Hamilton's plan gave me pause. I was done biding my time and ready for some action!

On January 19, 1972, I gathered a few members of my New York cell, and we set out for Philly in two stolen vehicles: a six-wheel truck and an ambulance belonging to the Society for the Prevention of Cruelty to Animals. We drove first to Germantown, to a safe house that my sister Beatrice had secured as the base for this particular operation. Hamilton was already there with his team, which included Danny Weston, the brother of my old Corner boy TZ, a Moon Gang member who was now my brother in the struggle. Turned out Danny had converted to Islam and now went by the name Tariq. He'd recently been locked up in Graterford Prison, but had managed to escape while on a furlough program. There was also another devout brother, named Sharif Rahman, who had just returned to the streets after serving sixteen years in prison. The fact that two men fresh out of the penitentiary were willing to risk their freedom to free their comrades was all the proof I needed that this cell was worthy of my commitment. I quickly assigned Randy to the bank raid and agreed to join Hamilton's team for the attack on the prison.

At the time, none of us had any comrades inside the House of Correction. Everyone we knew was being held in another facility across the expressway, known as Eastern Penitentiary. But striking the

House of Correction would allow us to gauge the guards' response to an attempted attack, while simultaneously putting them on edge. This would keep their attention trained on the wrong institution, which might give us a fraction of an advantage during a future breakout from the Eastern Penitentiary.

At the appointed hour, in a revolving convoy of hot wheels, we shot up the guard station located directly outside the Philadelphia House of Correction. This brought ground and air police units by the dozens, swarming and converging on the prison and leaving an open path to the Beneficial Savings Bank, which was in the same neighborhood of Northeast Philly—a majority white community largely unaccustomed to Black people. Through some miracle, our team managed to get in and out of that bank with five thousand dollars in cash!

That was a big haul for us. We had grown accustomed to doing what needed to be done without anything in our pockets, so handling that much money was a heady experience. At the safe house we divvied up the booty, gathered our weapons, and slipped out back into a warren of alleyways that connected all the households of this poor Black neighborhood in West Philly.

It should be a more exciting story. But the truth is, a fugitive's life is rarely glamorous. The devil is in the dullest of details, human missteps that dot the line between liberty and capture. Maybe we let our guard down. Maybe we were snug in our small victory, or believed, foolishly for a moment, that because we were among "our people" we were safe. But a neighbor had grown suspicious of the comings and goings in our safe house. She made a phone call to the police that burglars were prowling the area. This brought a couple of overenthusiastic beat cops to the scene. It was a weekday evening and they were looking for entertainment. What they found was a cell of Black revolutionaries, flush with cash and weighed down with weapons.

And just like that I was in handcuffs, sitting in a cop car next to Danny "Tariq" Weston, whom I'd once warred with on these very streets, speeding off to Philadelphia's Eighteenth District Police Station.

CHAPTER 15

PRISONERS OF WAR

W hen we arrived at the police station, the first thing I saw were wanted posters of my own face, seeking me in connection with the murder of Sergeant Frank Von Collins. Bizarrely, none of the cops seemed to notice this. They were too busy looking over my false identification papers and booking me under weapons possession charges! For two years my photograph had appeared in the papers and on nightly television news shows. Now here I was, right in front of their eyes in handcuffs under fluorescent lighting, and not one of them recognized me. It just proved one thing: It didn't matter if we were peddling drugs or waging a revolution against their government, we were all the same to them, a bunch of Black criminals. They couldn't see our humanity if their lives depended on it.

They shackled Tariq and me to a wooden bench, and we sat there for a good hour before a passing cop stopped, stared, and then yelled out: "Hey, it's him! It's Shoatz!"

That was too much for Tariq. He laughed out loud, so loud he couldn't get a hold of himself for a couple of seconds. It wasn't the reaction the cops had been expecting, and it threw them off until Tariq said, "Finally, man! 'Bout fucking time!"

He was still laughing when they started punching and kicking us around on that bench. We tried to shield our faces with our shackled hands as best we could while they said things like "You're laughing now, but we're about to lock you motherfuckers up and throw away the key."

Maybe it was the adrenaline that allowed us to laugh in such a moment. But it was something else, too. Once you remove yourself from the moral universe of your oppressor, you're less impressed with their instruments of judgment and punishment. It becomes harder for the state to intimidate you. Places designed to evoke fear, guilt, or admission of wrongdoing, like police precincts and penitentiaries, lose a lot of their power. That was the very thing we had been fighting for, that feeling of liberation. And in that moment—even though I'd fallen into enemy hands after two years on the run—I felt completely free.

I was saddled with a host of criminal charges including theft and murder. Over the following days I was asked numerous times how I pled to these charges: innocent or guilty? I was shunted from interrogation rooms to courtrooms to visiting rooms where everyone from family members to prosecutors attempted to coax a response to this question, but I refused to answer.

There was, however, one charge that I acknowledged wholeheartedly: sedition. *The incitement of resistance to or insurrection against the authorities.* Yes! Guilty as charged! I was unequivocally involved in the war of the flea, an organized urban guerrilla revolt to overthrow an oppressive and unjust authority. I considered myself a soldier captured in combat, a prisoner of war. I was willing to submit to the international laws and covenants that governed conventional warfare—the accords and agreements that determine how belligerents from either side should be treated when they fall into enemy hands. I would not debase my motives by cooperating with civilian proceedings that tried to paint me as a common criminal. On that point I refused to budge.

However, it was a sobering reminder that even though we'd declared ourselves to be guerrillas, the government had never officially acknowledged it was embroiled in a conflict with its people. They had branded our civil war a Civil Rights Movement, and there was nothing civil about it at all. It enabled them to hound us and lock us up under criminal laws, bypassing all the codes of conduct that might have given me and my fellow POWs a fair trial or better treatment in captivity. Instead, they were able to portray us as pariahs, menaces to society, while at the same time discouraging others from following in our footsteps for fear that they would be subjected to the full might of the state if they were captured in the course of their duties for the movement.

I was never one to suffer from doubt or uncertainty. When they put that question to me—innocent or guilty?—I simply felt it was my duty to set the record straight. This was a decision I made not as an individual but as a member of a movement. Not all of my comrades took such a hardline approach. Hamilton and Sharif Rahman, for instance, pled guilty to some of the charges, gathered astronomical sums of money for their bail, and gained their release. There were only a handful of occasions when I was tempted to do the same: when my ageing parents gained access to the interrogation room where I was being held and questioned; when I learned that my sister Yvette was organizing rallies at City Hall on my behalf; and when Asani brought our first-born son to my trial. Not for nothing, though, had I passed through fire and steel, because not even the sight of my child in the courtroom, so little that when he sat on the bench his feet barely touched the floor, could soften my commitment or weaken my oaths.

My first place of incarceration was the Philadelphia Detention Center, but I didn't stay long. Less than six months after I'd arrived, the guards rousted me from my bunk in the middle of the night and shoved me off into the most secure section of the jail, a holding area behind the central control security enclosure. I knew something big was going on outside because I could hear helicopters circling the facility overhead and there was a lot of rushing around and yelling into walkie-talkies, but I had no idea how it involved me.

Next morning the guards outfitted me in high-security-prisoner regalia—handcuffs, shackles, leg irons—and pushed me into a police car that transported me across the highway to Holmesburg Prison. We stopped outside, sirens blaring and escort cars flashing their lights, until presently another prisoner was dragged out of that institution and flung in the back seat beside me: my main man, Victor "Sharp" Davis.

We hadn't seen each other in close to two years, and all the fetters in the world couldn't stop us greeting each other with delight and affection. Our last interaction had been on the day of the Fairmount Park attack, and ever since then, the closest we'd got to being together was having our faces side by side on most-wanted posters, in newspaper clippings, and in mug shots on the news. So even though we were in chains, we were grinning our faces off and there was a lot of "Alright man, you good? You good, man?" In the middle of a war there is nothing more heartening to a soldier than seeing one of your people in one piece.

As the convoy transported us out of Philadelphia, Sharp caught me up on what had gone down. True to the jailbreaking spirit at the time, the night before, Tariq and another former Panther named Stan Woods, who'd been unceremoniously expelled from the party by Huey P. Newton, had attempted to enter Holmesburg, arm our comrades, and gain their freedom. They were thwarted by a patrolling policeman who noticed some activity outside the prison walls and tried to summon backup. Someone shot him several times while he was using his car phone, but the dispatcher picked up enough from his garbled report to immediately dispatch support teams to the area. A quick investigation revealed forty feet of rope and a grappling hook hanging from the prison's boundary wall, along with scattered rifle casings that the police claimed had been fired from the same weapon used on the wounded officer. Before long the staff had cordoned off the entire area and launched an intensive search for anyone who might have been involved. Between the prison's administrative records and police intelligence files, the authorities immediately jumped to the conclusion that I was the target of this escape attempt, never mind the fact that I was being held in a completely different institution on the other side of the highway.

By the time the sun began to rise, the jailers had isolated me in the Philadelphia Detention Center and the cops had managed to locate and trap Tariq in a wooded area not far from Holmesburg. Later, following a tip from a couple who reported that a negro man with a rifle had commandeered their car and forced them to drive him away from the area, a police patrol hunted down and arrested Stan Woods. They also found a rental car parked on the lip of the woods close to Holmesburg. A quick check led them to discover my sister Beatrice's name on the rental papers, from which they gathered that Sharp was part of the plan.

That's when Sharp broke the news that he and Beatrice had both converted to Islam. To solidify their commitment to each other and to the struggle, they'd adopted the noms de guerre Hakim and Akila.

It was fitting that he delivered this news as we swung into the massive complex of Graterford State Prison, the largest penitentiary in Pennsylvania, for it was here, in this octagon-shaped fortress surrounded by thirty-five-foot walls, smack in the middle of coal country, that I would discover a new kind of faith, a religious calling that would fuel and fortify me for the ordeals that still lay ahead.

CHAPTER 16

ISLAM

Any man who hopes to survive a long prison sentence must learn to retreat into himself. Nothing about a prison is made to hold a human being intact. Every feature, every façade, every drill and daily routine is designed to destroy a man, break a man down. Your very life depends on studying this architecture and finding ways to move through it without being crushed against the stones.

When I arrived at Graterford I was in awe of the sheer scale of the place—nearly two thousand acres of farmland with a sixty-two-acre compound at its heart, which was closely guarded by eight enormous towers that sat at every point on the octagon. The prison complex itself centered around five interconnected cellblocks that housed 1,800 men. Each cellblock was about the size of your average city block in Philadelphia, and contained four hundred cells on two tiers, which were essentially foot-wide walkways providing the guards access to each prisoner. The cellblocks were labeled alphabetically from *A* to *E*, and were in turn linked up with the dozens of quarters and facilities that keep a prison running: kitchens, five dining areas, a commissary where prisoners spent their own money on food and toiletries, a laundry facility, industrial and craft workshops, maintenance shops, a hospital, a chapel, an

outdoor yard, a movie house, a visiting area, counseling and administrative offices, and a web of security checkpoints.

In addition there were two other buildings that no one liked to
speak of. They housed the Holes, those isolated sections of a prison
where men are sent for the most extreme form of punishment that
exists within a penitentiary: solitary confinement. One of Graterford's
holes, called Little Max, was situated at the end of one of its regular
cellblocks. The other, known as Big Max, sat apart, a horror away from
the horrors, a lone building in an otherwise intimately connected landscape, earning it the name Little House on the Prairie.

That's where they put me and Hakim.

Little House on the Prairie was a U-shaped building that contained forty cells in four separate sections. Each section contained
ten cells that were separated from one another by solid steel doors. In
essence they functioned like four miniature prisons. The only time you
could hear or get a glimpse of another prisoner not on your wing was
when the guards opened the doors to travel between them, or when
they opened the tiny windows outside of your cell. The cells themselves were small, about six by seven feet. They contained a steel rack
for a mattress and a combination sink/toilet. There was no hot water in
the pipes; hot water was delivered twice a day in the kinds of carriers
service stations use to fill up car radiators. A guard stuck the nozzle
between the bars that fronted your cell and poured it into the sink. In
the middle of the Pennsylvania winter, this tiny quantity of hot water
didn't do much, or last long.

The chow—what they called "hot" meals—was terrible, barely discernible as food. There were no light fixtures in these cells; all light
came in from a forty-watt bulb outside. We were allowed nothing
except a few personal books, magazines, newspapers, writing paraphernalia, and a change or two of socks and undergarments. No one
in this unit had any access to anything like radios, TVs, or typewriters.
The routine was called Three Hots and a Cot, in reference to the three
hot "meals" and a place to sleep. That was it, along with thirty minutes

of exercise five days a week in a small yard overlooked by a gun tower, and two fifteen-minute showers a week, or whenever the guards felt like we deserved one.

It was a good introduction to my new life. No perks or privileges. No polite pretending.

I knew from past experience that prisons are dangerous places. If you enter with the notion that you can rely on the guards for protection or your fellow prisoners for support, then you've already lost. Your own mind, body, and determination are the only sure things. The guards are of course the dominant force within a prison, but at that time most guards were armed only with a policeman's stick. This meant that in an unusual situation like a riot they were reliant on their numbers and on the speed with which the state could dispatch backup or heavy artillery. In a one-on-one confrontation, however, a prisoner stood a good chance against a guard with one of the homemade knives we called shanks or any of the numerous other crude weapons we learned to fashion from the most basic materials. So in reality, all prisons in the 1970s hung in a delicate balance based on a brutal understanding between the jailers and the jailed. Prisoners and guards alike spent most of their time trying to determine where that balance lay and doing everything in their power to ensure it didn't shift in a direction that was unfavorable to them, because if that happened, one would be bound to experience some extreme discomfort, if not severe injury or even death.

Because neither Hakim nor I had ever been at Graterford before, we were soon released into the general population, though of course we were housed on different blocks. After we were separated, it took me a while to track him down, but in the meantime I discovered that Graterford State Prison was filled with familiar faces—dudes I'd been locked up with as a young gangbanger, men I knew from the streets, guys I barely recognized and guys I knew really well. No matter what path we chose to follow, this was just where a lot of Black men in the state of Pennsylvania ended up. It didn't matter whether we had educated ourselves on world history or shot up the local liquor store or organized a food drive or embezzled money. Our presence in their schools and cities, our politics, our power to survive everything they threw at us was something white people feared beyond imagining, and so our very existence was criminalized.

They built the prisons for us. Soon, whole towns sprang up around these places of incarceration, creating large white communities whose livelihoods and futures depended on our confinement. It bred generations of jailers, administrators, and bureaucrats who, because they saw us only behind bars, came to associate us with animals in cages. It is a system that takes on a logic of its own that is indifferent to innocence or guilt, truth or honor.

I had come to these conclusions after many years of political education as a revolutionary; very few of my fellow prisoners shared my views. As I went about the process of assessing each individual I met, as was my habit, I realized that it would take an immense degree of time and effort to raise their consciousness enough to bring them into the struggle or even to rely on their commitment in a liberation attempt. But though they lacked political consciousness, many thousands of prisoners in the 1970s were discovering something else on the inside, something perhaps even more powerful: Islam.

Even before I arrived at Graterford I became aware of this phenomenon because dudes I'd rolled with for years, like Tariq, had converted on the inside. I was also struck by how the Muslim faith had influenced scores of people on the outside, mostly women. I'd observed all this from a distance. I've never been drawn to religion and my studies so far had focused entirely on the need for men to change their own circumstances, not wait for God or the White Man to hand us our freedom. If not for Hakim I would probably have stayed away from the whole thing.

Hakim was one of the coolest dudes I knew, because he never lost his composure. He had a firm head on his shoulders and a thoroughly meticulous manner. His curiosity for how things worked—I suppose you could say the mechanics of the world—made him both an excellent student and the perfect teacher.

From our many discussions in his cell I began to understand that this wasn't just some Sunday school bullshit. According to Hakim, not only were the teachings in the Qu'ran deeply connected to our ideas of liberation, they would actually provide a stronger foundation for the entire movement. He felt that many of our failings until that point were caused by the inability of the Black revolutionary leadership to truly win the hearts and minds of its members, leaving many people open to vacillation, treachery, and failure of will at crucial moments. I had never concerned myself too much with such questions. Though I knew and shared the frustrations of many Panthers and other revolution-aries, I saw myself as a mere foot soldier, and believed my only job was to continue to fight until either we achieved our goals or I was killed in connection with the struggle. But now that Hakim and I had so much time on our hands, I gave myself over to a rigorous debate about the role of Islam in the Black Liberation Movement.

Whenever I do something I give it a 110 percent. After a while I was not content to simply ask Hakim questions and receive answers. I slowly started to stockpile all the Islamic religious texts that I could lay my hands on. I also began to learn the Arabic language and embarked on an intensive study of geography and world history. I believed both subjects were necessary for me to properly understand the part Islam had played in shaping global events over the centuries. I obtained access to a world map and, over time, reproduced it on my cell wall by sketching out the longitude lines from north to south and the latitude lines from east to west and then filling each block with the correspond-ing geographical features. It was like doing a giant puzzle. Looking at this five-by-five-foot map on a daily basis soon burned all of its features into my mind.

Back then, Graterford was big on utilizing prison labor, and an inmate could land just about any job you could imagine. We worked as plumbers and carpenters, farmers and foresters, masons and firefight-ers, cattle herders and tractor drivers. I got myself a job in the prison's machine maintenance shop, where I was supposed to work six-hour days repairing farm or laundry equipment. Often I'd have a lull in my workday, when I could just sit quietly and study my religious or history texts, sometimes for five hours at a stretch.

At that time there were three different Muslim groups at Graterford: the Sunni Muslims, which was the group Hakim belonged to; the Ahmadiyyas; and the Nation of Islam. There were no more than twenty Sunni Muslims, about eight to ten Ahmadiyyas, and close to seventy-five members of the Nation of Islam. Each of these groups had followers in a number of other prisons and jails in the state. At Graterford they all had separate areas for worship in the chapel, which they could visit periodically during the week. The Nation, being the largest, occupied the main sanctuary while the other two utilized smaller, adjoining rooms in the basement.

The very first Sunni Muslim prayer service I attended had a profound impact on me. I was instructed to take off my shoes at the entrance of the "mosque" and sit on the side while the men prepared themselves to make their salat, or prayers. This entailed washing their hands, faces, and feet to rid themselves of external impurities before lining up in neat, even rows. Led by one individual, whom they called the imam, they went through the entire ritual with military precision. It was like watching a beautifully choreographed dance; better, because the men were clearly deep in a spiritual state as they performed each motion of kneeling, bowing, touching their foreheads to the floor, and speaking their words of faith in unison. When it was over everyone got to their feet and hugged and shook hands with one another. There were smiles on everyone's faces. Eventually the imam directed us all to sit in a circle on prayer rugs. We spent several hours reading and discussing passages from the Qu'ran before moving on to community-related business—primarily the question of whether or not Hakim, whose reputation in the Sunni Muslim community preceded him, would accept the post of imam. He was initially reluctant, feeling that he had not been a part of the community long enough to come in and try to rearrange their affairs, but he was gradually won over. I had never witnessed the level of humility or dignity these men expressed during this discussion. Everyone spoke without a trace of rancor. It was completely unlike the petty squabbles over leadership positions that had become common among the Panthers. Though it would be some years before I stood before Hakim and made my declaration of faith, the vows that all Sunni Muslims undertake, I knew then that I had discovered yet another path, one that would define my journey for several years.

I took the name Harun Abdul Ra'uf, and continued to read widely. I observed the rituals, and dedicated myself to prayer. I found tremendous solace in turning to a higher power—it was balm to the chaffing reality of life in Graterford, where, to the guards, we barely qualified as human beings. Soon I was asked to be the emir of security, a position that earned me a solid place in the community but also put me at the heart of a hugely complex and highly explosive social system. My job entailed coordinating the efforts of my fellow Sunni Muslims to protect themselves in a hostile environment, since the general attitude toward other sects of Islam was deep distrust and antagonism. Though each community pointed to doctrinal differences in their religious practices as the root cause of this hostility, my experience with gangs told me that it was more to do with masculine rivalry, frustration, and ignorance.

But there wasn't time or space to hash out these ideas. If I had felt a sense of urgency on the streets, a notion that action was more important than theory, that feeling was magnified tenfold inside Graterford. It's difficult to describe such a compressed and concentrated powder keg to someone who hasn't lived inside it. There is an intimacy to prison life that doesn't exist anywhere else on this earth, and it renders you naked and vulnerable 24/7. Men got raped in the showers, knifed in the chow hall, beaten to death in the yard. Prisoners killed for little and died for less. This whole situation suited the guards just fine. As long as our pent-up rage was directed against one another and not at them, they were willing to turn a blind eye to brawls and bloodshed. So although I was desperate to bring representatives of the different religious communities together to hash out our ideological disputes and join forces against the racist staff and administration, I found myself instead making weapons, gathering intelligence, and doing whatever was needed to protect our membership from brutal attacks by other Muslims.

We also had links to Sunni Muslim groups on the outside, including a large mosque based in North Philadelphia that was approved for visits. Periodically, learned men from this mosque came to deliver sermons and services, and because they had access to far more reading materials and resources than us, we came to view these individuals as theological guides. They exerted a tremendous amount of influence on our lives, including how we managed our relationships with our families and communities on the outside—particularly women. It became incumbent upon us to urge the women in our communities to convert, a mission we took very seriously.

By that time, Asani had begun to pay me regular visits. She was usually accompanied by our kids and one or more of my faithful sisters, and I used these sessions to press my case about religion. It wasn't easy. These were all fiercely independent and strong-willed women who rarely did anything simply on the strength of a man's words. Asani, as I recall, fought back, saying she had no desire to subject herself to the strictures of Islam like the dress codes that required women to conceal everything but their hands and faces. Already women were coming under pressure from various quarters, not only their husbands on the inside but other women in the community. The visiting room at Graterford became an exhibition of whose family members had crossed over to "our" side and which ones were stubbornly holding out against conversion.

The worst part of all this was when our religious guides raised the notion that Muslim women should have husbands who could "satisfy their needs and desires." For those of us in prison, especially those of us serving long sentences, this essentially meant encouraging our loved ones to find new partners. This was a very bitter pill for me to swallow.

Asani and I had never been just your average couple. We'd been comrades in a struggle, meaning we'd shared the highest form of love that exists. All the trials we had endured had strengthened our passion and commitment, and even though we were deprived of our physical relationship we were closer than ever. Such a bond is not easily broken. So I struggled with this new edict, maybe harder than I have with anything else in my life.

I don't know if it's a blessing or a curse but I am possessed of an iron will, and once I had committed myself to the religious path I had no choice but to follow it to its terminus. I also don't allow myself to waver when a decision has been made. There was only one way for me to handle the situation: communicate my decision to Asani and then cut ties with her completely.

It happened overnight. I stopped writing letters. When she showed up at the visiting room I refused to see her. Sometimes she sat there for hours. Like I said, she was a highly determined individual and didn't accept this state of affairs quietly. On either side of the prison walls, my decision crushed us both. I started to get reports from my sisters about what my actions were doing to her, but by then I had begun the process of steeling myself against my feelings by immersing myself completely in my studies and religious rituals. In essence I put myself in a sort of trance, alert to the day-to-day dangers of prison life but otherwise numb to everything else. I can describe it only as locking my emotions away in cold storage—over time I would come to refer to this method of dealing with things as "going to the north pole." It never occurred to me that I was playing right into the hands of our enemies, who do everything in their power to destroy our foundations, which is to say, our families. Despite all my reading and studying, I possessed very little emotional literacy, and was unable to fully acknowledge the massive amount of harm I inflicted on the psyches of my loved ones from which I believe many of them may still have not recovered. I felt that to suffer in the course of a revolution was a normal and necessary process, so I embraced it. I failed to see the importance of staying together, or suffering together—as a couple, as a family. I didn't try to make my situation tolerable. I simply taught myself to bear the unbearable.

This hit home for me sometime in February of 1973, a year after my recapture. I was walking down the tier of E Block when this dude stepped out of his cell and silently handed me a newspaper. It was turned to page three, where a banner headline informed me that my sister Yvette had been murdered by her own husband. He'd shot her in the face five times and once in the abdomen before turning the weapon on himself and committing suicide. Yvette was five months pregnant at the time. I didn't think it was possible for me to grow any colder than I was, but that news just froze me completely. I tried to gather more information, but it was hard to get access to newspapers on the inside. I appealed to the administration to allow me to attend her funeral, though I wasn't surprised when the request was denied. In the weeks and months that followed I pressed other family members for details about what led up to this tragedy, but the whole thing was too fresh and painful to discuss during our brief visits. Eventually they began to shy away from the subject altogether. But the longer I reflected on it the more I realized I had seen signs of trouble whenever Yvette and her husband came to visit me. He was a tall, fearsome-looking guy with a black belt in karate, and he was very controlling over my sister. Later on some reporters interviewed her colleagues and her students, who revealed that Yvette's husband had been maniacally obsessed with her, refusing to let her out of his sight. He would actually accompany her to the school every day and stand at the back of her classroom while she conducted lessons. In October of the previous year, she'd taken a leave of absence due to stress and never returned to her duties, which led everyone to believe that he had forbidden her to leave the house at all. And I had been too concerned with my own troubles, too dedicated to sticking it out at the north pole, to intervene when I saw hints of this terrible state of affairs or try to help them somehow work out their problems.

Once again I sought refuge in the Islamic faith and my Muslim community, which was growing in numbers and in daring by the day. As more and more men converted and the violence inside various facilities continued to rise, it felt like the entire state prison system was moving toward some kind of showdown.

This eventually did happen, thanks to the actions of a tiny little guy named Kevin "Ko Ko" Turner and another dude named Abdul Malik—my old Black Unity Council member who'd once gone by the name John King and was my codefendant in the Von Collins murder trial.

CHAPTER 17

TIPPING THE BALANCE OF TERROR

I was never hopeful that I'd get a fair hearing. A Black man on the stand for the death of a white police officer meant one of two things: the death penalty or life in prison.

The year was 1973 and I'd been transported to Holmesburg prison for the duration of my trial. I was held in isolation and taken out only to be ferried to and from the Philadelphia courthouse. My sisters Maria and Akila were frequent visitors. For several years they'd been visiting BUC members at Holmesburg, including guys from my former cell who were also accused of being involved in the Fairmount Park attack. During my incarceration both of my sisters had become highly respected individuals within the Sunni Muslim community, and through this network they had become acquainted with a large number of Muslim prisoners, among them the phenomenal Kevin "Ko Ko" Turner.

Before I even laid eyes on Ko Ko I'd heard rumors about him. He was what we called a Revolutionary Freeshooter—a reference to a German folktale in which a marksman, by contract with the devil, receives a certain number of magic bullets that are destined to hit their target, with the final bullet answering only to the devil himself. In a previous life Ko Ko had been a Heart with the Thirtieth and Norris Street gang, which meant he was viewed by all his fellow gang members as being the most courageous man in their midst. His exploits on the streets led him to Holmesburg prison sometime in the 1960s, where, rumor had it, he undertook a period of intense self-directed study on revolutionary politics and dedicated himself to the Black Liberation Movement. They said he had read every military training manual there was, and then he read them again. Upon earning his release he sought out the most militant formations in Philadelphia, but by then the movement was disintegrating thanks to the betrayals of the Newton-led West Coast clique and subsequent police repression. Not content to return to gangbanging, he skirted around between different formations until one day he ended up in a gun battle with a policeman on the streets of Philadelphia. Bullets flew both ways, and when backup units arrived on the scene, the cop was dying from his wounds and Ko Ko was on the run. He was captured in that manhunt and returned to Holmesburg to await his trial right around the same time I was also transported there.

Holmesburg was one of the most notorious prisons in the country. It was there that a physician named Albert Montgomery Kligman conducted a series of barbaric medical experiments on Black prisoners. For over two decades, between 1951 and 1974, he exposed them to a range of cosmetic products, chemicals, pathogens, and even viruses, for his own research and on behalf of huge pharmaceutical corporations and several government agencies. Black prisoners desperate for money signed up for these clinical trials without really knowing what they were signing up for. They were paid anywhere from ten to fifty dollars for their participation, which included the application of highly toxic and sometimes even carcinogenic substances such as dioxin. Participants developed lesions, abscesses, and wounds, which Kligman studied but did not treat. Some men reported enduring excruciating pain, long-term skin sensitivity, and a whole host of other sicknesses and side effects. Participants were easily identifiable to the rest of the prison population, as they often walked around wrapped in gauze or surgical dressings. It was just another example of how the prison system refused to view Black people as human beings. When Kligman first visited Holmesburg, his impression of the mostly Black prison population was this: "All I saw before me was acres of skin. It was like a farmer seeing a fertile field for the first time."

That was the environment into which we were thrown. That was the institution in which I encountered Ko Ko.

He was not, at first glance, a particularly impressive-looking guy. He stood about five feet eight inches tall and couldn't have weighed more than 130 pounds. If he'd shaved the whiskers from his face, his delicate features would have allowed him to pass for a very young man. But underneath this deceptive outer appearance lay a will of steel, guided by a mind that I believed bordered on genius.

By the time we glimpsed each other in the corridors of Holmesburg, we had each heard enough about the other to make us both pretty curious. Of course we were never allowed to meet properly or sit down and talk face-to-face—both of us were considered "high risk" prisoners, so we were kept isolated in distant corners of the prison. Like me, Ko Ko had converted to Islam and become a respected figure among the Sunni Muslims, another reason why the guards were reluctant to allow us to interact. As I got to know him I came to realize that while he was a deeply religious person, he did not hide behind the Almighty. He was always very clear that his deeds were his own. He made no excuses, and named no names. If he undertook something, he did so with absolute integrity.

For a long time I had to be content with sizing him up from a distance. Those were trying days for me. My sister's death and my abrupt separation from Asani had frozen me completely and I wasn't ready to come back from the north pole. I found solace only in my religion. The Islamic faith took me through my trial, which lasted six months and was pretty much a sham.

As far as I recall, most of it rested on the testimony of a family member of one of the BUC, who claimed to have been privy to meetings that took place in the basement of their home in which Hakim

(Victor "Sharp" Davis), Wes Davis, Lewis Young, Abdul Malik (John King), and I had discussed plans to "off some pigs." The witness handed over a Panther Party propaganda poster depicting a policeman bleeding on the ground, and a Black man towering over him with a banner headline that read *This, Now*. Again and again the prosecuting attorney referred to the alleged conversation the witness had overheard from the basement of their home. Again and again, he displayed that poster, since he had no other evidence that would have placed us at the crime scene. If I hadn't been fixated on deeply spiritual questions I might have been disheartened by my defense attorney, who in my mind was ill-prepared, the all-white jury, the constant presence of the lackey press in the courtroom, and what I believed to be blatant bias and racism on the part of the district attorney—but I had been prepared for all of it and I accepted the outcome calmly.

I was convicted in the attack on the police station and found guilty of the death of Sergeant Frank Von Collins. The prosecution wanted me sentenced to death, but the presiding judge, realizing that Pennsylvania's death penalty laws were soon to be ruled unconstitutional by the Supreme Court, instructed the jury to hand down what she called a "natural life sentence" instead. On top of this I was slapped with a couple more sentences, years upon years, back-to-back, that I would presumably serve if I could somehow overturn the original life sentence.

That's how they buried us. No pallbearers or gravediggers, just a scroll of paper rippling out of a court reporter's machine. They were not content with putting us six feet under, so they poured concrete over the top to make damn sure that we would not only die, we would well and truly rot.

It wasn't just me and my codefendants. All around the country soldiers who'd committed themselves to the struggle were being shoved into cages and watching while the doors were welded shut. White lawyers told white juries that it was all about keeping White America safe: Put the "animals" away, and children will sleep better at night. Throw away the keys, and no one else would get hurt. There was only one place for us: out of sight, out of mind. Maybe they hoped we'd grow complacent in captivity, that the handcuffs would paralyze our trigger fingers and the leg irons would make docile creatures of us.

It was men like Ko Ko and Abdul Malik who busted that kind of mindset wide open.

I was back at Graterford when it happened, nearing the end of the month of May. News reached us through the grapevine, which as always was shot through with rumors, but the true story needs no additions or embellishments.

Abdul Malik—who also received a life sentence for the Von Collins attack—and Ko Ko had been elected as the leaders of their particular Muslim community. At the time, however, all Muslims at Holmesburg were severely restricted in their religious practice. Under the heavy fist of Holmesburg's warden and his deputy, many of the rituals that Muslims considered mandatory were banned, and could be performed only under threat of being caught and afterward subjected to harsh punishment. For a long time the community had tolerated these conditions, trying to use rational arguments to convince the prison staff to allow them to undertake their sacred rites. But the warden and his deputy, as well as a captain of the guards, were all old-school administrators. They had no intention of changing rules and traditions that had been in place for generations to accommodate what they considered a strange new "cult" among the prison population. Through sustained efforts and a tremendous amount of community pressure, Ko Ko and Abdul Malik managed to secure a meeting with the warden's deputy to air their grievances. They were escorted into his office, where, behind a closed door, a heated argument soon ensued.

Nobody will ever know the truth about what went on inside that office because two of those present at the confrontation are now dead and the other two have vowed not to speak of it. Those who were later called as witnesses to the incident say that the warden and the captain of the guards, on hearing sounds of a serious commotion, rushed into the deputy warden's office to investigate. Shortly thereafter the captain dragged himself out, his body a bloody mess of stab wounds. Dozens of guards in riot gear quickly converged on the scene and after a terrible struggle, managed to extract four people from the office: Ko Ko, Abdul Malik, the warden, and his deputy. The deputy was already dead. The warden succumbed to his injuries while lying in the corridor awaiting emergency medical response teams. Ko Ko and Abdul Malik were delivered to the Philadelphia General Hospital with broken bones, internal hemorrhaging, fractures, and ruptured organs, all caused by severe beatings.

Immediately afterward, Holmesburg prison was subjected to a reign of terror. Frank Rizzo, who had risen in the ranks to become the mayor of Philadelphia, sent legions of his cops to join Holmesburg guards in beating and intimidating the entire population. Speaking to his new police chief, Joseph F. O'Neill, on a car radio on his way to the prison, Rizzo said simply, "Go in there with clubs and all the force we need to put them back in their cells." It went on for weeks, and we could only watch and listen to the news reports from our respective penitentiaries.

For the first time in years I felt something like what I'd felt the day I read about Jonathan Jackson's death following the storming of the Marin County Courthouse; something like the stirrings of a forgotten pride. I'd been on the run for two years and in prison for nearly another two, and in that time I'd realized how quickly people adjust to oppression. Fugitives and prisoners feel this more deeply than anyone else since every aspect of our daily lives is dictated by the authorities. Even those of us who view ourselves as refusers and resisters are forced to bow to the demands of our oppressors. Without even knowing how it happened, you find yourself acquiescing to all kinds of indignities, like offering up your wrists for cuffing, responding to bells and whistles, walking when they say go and stopping when they say freeze. On the other side of the water, your oppressor also adjusts to his power, comes to assume that his orders will be obeyed. They grow cocky while we become crippled. So when men like Ko Ko and Abdul Malik suddenly refuse to play nice, the status quo operatives are caught unaware. It's a terrifying moment for both sides because it signals the end of a long and familiar relationship, that of the slave with his master. The event is not quiet, like the shedding of a skin. It's more like an explosion that shatters everything and everyone involved, and both groups must be prepared to function in the new, altered landscape. Often, when the oppressor learns that we will not always receive his blows with a bowed head and crooked spine, his response is to lash out worse than ever, and this reaction on the part of the authorities has never failed to reinvigorate me.

The incident at Holmesburg was a reminder that some of our fighting formations were still fighting—and winning. The proof of this lay in the fact that, less than a year after Ko Ko and Abdul Malik were carried out of Holmesburg prison on stretchers, all the demands that Muslims had been petitioning peacefully for over many years were suddenly being granted to prisoners throughout the state of Pennsylvania, including the right to fast during the holy month of Ramadan, acceptance of the Qu'ran as a religious book on par with the Bible, and permission to pray five times a day.

It therefore came as a huge shock to me to learn that most Muslims on the outside, including men I considered to be my spiritual guides, did not share my respect for Ko Ko and Abdul Malik's actions. Even worse, I began to read accounts in various newspapers of religious leaders in the streets denouncing them outright, saying they were "not true Muslims," and going out of their way to assist police and the courts in their planned retaliation against these two men. A horrible sense of déjà vu came over me. I saw a shadow of the old self-serving ways of the Black Panther Party leadership that I had come to detest. I confided these misgivings to Tariq and a couple of other revolutionary brothers at Graterford, and they all agreed that the religious leaders on the streets seemed to suffer from the same malaise that overtook the West Coast Panthers: fear. They were free, and so they had too much to lose. They could not accept and embrace a path of armed struggle, even when it had proved itself to be effective. They weren't ready to seize the opportunities that follow the momentous event of a slave slaying his master.

Things soured even further when, on the heels of this, a couple of Philly Muslims approached me and Tariq about using our connections on the outside to help them acquire hand grenades and other heavy weapons to attack some neighborhood bars that they believed had become a nuisance. I was incensed. In my opinion these were definitely not the kinds of problems that we should have been trying to obtain hand grenades to eradicate. It was one thing to try to clean up our neighborhoods, but to use weaponry to wage war on our own community rather than against our oppressors wasn't just escapist and downright cowardly, it was completely against the teachings of the Qu'ran. By that time I had reached a stage in my religious education when I was no longer taken in or thrown off my game by the blizzard of quotes and verses that my so-called spiritual teachers were in the habit of throwing at me. I had studied all the texts myself and, owing to my habit of devoting myself completely to any pursuit I would undertake, I had developed a thorough understanding of Qu'ranic principles, which I found were often at odds with the opinions expressed by many of our religious leaders. By then the number of Muslims behind bars had more than tripled. In Graterford alone the Nation of Islam had close to five hundred members, and Sunni Muslims numbered nearly one hundred. I saw this as a potentially unstoppable force if only they could stop squabbling over who was closest to the Creator and instead join together to try to liberate themselves. But for the most part all these devout men were enamored of the teachings of our misguided guides, and any conversation I attempted to have with them was like talking to a brick wall.

I felt the moorings of the religious community that had held me close for two years start to loosen. No matter what his circumstances, a revolutionary's compass will always point due north, toward liberation for himself and his people, and I had reached the stage where I was no longer content to just sit in prayer. Of course I still adhered to the vows I had taken to the Muslim faith, but at the same time I was aware that I needed more, a goal to work toward with the handful of men I could count on and who were also ready to make a move.

CHAPTER 18

A REFRAIN INSIDE A COFFIN

O nce you make up your mind to get free, you stop seeing obstacles and start seeing opportunities. No matter how closed it seems from the outside, every system has holes, weaknesses—openings. A garbage can filled with rotten food and broken glass. A light fixture in the ceiling. One man's job in the laundry, the fog that gathers over rural Pennsylvania in the early morning, the metal slats from your cot—all these things become tools. Tools to achieve a life beyond prison walls.

Tariq and I were solid. We trusted each other as brothers and could communicate without exchanging a lot of words. We were both quick to size up the guys around us. Tariq had a simple rule for bringing anyone on board with our plans. They had to be "cool," "right on," or "thorough"—meaning we had to know, in our gut, that they were men of their word. Men of honor.

Based on this principle, we finally recruited two other Muslims, both young men from Philadelphia who we knew desired their freedom deeply, a dude named Raheem and another named Amir who was known to everyone as "the Cobra" owing to his slender stature but fearsome ability to attack when cornered.

The plan was pretty straightforward. I had secured a job in the kitchens, and during my shifts I'd observed one particular trash collector paying regular visits to the prison with a hydraulically operated truck. At first glance it appeared that this unit exerted a crushing force on all of the trash placed within. But during a closer study of the vehicle during one of my shifts, I noticed that the operators didn't always engage the mechanism to crush the trash before leaving the prison. Further inquiry led me to discover that this particular model of truck was equipped with a massive blade that rotated in a manner that forced all the trash to tumble over itself, thereby helping fill the cargo area to maximum capacity without leaving any dead spaces. It was set at an angle of about forty degrees to the rear of the cargo bay, which meant that it never completely touched the truck's rear doors. So unless the cargo area was completely full there was no real danger of an individual being crushed by this blade. I'd noticed that the drivers often didn't even engage the compacting blade until a certain quantity of garbage had been dumped into the hold. That was all I needed to know.

Plans of this nature always involve a wide margin of risk. For years now I'd been in the habit of weighing such risks to determine the precise point at which a plan passed from feasible to foolish. Knowingly entering a confined space where there was a chance you'd be crushed by a six-foot blade might seem to some people like a foolish plan. To me, it was our way out of that prison. First we would bury ourselves inside a couple of those huge kitchen bins, underneath some mattresses that we would bring with us. Once the truck had picked up our bins and dumped them into the cargo bay, it would be up to us to scramble to stay on top of the trash, using the mattresses as shields against any sharp objects, metal or steel from the workshops, broken glass, or rusted tin cans concealed within the mountain of rubbish. We calculated that we'd be offloaded in one of the dumps that surrounded the prison, most of which were located at a reasonable distance from urban centers. The thought of spending hours being tossed around in trash, being emptied into a garbage mountain full of rats and flies and possibly worse, of having to stay very still within this heap, choking on rotten refuse until the truckers drove away, did not come close to eclipsing the outcome: freedom.

We made it as far as the kitchen trash cans and would have gone further if not for the fact that another prisoner named Eddie "Eagle" Preston had launched his own freedom bid that same morning and his actions had put all the guards on red alert. A whole platoon of them found us buried beneath our mattresses. They hauled us out, beat us down, and marched us off to Little House on the Prairie. Raheem was shipped off to the state prison at Huntingdon, and Tariq and the Cobra were moved to Pittsburgh. I stayed in that Hole, in solitary confinement, for a couple of months, but instead of being crushed by the isolation I found myself riding high on our freedom bid. Going over every step of the attempt didn't just help to pass the time. It imprinted a whole lot of details in my mind, stuff I could use, things that would bring me closer the next time. It was my refrain inside that coffin: *Next Time, Next Time.*

When I was released back into the general population I found that tensions between the different Muslim communities were worse than ever. The larger each sect grew, the more pressure built up inside that facility. It's hard to paint the scenes of daily life. You have to be able to imagine hundreds upon hundreds of men dressed in identical maroon jumpsuits, most of them bearded, almost all of them wearing different-colored prayer caps, just existing side by side. Some of them are scrawny and scrappy, some of these guys are massive, and one thing they all have in common is that they can fight. Every hour of the day and night they're forced into close quarters, if not into outright contact with one another, and anything can light the fuse: someone brushing against you, someone making the wrong kind of eye contact, someone stepping out of line. Then one day one of the Nation of Islam members allegedly stabbed a Sunni Muslim in the shower and it broke loose, declarations of all-out war.

As always, no one was happier about this than the prison administration. This was how we did their job for them, by despising and conspiring against one another. Shortly after the stabbing, the staff arranged for all the Muslim prisoners at Graterford to be released into the exercise yard at the same time, over six hundred men in total, something they had never allowed before. It wasn't until we'd been corralled into that barbed wire–topped enclosure that we noticed the state police had been called in and their sharpshooters placed in the towers surrounding and overlooking the yard. A couple of minutes later a state helicopter appeared overhead, dipping and hovering low over the scene. It was their idea of a battle royal. They would watch while we killed one another, then, in the name of breaking up the brawl, they would kill or maim those still standing, picking us off one by one. But nestled within all the bravado and passionate hatred between the groups was a handful of highly evolved and educated individuals who were capable of talking their men down. These cooler heads stepped out in front of the opposing armies and prevailed. To this day no one has acknowledged the role they played in preventing a massacre. The archives of the White Man have a habit of filling themselves up only with stories of Black men who start riots, not those who stop them.

Meanwhile, the escape attempts continued. A comrade of ours named Jarrod "Azhari" Anderson managed to maneuver himself onto a work detail that labored on Graterford's huge farm, a job usually reserved for what the staff called Short Timers: prisoners whose sentences are nearly up and who are considered less of a flight risk. The only inmates who get more perks than Short Timers are Old Timers, prisoners who have spent twenty or more years in prison. Staff believe these men are so broken in and broken down that they can be trusted to work outside the prison walls, without chains, overseen by a small, lenient group of guards who are not even equipped with firearms. Now, Jarrod was a Short Timer with just two more years on the books, but he was also a revolutionary, and when he learned of our plans he decided to use his privileged position to make a freedom bid of his own, and then return to help the rest of us out. I wasn't privy to the details of how he arranged for a getaway car to meet him on the perimeter of the farm—all I know is that he made it as far as Philly before he was rearrested.

During this time I began to make the acquaintance of a prisoner whose life had been on a track parallel to mine since we were kids: David "Mustafa" Richards. We'd been informed of each other's exploits through mutual comrades. Every time his name came up, the suggestion was made that Mustafa and I would hit it off. He was just as committed to revolution as I was. He had been in prison six years and earned himself a reputation as a fearsome individual and a brave fighter. Like me, he had converted to Islam under the Sunni faith, and devout members of that community had similarly high praise for Mustafa that was always somehow paired with a comparison between the two of us. Before I even came face-to-face with him, I had begun to think of the two of us as long-lost brothers who'd been separated or kept apart for reasons we would never understand.

When we finally sat down together, we took a good long look at each other. I don't know what his first impressions were, but my immediate thought was *Damn, this is not a dude you can forget in a hurry!* He was handsome and charismatic and capable. This was a world away from how I'd perceived him in the past. Maybe he was going through a similar thought process, because we both burst out laughing at the exact same moment. We started talking about our Corner days and our old ways, the wasted time, the effort we put into killing each other. Laughing it off was the only way to ease any regrets or memories of guys who'd perished needlessly in the street violence that we indulged in as a way to take ownership over our lives. Maybe that's what strengthened my and Mustafa's resolve, and our loyalty to each other: the knowledge that we weren't doing this just for ourselves, but for all the guys who couldn't do the same.

Friendships forged in prison are not like regular relationships. For one thing they happen against all odds in a place that's designed to force people apart, not bring them together. They're built on stolen time, clandestine conversations. They teach you to communicate without too many words and to read signs. They also force you to strip a person down to their bare essentials. Before you trust someone with your life you have to first look hard at their core and understand what makes them tick. From then on, everything else happens automatically. You find you're ready to die for another person without even thinking twice about it. We call it "falling into step." That's how it was with me and Mustafa.

Mustafa had what I perceived to be almost supernatural stores of energy, which he used to transform his body into a streamlined machine, ready for anything. He had a great deal of respect for what he called the "competent enemy"—and he believed we should not only match our adversaries' abilities but surpass them in every way. In this regard, he reminded me of the old RAM leadership, whose directives to their Black Guard had always been: *You must be worth ten or more of the enemy. You must be politically, psychologically, physically, and spiritually superior to a Green Beret* [the elite special force of the US Army] *or the Navy SEALs. You must look death calmly in the face. You must be ready to make the ultimate sacrifice without the slightest hesitation.* He hated waste: wasted food, wasted materials, wasted time. If someone said, "Let's do this tomorrow," he'd return with, "What's wrong with today?"

There were only two things Mustafa was not prepared to do—attack someone whose back was turned. And turn the other cheek. For him, every action must provoke a reaction. Like breathing in and breathing out, you could not have one without the other. To fail to retaliate against an attack was like holding your breath until you died.

And there was another thing about Mustafa. He had a laugh that could shake the world. No matter what we were up against, he never lost that big, huge, honest laugh.

About a year after arriving at Graterford, Mustafa managed to secure a job on the farm, but unlike Azhari he wasn't in a position to simply walk off his work detail. He was assigned to the water filtration plant, where he and several other prison workers were locked inside a building until their shift was up. If he wanted out, he would have had to take over the entire facility by force. When I learned of his plans, I volunteered to use our contacts in Philly to arrange for an escape vehicle to pick him up outside the farm, a task that would require some time and coordination. But Mustafa was impatient. He and another prisoner named Milo Parker decided it would be easier to simply commandeer one of the farm trucks, again using force if necessary. I was still working in the kitchens as a cook, so my contribution to the plan ended up being nothing more than a big bag of food I prepared to keep them going on their journey. Sometimes you do what you can and then just step back and hope.

Between them, Mustafa and Milo managed to take over the filtration plant using shanks. I didn't witness it, but usually this entails taking one or more hostages in order to force compliance from everyone else. They apparently tied up the prison staff and a couple of Short Timers who they believed might try to hinder their efforts—a suspicion that was later confirmed when news reports of the incident revealed that these two particular prisoners were the ones who eventually got loose and summoned help. From one of the staff members in the plant Mustafa allegedly stole a set of keys to a farm truck that was parked nearby. What he didn't know was that all prison vehicles at the time had serial numbers stenciled in big white letters on the roofs of their cabs. By the time Mustafa and Milo reached Philly, state police helicopters had located their position and called in ground reinforcements. Realizing that their captors were closing in, Mustafa and Milo abandoned the truck and commandeered a mail truck—but by then there were too many police on their trail.

News of their recapture came to me through the prison grapevine, and you better believe we talked that story to death. Every movie buff knows that prison breaks and car chases make good entertainment, but for us prisoners an escape wasn't just some thriller. It was the biggest event in our lives as prisoners. It shook up the whole system, and every day that a prisoner remained at large, on the run, was considered a victory. We stacked those victories up against the loss of our freedom and stacked 'em high. Even if the individual or individuals were eventually hunted down and dragged back with a noose around their necks, nothing could quell the euphoria, the pride that lit up our dismal surroundings just for a little while.

CHAPTER 19

TURNING YOUR BACK ON THE WALL

No one was running a marathon. It was more like a relay, where there was always someone behind you who'd just completed a lap and someone waiting up ahead to take the baton. It was probably the greatest thing we had going for us. It was also the thing that frustrated our captors most. All punitive systems rely on the power of deterrence, of making an example: whip one person badly enough that the others won't even try. This system crumbles when it confronts a movement, which can in essence be defined as a group of people who *will not be deterred*. Such a group requires different handling, more sophisticated techniques of obstruction and destruction. While the prison staff were trying to figure that out, we were busy trying to get free.

Both Mustafa and Milo ended up in Little House on the Prairie with fresh prison terms pertaining to their escape slapped on top of their existing sentences. By then, Tariq, Azhari, and I were ready to launch our second liberation attempt.

It was the summer of 1975, and we were becoming intimately familiar with Graterford's geography, architecture, routines, and rhythms. For all their cold deadness, prisons are living creatures. More than on stone walls and steel doors, they rely on the discipline and diligence of a couple of hundred guards, who are after all only human, and therefore prone to mistakes, lapses in attention, laziness. For a long time most prisoners had been aware that two of Graterford's nine security towers were generally not occupied in the early morning hours. Apparently, since over 98 percent of the prisoners were locked inside their cells between nine at night and six in the morning, and any remaining prisoners were closely supervised by prison staff, the administration had reasoned that they could cut some operating expenses by leaving a couple of stations empty during those hours. This information alone was not worth much. You would still have to find a way out of your cell during lockdown and then try to discover which two towers were empty before attempting to climb up into one—obstacles that discouraged all but the most audacious prisoners from even considering taking advantage of this lapse in security. But Tariq, Azhari, and I were systematic thinkers and problem solvers. We worked through the steps one by one.

For my part, I befriended a prisoner who did most of the clerical and grease work for the kitchen staff. He initially worked under the supervision of a guard who, having no desire to do any actual work, offloaded most of it onto the prisoner. This dude turned the whole situation into a side hustle for himself by "selling" some of the jobs in the kitchen. I, in turn, "purchased" from him a new job as a breakfast cook, which got me out of my cell at two o'clock every morning. I paid him a carton of cigarettes for that job, a steep price but well worth it as it would allow me to perform two crucial tasks: keep a close watch on the fog that gathered outside the prison to determine if it was dense enough to provide us with adequate cover, and use the kitchen phone to systematically call every single guard tower so we could be damn sure which ones were empty.

Tariq and Azhari, meanwhile, discovered they could use a hacksaw blade to remove part of the steel window frames in their cells, creating just about enough space to shimmy through them and out onto the roofs that connected our cellblocks to every other wing within Graterford's main compound. They also got hold of some quick-drying paint and putty, which they could use to "patch up" the windows behind them so there would be no trace of them having been tampered with. They would then join me in the kitchen, and together we'd make our way to the unoccupied tower, up into it, and down the other side.

This plan called for a lot of gear. Most importantly we needed to fashion a sturdy rope, along with a strong grappling hook and belay device. We also required some kind of pole that we could use to hoist the whole rope-hook contraption to the top of the tower, since it was far too heavy to simply be tossed up there. We also needed secure places to store our supplies, work on assembling our gear, and finally conceal everything until we were ready to move.

The chapel ended up being the ideal place for most of our needs. Although the main section was occupied by the Nation of Islam, we discovered we could claim a small corner of it undetected and use the messy, cluttered storerooms in the rear of the mosque as a holding area. We created the pole using broken-off mop and squeegee handles, and the grappling gear was made from bits of our metal bed slats. We removed some panels from the ceiling, which gave us ample storage space among the rafters and also allowed us to move in and out of the chapel by traversing the ceiling instead of using the front door. By cutting out a section of the stained-glass windows that was hidden behind some elaborate brocaded drapery, we could enter via the ceiling, drop down behind the window, slip in past the drapes, and from there blend in with the throngs of worshippers that were always coming and going from this space.

Our activities definitely sparked some interest and suspicion from other Muslim prisoners. A dude named Max, who had been part of my underground cell in Philly and was now highly influential in the Sunni community at Graterford, became our de facto security guard—his job was to keep unwanted noses out of our business, a task he fulfilled diligently! That's how it was with escape attempts—there were always people willing to help. At the same time, there were those who became a hindrance.

One such individual was named Roy Forna. Now, Roy was a monster, six feet five and pure muscle. There was a two-word rumor about him: "Seventeen bodies." Tariq, who knew Roy from Philadelphia, always joked that "Roy would cut your neck as quick as look at you—but he's a nice fucking guy!" The rest of us knew him only as one of the prison boxers who had all the signs and scars of a wild life on the outside. We used to compare him to Ali, saying he could float like a butterfly and sting like a bee. He was one of those people you'd rather not tangle with, someone who was best respected from a distance, never allowed into the inner circle. You couldn't just say no to Roy Forna. But we had to.

As we got closer to our anticipated departure, we had started doing some of our prep work in our cells. If we timed this to fall between the guards' scheduled checks, we could simply hang a sheet in front of one person's cell and sit around doing various tasks. One evening Tariq and I were working on our rope using torn and plaited bed sheets when Roy just showed up in Tariq's cell. As soon as he learned of our plans he wanted in. This was less than ideal because by then we just didn't have the time to vet him or fill him in on the all the details we'd been working out for months. Tariq knew him better than I did, so I left him to manage the situation. At first he tried to reason with him. "Keep it down, man," Tariq said. "The guards come around here, we busted." But Roy was adamant as a fly. "Come on, man," Roy kept saying, "I got this, I got your backs, just let me come along, Tariq." To which Tariq had to reply, "No, man, we already halfway there. You know I got you, man, but we about to *do* this shit." At that point Roy just muscled his way into the cell, picked up our rope, and said, "Man, you motherfuckers *need* me, you can't even fix a decent rope." Fortunately for us Tariq has the kind of temperament that can neutralize people and situations. He's just chilled out like that, and after much wrangling he got Roy to back off. In the end, Roy even volunteered to make the rope for us, flipping the cast-iron bed frame over like it was a doll's house and using those slats to test the strength of the rope while plaiting it tightly.

We pooled our meager wages and used those funds to purchase whatever could be procured from other prisoners. Every single prison in the state of Pennsylvania at the time was known for producing goods using the free labor of thousands of inmates. Each facility specialized in something, and they traded those products among themselves. Rockview had dairy farms that churned out milk and eggs, which supplied towns and cities for miles around. Huntingdon produced soaps, Western manufactured license plates. And Graterford had the shoe shops and tailor shops, huge factories that knocked out uniforms for prisons all across the state. By befriending a guy who worked on this production line, we purchased three brand-new guard uniforms, and supplemented them by picking up a few guard hats whenever one of the staff left theirs unattended. We pilfered canned goods and other nonperishable food supplies from the kitchens. But we also needed money to keep us going on the outside. That was a harder task, since most transactions in prison rely on bartering goods, services, and favors rather than dealing in cash. So we embarked on a major side hustle: selling Swag.

In my previous life *swag* had always referred to a lifestyle, the accessories and trappings of a pimp, a gangster, or a hustler. On the inside it referred to something much more basic: edible food. Like all prisons, Graterford served up atrocious chow. It didn't just taste horrible, it was also nutritionally barren, killing us slowly, a mess of fried, starch-heavy, pork-laced items that made people fat and sick. This was particularly hard on the handful of vegetarian and health-conscious prisoners as well as on the hundreds of Muslims who were required by religion to follow a certain diet. So there was already a hungry market for our Swag sandwiches, which grew along with the success of our hustle. Tariq's egg salad sandwiches in particular were a huge hit with the Nation of Islam: he got more orders than we could fill!

The great thing about this whole operation was that it was only semi-illegal. In theory the guard cooks knew what we were up to, and they even supplemented our efforts by giving our work detail close to a dozen raw eggs every day. Sometimes we would even make the Swag right in front of their eyes at the end of our shift. It was like during slavery, when there were two types of slaves: Field Slaves and House Slaves. The House Slaves, being in such intimate proximity to their masters, always got a few perks, some scraps off the table. Maybe it was guilt, or maybe it just let the masters sleep better at night. Either way, those of us who worked in close contact with the guards always got a little something extra—they knew we were not being paid or fed right, so this was a small attempt to offset that and win greater cooperation from us.

Most guards were involved in such elaborate side hustles of their own, and they made our Swag trade look like kid's play. At Graterford the guards pilfered supplies, from toiletries to medicines; received kickbacks from vendors; took portions of meals off of prisoners' trays in order to resell them on the outside; diverted the interest from prisoners' personal bank accounts; took payoffs from the well-off prisoners in exchange for privileges or to turn a blind eye to violence and abuse; and even smuggled drugs. I witnessed racket after racket, some of them degraded enough to make you sick. So whenever we stole a box of cereal, or a jar of pickles or peanut butter, we never felt any kind of way about it, except that we were taking a very tiny portion of what was already owed us. Though I eventually lost my job in the kitchen for stealing, no guard that I am aware of has ever been fired for his role in the numerous criminal enterprises that take place inside a prison.

By now we were too close to our attempt to even think about turning back, so though my termination from the kitchen was a blow, it didn't dampen our resolve. Like with everything else, we just worked around it, waiting only for the perfect weather conditions. My cell was on A Block, where I could look across the main yard and see two of the guard towers. When the fog became so thick that I could no longer make out the towers, it would be time to make our move.

This finally happened in October 1975, on a cold fall morning. I had been staring through my window all night, watching the fog sneak up on and around the prison from the surrounding countryside. It always happened gradually, a slow enveloping of the gray stone like an optical illusion until all you could see was a thick wall of silver smoke. Brick by brick the guard towers disappeared from view. I started punching out my window slats, shimmying through the gap, lowering myself onto the roof. I had wrapped cloths around my knees to protect them as I crawled the nearly one hundred feet between my cell and the kitchens, and also to muffle the noise from the gravel that somehow accumulated on the roof. It was cold, the fog like a wonderful icy skin, concealing me from view. I got in through a dining room window, ran silently into the kitchen, grabbed the receiver off the wall, and started making calls to the guard towers until I reached a number that rang and rang with no answer on the other end. To make sure, I tried the number again. *Ring. Ring. Ring.*

I dropped the receiver and raced for the window and back out onto the roof, then crawled along painfully on my bandages toward Azhari's window to give him and Tariq the all clear. But the fog was lifting as fast as I was moving. It thinned and drifted away in half the time it had taken to accumulate, revealing the guard towers and exposing me to whoever was on duty. At the rate it was clearing I wouldn't even have time to make it to my cell. Not knowing what else to do, I went backward, in the same direction I'd just come from, telling myself I'd be better off hiding in one of the main buildings than risking being caught on the roof. I'd just climbed back in through the window when I heard someone approaching from the kitchen corridor. Peering out through the door, I glimpsed the morning shift of prison cooks and guards taking up their stations in each of the five dining rooms along the corridor.

In a panic I dashed for the long, broad kitchen counter and crouched underneath—a hiding place that would have been useless after a few seconds if the cook assigned there hadn't been a comrade and a staunch supporter of our plan. He was startled to see me, but I kept my cool and talked him down until he suggested I remain where I was, concealed behind the counter, until the staff started serving breakfast. That way I stood a good chance of just blending in with the crowds of inmates queueing up for the morning meal. But already I could tell that something was amiss. From my crouched position under the countertop I detected a flurry of activity outside that was unusual for this early in the morning, a divergence from the regular breakfast routine. Instead of beginning the new day with their customary lethargy, the guards seemed to be moving up and down the corridors in that quick, purposeful way that signaled suspicion on their part. Something had put them on red alert. Footsteps came closer, entered the room. I felt suddenly naked, exposed, realizing that everything hung on this other prisoner keeping my position a secret. A couple of feet of floor space and the loyalty of a dude who had as much to lose as I did and less to gain—that's what stood between me and capture.

I heard the guard's voice, bullying and arrogant. He'd gotten a call from one of the guard towers; someone had been spotted on the roof. Had the cook seen anyone who shouldn't be out of their cell at this time? Any inmates in an unauthorized part of the prison?

"Nah, chief," the cook said. "Just me, same as always."

It's not easy to lie to the guards. They may be a lazy, thieving bunch, but most of them can be razor-sharp when they need to be. They don't always have to strip our clothes to strip us down; sometimes just their gaze can bore right into you. But the cook was rock solid, and pretty soon I heard the guard walking away. There wasn't time for hugging or hand shaking or even thanking the other prisoner. In a situation like this all those gestures are understood. I just had to keep moving.

I knew that the doors leading back to the cellblocks were opened half an hour before the entire population was let out for breakfast. If I could hide until then I might be safe. I took refuge in a dark, empty dining room that led directly to my cellblock. By now it was close to five thirty and the only sound that could be heard up and down the corridor was metal doors clanging open, but I knew I couldn't be seen on my block until I was sure every cell door had been unlocked. At the same time I knew I couldn't stay in the dining room much longer. Soon a guard would take up his position here in preparation for the flood of inmates carrying breakfast trays. I calculated that I would have to risk outright exposure yet again by making a dash for the nearby cell of a guy named Grey, who I knew was on early-morning kitchen duty. His cell door would be open and his bed would be empty. I needed to get in there and hide myself under his bedclothes. I was counting on the fact that the guards' search teams were currently not conducting a headcount—they were first trying to determine who had been on the roof by sneaking up on whoever was out of their cell without authorization, meaning that anyone inside a cell was free from scrutiny for the time being. I was also banking on the knowledge that Grey wouldn't return until after breakfast, and that even if he did, he wouldn't give me away. Every single one of these moves was a split-second decision, like someone playing chess on a timer.

I don't know how long I lay frozen under Grey's blanket running through every possible scenario in my mind. All I remember is the breakfast bell going off, me calmly rising from the bed, straightening the bedclothes, and falling into step with a long line of prisoners heading for the chow hall. By the time Tariq and Azhari joined me at a table, I was ready to let them laugh about my narrow escape. That was part of surviving. Tariq kept making me repeat how I'd scuttled back and forth between the dining room and my cellblock, saying, "I can see it man: there goes Harun thinking he some kind of Mandingo warrior gettin' ready to bust out the slammer, patched up knees, on the roof again, damn man!"

But there were lessons, too. We now knew that even when it was at its thickest the fog could clear in a matter of minutes, so we couldn't afford to take all the safety precautions we'd planned. No more wasting time having an advance scout making phone calls to guard towers before rallying the others to move. Next time we would leave together, make our best guess as to which tower was empty, and just go for it. *Next Time. Next Time. Next Time.*

Our chance came a few days later. Fog so thick we could hardly see our hands when we held them up in front of our faces. Before the sun rose we were on the roof heading for the chapel on bandaged knees. Down below we could detect the movements of a two-man guard patrol making their rounds inside the prison with a flashlight that cut a thin ribbon through the fog. If we were silent, there would be no reason for them to shine that light up to the roof. We made it, and shimmied down through the loosened panels in the ceiling into the space behind the stained-glass window. We changed into our guard uniforms, psyching ourselves up and calming one another down. Then we gathered our supplies, food, hoisting mechanism, grappling hooks, and finally the hefty rope courtesy of Roy Forna, the thing that might have looked to anyone else like a crude mess of scrap cloth and fraying fibers but was to us the lifeline that would bear us away from this place.

Outside the chapel we lay in the grass waiting for the ground patrol to pass. God knows how long we lay there, barely breathing. My mind was racing but also surprisingly empty of all thought. It was as if all my brain power was being redirected to the most primitive senses, listening for the approaching guards or trying to make out any movement through the fog that would tell me how close they were, how close *we* were. They were talking softly, but to us their voices were thunderous, the light from their flashlights grazing the tops of our heads blinding. And when they finally passed within less than thirty yards of us, their footsteps echoed through the earth and pounded in my chest. *Going. Going. Gone.* We had just cleared our first major hurdle; it would take these guys at least an hour to return to this side of the prison.

We made for the tower that we all suspected was empty, and this time we didn't trouble to keep silent. In a clatter of metal and steel we began to prepare our gear, reasoning that if the tower was manned, its occupant would either call down to us or lean out of the window to examine the source of all the noise—at which point, we hoped, our guard uniforms would allow us to pass for any other patrol. Nothing. No one looked out, no one called down. At one point Tariq turned his face up toward the window and yelled something, I don't remember what, but it yielded no response. The tower was empty.

I started to hoist our contraption toward the window, giddy with adrenaline. I had to take a couple of deep breaths to steady my hands because although the next part called for pure core strength, the task of hitching everything up balanced on the end of a thin, makeshift pole was a delicate one. I finally got it up there, and as soon as I felt the hook catch on the other side of the wall, I tugged on the rope to test its sturdiness and began to climb. Every movement was pure ecstasy, an inch closer to freedom, then a foot closer, then another. I was about seven feet off the ground when the rope broke.

I came crashing down, shook off the fall, and had turned my attention back to salvaging the rope when I realized that our hoisting mechanism had also come apart about fifteen feet up the wall. Tariq began to hurriedly heave what was left of it back up the wall in order to use its end to jog loose the section of rope still attached to the hook. If we could dislodge them both, they would fall back down to the ground and we could try to reattach the whole system. But this wasn't an easy task because the hoisting pole was now nowhere near as tall as it needed to be. Tariq worked frantically. Azhari and I stood there in silence. And all the time a new threat was rushing up on us: the fog was lifting. When your whole life depends on darkness, it's difficult to explain how much you dread the light. The dawn sun creeping up along the horizon was to us in that moment a terrible reminder that all our efforts might soon come to nothing. As soon as it was daylight all nine towers would be occupied, and without the protective cover of the fog our "disguise" uniforms would be useless; there were no Black prison guards at Graterford in 1975.

Even as Tariq made a few last desperate efforts to retrieve our gear, all three of us were fast reaching the same conclusion, which was *God damn, this shit is aborted like a motherfucker.* We needed to abandon everything and retreat to our cells. If, by some miracle, we achieved this without revealing our identities, we could conceivably launch a fresh liberation attempt in the future.

Anyone who has come tantalizingly close to freedom will understand how hard it was to turn our backs on that wall. After months of preparation we were so near our goal we could almost taste it, but at a certain moment Tariq just dropped that hoisting device and all three of us ran for the chapel. Everything happened in a nightmarish rewind, the uniforms coming off, our gear going back up into the rafters, the three of us hauling ourselves back up through the ceiling panels and onto the roof, where, on bandaged knees, we crawled as fast as we could back to our cellblocks. We managed to lower ourselves down into an interior courtyard that would give us easy access to Azhari's window. We knew that since it was now past five thirty in the morning, the cell doors would have been opened, so Tariq and I would be able to simply walk out of Azhari's cell and into our own. We were almost there, Azhari first, then me—but before Tariq could shimmy between the bars, a lieutenant on duty in the kitchen spotted him.

The lieutenant yelled out, but we kept going—after all, he'd gotten only a back view, so we still had a chance. Leaving Azhari where he was, Tariq and I raced back to our respective cells, which were on an upper tier. My whole body had seized up, every single muscle taut and tense and trembling as I began to replace the bars in the window and apply the quick-dry paint around it. I was about halfway through this operation when the bell sounded for the entire prison to go back on lock-up status. This is a shrill bell, a screech of warning that grates on your very nerves. It never means anything good, and it's followed by a frantic clicking—a *click-click-click* of cell doors locking people back in.

I worked fast, trying to handle the glass, metal, and putty gently so that the cover-up job would be convincing, trying to steady my hands as I applied the paint. All around me were the sounds of steel doors being wrenched open and slammed shut as the guards herded several hundred prisoners out of the dining halls and back into their cells. Luckily such a procedure requires time, enough of it that when the guards converged on me I had finished the job. I sat on the edge of my cot while they used hammers to beat on the metal air vents that ran across the top and bottom of the window, but since I hadn't messed with those I passed the test. The whole structure held, and after throwing some of my personal belongings on the floor and kicking them around for good measure, the guards moved on to the next inmate.

I didn't want to believe I'd gotten away with it. I spent the next thirty or forty minutes sitting exactly where I was, not yet able to breathe freely. Sure enough, the guards returned. It turned out they'd conducted a more diligent inspection of the cells on the lower tier since that was where Tariq had been spotted, and in doing so they had discovered Azhari's tampered window. This time around they knew exactly what they were looking for, and a couple of blows sent my loose slats and makeshift glass window sailing down into the prison yard below.

Guards are always of two minds about foiling an escape attempt. On the one hand, nothing gives them a bigger or more sadistic thrill than crushing a prisoner's hope, and they savor the moment as much as they can by taunting, mocking, and humiliating us. *Bet you niggers thought that was real smart, huh?* And all that kind of shit. But uncovering one of our convoluted plots also pricks at their arrogance, deflates their egos just a little when they realize what they had to have overlooked for us to even get as far as we did. Outsmarted. Fooled. It stings, and that makes them lash out. Which meant that before we received any "official" notification of the penalty resulting from our escape attempt, Tariq, Azhari, and I were subjected to the customary torture. Boots and batons and fists. Two, three, four against one, while we remained handcuffed and shackled.

Only when the guards were spent did they pull us to our feet and march us off to Little House on the Prairie—and this time they put us on Death Row.

CHAPTER 20
THE BADDEST BROTHERS ON THE BLOCK

You hear the words *Death Row* and you might imagine a bleak, silent place where emaciated men in chains sit around or waste away while waiting for death. That wasn't us.

To picture us you need to imagine a group of men at peak physical fitness, hungry for knowledge, inspired by one another, and determined as hell to keep fighting, to keep living. We prayed five times daily. We worked out every chance they gave us. We learned to play chess. And most importantly we embarked on a serious study of current events, revolutionary theory, and world history. We went from being students to being scholars, and our discussions and debates were nothing short of volcanic. *Death Row* was simply the name of our university.

Since Pennsylvania's death penalty had recently been ruled unconstitutional, the cells on this block were no longer occupied by prisoners scheduled for execution. It was, however, reserved for those whom the guards referred to as "hardened criminals": men like the avowed white supremacist Terrence Whitaker, who'd been imprisoned for rape. He'd escaped from prison, and upon his capture had been locked up in the state prison at Pittsburgh, where he and a couple of other white dudes beat a Black prison guard to death, resulting in his transfer to Graterford.

But there were also ten highly political prisoners on that wing, including David "Mustafa" Richards, Ko Ko, Tariq, Azhari, and me. Some of the baddest brothers in the state finally united on a two-foot-wide cellblock! There was also a young Black guy who would become one of my closest comrades: Carter "Nkosiyabo" Clark. He was just seventeen years old, and serving a natural life sentence. Out on the streets he'd been a member of the Seybert Street gang in North Philly. He'd been imprisoned over the killing of a rival Black teenager in a gang war. Barely a year into his sentence he'd become highly influenced by some prisoners who'd educated him on African culture, the Black Liberation Movement, and other revolutionary ideas, which had prompted him to take the name Nkosiyabo. Like the rest of us, he identified himself as a revolutionary Black nationalist—meaning he saw the necessity for Africans born in America to operate as a separate and self-governing people, while also recognizing the need for a social revolution amongst ourselves to deal with the lingering problems inherited from our enslavement in this country.

Nkosiyabo was relatively new to these ideas, but the rest of us had been grappling with them since the 1960s, so we took him under our wing as we began a tenacious investigation of what had caused the virtual disintegration of the Black Liberation Movement in the streets over the last six or seven years. We studied everything we could get our hands on in order to develop our own comprehensive analysis of where we'd gone wrong and what had provoked such a sudden retreat of the revolutionary upsurge we'd witnessed in our early twenties. We no longer had the luxury of viewing ourselves as foot soldiers. We needed an in-depth, sophisticated understanding and theory of where we had been, where we were at, and where we should be heading. We could not depend on getting this information from the streets. To be sure, there were still organizations active in these areas, yet almost without exception they were rapidly changing their ideologies and programs to fit into a mainstream mold, had been stripped of their revolutionary bases, or were exhibiting infantile tendencies and methods of operating that we rejected as being inadequate to the task at hand. In a way, we were converting ourselves into political strategists, becoming the ideological leaders we didn't have.

Before his death Malcolm X had said that there were a lot of people who were running around calling themselves revolutionaries, and preaching revolution to the masses, who didn't quite grasp that revolutions are terribly bloody affairs in which there is no space to "love your enemy." He rejected the nonviolent tactics adopted and embraced by much of the Civil Rights Movement, and its emphasis on electoral democracy as the pathway to liberation. "It's got to be the ballot or the bullet," he famously stated, "the ballot or the bullet. And if you're afraid to use an expression like that...you should get back in the cotton patch, you should get back in the alley." He predicted the retreat of many self-professed revolutionary organizations when it finally dawned on them that what they were demanding would not be handed over in a polite ceremony accompanied by pomp and pageantry. It would have to be snatched from reluctant hands by force, as Ko Ko and Abdul Malik had demonstrated, and as so many martyrs had proved.

So there we were, locked up in isolation, never allowed to interact beyond yelling to one another through the bars of our cells, urging one another on to new intellectual heights, pushing ourselves to become the best possible grade of revolutionary theoreticians, strategists, and tacticians that existed because by now we were convinced that if we didn't do this, no one would. Nothing we discussed was purely academic: it was all part of a practical course toward liberation that would soon involve fresh efforts to break out if we didn't want to die on Death Row. All our pent-up energy went into these study sessions, which quickly turned into verbal sparring matches that kept us all on our toes. When we disagreed, Death Row exploded. But in the end we shared a goal. We were all intensely committed to what was being proposed and planned, and every man there would either stay true to these ideals and principles all his life or would die trying to implement them.

But we also had moments of great levity, like the day Roy Forna was brought onto the block in retaliation for an escape attempt of his own. Until that moment we'd never had a chance to tell him how his attempt to "assist" us had ended up foiling our entire plan. So as soon as the guards were gone, Tariq started to rag on him, joking about how this "expert fucking rope maker" had provided us with a rope that couldn't even take my weight, which at the time couldn't have been anything more than 160 pounds. We had a huge laugh about that, including Roy himself.

It took the prison staff a few months to realize that housing some of the most politically conscious prisoners in the state of Pennsylvania on one cellblock probably wasn't the best idea. As they came and went with our food and clothing, I'm sure, the guards were privy to enough of our conversations to alert their supervisors, who finally broke up the party. A few months after I arrived on Death Row, in the late fall of 1975, Mustafa was transferred to Huntingdon and I was moved to the state prison at Pittsburgh, otherwise known as Western Penitentiary.

I was placed directly in the Hole, in a completely separate, walled-off section of the prison known as Home Block. I don't know how it came by that name, but by the time I arrived it had a fearsome reputation for the harshness and brutality of the guards. Ever since Terrence Whitaker and his two white companions had beaten one of the guards to death, the place had become a house of horrors, overseen and supervised by a man named Lieutenant Edward. Edward didn't believe in one-off punishments or incremental use of force: instead he favored the use of constant and systematic terror to subdue the entire population. I arrived at Western thinking I'd seen it all, or nearly all, but during my time there I would witness and learn more about the expert use of fear to control and divide people than I previously had any idea about.

On day one Lieutenant Edward ordered five of his guards to strip me naked. He then forced me to submit to the most rigorous physical examination I have ever endured: they inspected the soles of my feet, they ran their hands roughly through my hair and along my scalp, and finally they forced me to bend over and spread my buttocks open. While Edward snapped out the orders, his men stood around swinging their long black riot sticks menacingly. When he was satisfied with my body search, the whole battalion marched me off to a seven-by-five-foot cell with nothing in it but a concrete slab that served as a bed and a concrete-encased sink and toilet. Instead of locking me up alone they all piled inside with me. One of the guards jumped up on the mattress that lay on the concrete block, purposefully sinking the soles of his boots into my bedclothes. Edward proceeded to recite a list of draconian rules that I would have to abide by unless I wanted a "clubbing," stuff like always having my hands on my head when I stepped out of my cell or submitting to frisks and strip searches before virtually any activity. Then he started on my prison record, saying things like, "I know all about you motherfuckers from Philly, and your Black Panther bullshit. I've had guys like you in here before and I will again, and I don't care how many of you come my way—on Home Block there's only one person who matters, and that's me. You get that, you sack of shit?"

They departed with a flourish, leaving nothing but black boot prints on the white sheets.

I'd been surrounded by hostile forces plenty of times in my life. From my gang war days to my revolutionary activity on the streets of Philadelphia, I'd encountered my fair share of threats. But I have to admit that standing there in that cell in my underwear, clutching my prison uniform in my hands and listening to those guards' footsteps echoing down the block, I was suitably impressed. There wasn't a doubt in my mind that these guys wouldn't think twice about seriously maiming me if I put even one toe out of line.

After a couple of minutes I regained my composure, suppressed my fear, and took a good hard look at my surroundings. A door made of close-set steel bars led out onto the cellblock. A horizontal slit served as a food slot. Outside, out of reach, was a forty-watt light bulb. I couldn't see or touch anything in the adjoining cells—in fact, the bars of my door were so narrowly spaced I couldn't even slip my hand between them. In addition to my blue-striped, concentration camp–style canvas jumpsuit, I was allowed access to two sets of undergarments and socks, writing paraphernalia, two books at a time, some basic toiletries, and a single earphone that I could use to listen to four prison-selected stations. This was all possible only if I wasn't on what they called Punishment Status.

Within a couple of days I'd memorized the routine: three awful meals a day served on small paper plates, two fifteen-minute showers a week, fifteen to thirty minutes of yard time on weekdays, and weekly visits from family, friends, or an attorney. If I managed to save any of my chattel slavery–like earnings, I was permitted to spend this money on commissary items without actually visiting the commissary; prisoners in the Hole had these personal items ordered and delivered. Smokers had to save and present the burnt ends of their matchsticks in order to receive fresh supplies. You walked *everywhere* with your hands on your head, including to and from the exercise yard. If they left your head even for a second, guards would club you on the spot.

There were about 1,500 prisoners at Western, housed in two blocks called North and South, each of which towered five tiers high. Soon after I arrived I learned that Abdul Malik, my codefendant in the Von Collins trial and the comrade to Kevin "Ko Ko" Turner, was locked up in the cell directly above mine, but we couldn't really communicate by yelling to each other, so he managed to arrange a meeting in the exercise yard. This wasn't a simple matter. The rule on Home Block was that only two men were permitted in the yard at any given time and it was always the guy from a neighboring cell—unless that prisoner for some reason didn't take his allotted time, in which case the opportunity passed to the dude in the next cell, then the next and the next and all the way along the tier, then up to the tier above. So Abdul Malik went down the line and systematically convinced each prisoner to give up their half an hour of exercise so he and I would be paired in the yard. It was a testament to how much respect he had among the prisoners that he was able to pull this off, because an inmate, especially someone in the Hole, treasures his time in the yard above virtually everything else.

Even though Abdul Malik and I were thrilled to see each other after five years, we had to play it very cool so the guards wouldn't realize we were comrades and put a stop to any future meetings. But by jogging and working out alongside each other we managed to quietly communicate some of the highlights of the last couple of years. After the death of the warden and his deputy at Holmesburg, Abdul Malik had spent several years in Holes across Pennsylvania. His reputation among the guards as a fearsome individual was superseded only by his reputation among the prisoners. Politically awakened inmates recognized him as a true revolutionary. Most other Black prisoners simply saw him as a man who was not to be tangled with and kept a respectful distance. But Abdul Malik was pretty much doomed to spend his days in the Hole.

I, however, was released from Home Block within a month, after agreeing to abide by a "contract" while in the general population. It stipulated that I would work a prison job during the day and then, after the last meal, return to my cell to be locked in by six, three hours before all the other prisoners. If I followed this routine for six months, I could join the regular population's routine. Any infractions and I'd be back in the Hole. On my very first night out of Home Block, Tariq paid me a visit.

Strictly speaking, prisoners were not allowed to linger on the cellblocks, but every hour all the cell doors were opened in order to permit inmates to return from their various jobs or activities and use their own personal toilets. Afterward you had to either leave the block or remain locked in your cell until the doors were opened again an hour later. Tariq was so glad to see me he managed to conceal himself behind my cell door until I was locked in, so that we could spend the hour catching up. He and the Cobra had been here a few months longer than I had, and they knew how things worked: outside of fleeting meetings on the yard, the three of us should avoid being seen together so the guards wouldn't make the connection with our past escape attempts. We should communicate by notes whenever in the presence of the staff, or try to arrange clandestine opportunities like this one. He also told me that, owing to Western's diligent guard force and inflexible routines, he and the Cobra had reached a dead end in their efforts to find a way out of this place. If I came up with something—anything that gave us a decent chance—they'd both support me.

I got a job in the kitchens washing and sterilizing the plates, food trays, and utensils of Western's 1,500 inmates. I earned fifty cents a day. By now I was accustomed to paltry prison wages and I had come to view these "jobs" as ways to pass the time, to get to know the inmates, and to observe the staff on a daily basis without drawing any unwanted attention to myself. It was while on this job that I discovered Nkosi-yabo had also been transferred here. Since we had no history of past escapes together we were able to communicate and associate freely, and even work out together. I didn't even need to query him about joining a future liberation attempt—it was just a given, and it was pretty much all we talked about, weighing options, evaluating weaknesses in the security system, and sifting through scraps of information that came to us from the outside world. I remained in my one-track state of mind, fixated on liberation. I thought about it day and night, while hosing down those food-encrusted utensils, while running laps in the yard, while standing under the shower. And I can tell you that when you apply all your mental energy toward one single goal, the chances of achieving it are very high.

One evening I was lying in my bunk gazing up at the light fixture attached to the cell's ceiling when it just struck me: If I could detach that fixture and chop a hole behind it, there would be enough space for me to climb through. Which meant that if this could be accomplished in a cell on the topmost tier of the block, we could either exit into the gap between the cellblock and the roof or directly onto the roof itself. If we ended up in the space between the ceiling and the old tiled roof, we would be well concealed to keep chopping through until we could haul ourselves onto the roof. From there it would be a simple matter of lowering ourselves five stories to the ground. Of course we would have to avoid an armed patrol that was stationed on the roof and another stationed in the outside parking lot below, but I didn't see this as an insurmountable challenge. In any case, if we worked from a cell near the end of one of the blocks, using the night as cover, we could in all possibility avoid these guards altogether. I had a huge smile on my face that stayed with me until I laid the plan before Tariq, the Cobra, and Nkosiyabo the following day.

We had to work methodically. First it was a matter of divvying up tasks. The Cobra was assigned the job of trying to acquire a cell on the top tier, as close as possible to the southernmost end of the block. Tariq would use his contacts among the Sunni Muslim community to acquire the tools we'd need to chop through solid concrete. Meanwhile we all pledged to adjust our exercise routines to include daily intensive upper-body workouts. If we all wanted to make it to safety, it was essential that our arms and hands be strong enough to allow us to down-climb five stories on a makeshift rope as fast as possible. We could trust one another not to renege on this aspect of the plan since every single man understood the importance of pulling his own weight.

Things began to fall into place. First the Cobra received permission to transfer to a cell exactly where we'd hoped, at the rear end of the topmost tier of North Block. Quickly afterward the rest of us managed to secure bunks on various tiers of the same block, which would give us relatively easier access to the Cobra's cell, where all the heavy lifting was being done. Nkosiyabo and I set about recruiting supporters and sympathizers in a number of strategically placed cells on multiple tiers of North Block who would be willing to act as our early warning system against guard patrols. This was an elaborate security apparatus that involved coded messages and signals being passed from cell to cell, which would allow us enough time to either conceal ourselves beneath the bed in the event of a raid or return to our own cells before the guards had time to register our absence. These same brothers also agreed to play their radios at maximum volume to mask the noise that was necessary in order to hack our way through a cemented ceiling. Taking down the light fixture wasn't a problem; nor were we overly concerned about guards discovering the hole in the ceiling, since they almost never entered our cells during routine inspection tours. They just did headcounts, satisfying themselves with a cursory glance at our surroundings. Western was a sturdy old penitentiary, and as far as we knew no one else had ever attempted to escape from it through the concrete ceiling. Plus the staff were so secure in the harsh regime imposed by Lieutenant Edward that it probably didn't occur to them that we would be audacious enough to try something like this, which would only result in a longer sentence under harsher terms than the ones we currently lived under. But there were plenty of stringent rules that we had to work around, including the one that the lights in your cell had to be on at all times so the guards could easily determine what any inmate was up to at any given moment. To get around this little obstacle we jerry-rigged a separate light bulb to hang over the Cobra's bed so that we could then sever the wiring on the original light fixture before hacking around it. We also quickly discovered that our cold chisels would take us only so far in this process. Even if we kept it up for hours, we could do no more than make tiny dents in that rock-hard ceiling. So we had a supporter smuggle an electric drill out of the plant where the prisoners made license plates, and asked another dude to supply us with masonry drill bits. We taped a bath towel around the drill to muffle the sound of its motor.

So there we were. Every single day, after we finished our respective shifts at jobs that measured our labor in pennies to the dollar, wearing wool caps with eye holes cut in them pulled down over our faces, covered in concrete dust, drilling our way to freedom a couple of inches at a time. During the several weeks of this work we had a number of close calls, but the early warning system worked well; on every occasion we were able to take refuge under the Cobra's bed and resume our operation within a few minutes of the guards passing on. I have to admit, we grew a little complacent.

It's always the small things that mess up big plans, tiny miscalculations that end up costing you everything. For us, it was underestimating the zealotry of a guard named Lieutenant Polanski. He wasn't feared only by prisoners but by the other guards as well, to the point that they actually informed certain select inmates when Polanski was making his rounds so that these guys could in turn ensure that nothing was amiss. This was a win-win situation for the guards and prisoners alike since *no one* wanted to be caught on the pissed-off end of Polanski's truncheon.

A message came to us one morning from a cell at the north end of the tier that Polanski was patrolling the block, paying special attention to the cells in the back because he had information concerning some drug dealing in that area. It should have been our signal to head straight back to our cells. But now that we were actually making progress with the hole, it was always a wrench for us to abandon our work. Any delay in drilling meant one more day we had to spend in that hellhole of a prison. So with nothing more than a few glances at one another to confirm we were all on the same page, Tariq, Nkosiyabo, and I pulled our improvised ski masks down over our faces and crawled under the bed while the Cobra put on his kitchen whites and lay down on his mattress with a book.

It was nine thirty in the morning and very few prisoners were on the cellblock. Most were working their assigned jobs, or taking showers, so it didn't take Polanski long to approach the Cobra's cell. He snapped out a few routine questions: What was he doing here at this time of day? Didn't he have a job to go to? What did he mean, he had finished his tasks in the kitchens for the day? The prison wasn't paying its inmates to laze around reading at nine o'clock in the morning. Then he actually opened the door and entered the cell.

I peered out from around a blanket that was draped over the bed, hanging to the floor. The first thing I saw were Polanski's boots. Pushing the blanket aside to give me a better view, I watched the lieutenant giving the Cobra a thorough frisking. He seemed too involved in this task to notice that anything else was amiss, but all he had to do was incline his head upward and he would see a gaping, three-foot-long hole in the ceiling where the light fixture had once hung. There was nothing for it. I elbowed Nkosiyabo and Tariq, and in an instant all three of us were scrambling out from under the bed, taking the lieutenant completely by surprise. But he was a scrappy motherfucker. In a split second he had recovered from the shock and he beat us to the cell door. In the chaos of everyone trying to move in that tiny cell, he slammed the door shut, pressed his body up against it, and fumbled for his keys. But it was four against one. With a couple of collective heaves we sent both the door and Polanski flying—he was slammed against the adjoining wall. Again he recovered double-quick, and tried to yank the mask off my face as I came running out the door, grabbing at me and using the full weight of his body to shove me backward into the cell. Desperate to keep my identity a secret, I started punching Lieutenant Polanski in the face, over and over again, while advancing down the tier and away from the Cobra's cell. Finally I managed to subdue him enough to wrench myself free and race off down the tier behind the others. While Tariq, Nkosiyabo, and I scrambled to change our clothes and hide anything in our cells that might incriminate us during the raid that was bound to follow this incident, we heard the sounds of dozens of guards converging on the block. We knew they were headed directly for the Cobra's cell.

It's one thing to risk one's own safety. But when you have to flee, leaving a comrade to bear the brunt of your collective actions, you feel some kind of way. Of course this was an outcome we'd anticipated, discussed, and prepared for. Each of us knew that if we were in the Cobra's position we would not hold the others responsible for acting exactly as Tariq, Nkosiyabo, and I had just done. But it was tough sitting there in our cells not knowing for sure how bad he was getting it, or what would happen next.

Later we learned that the guards beat the Cobra, handcuffed him, and marched him off to Home Block, where they no doubt used a variety of "tactics" to try to extract information about our identities. As far as we could gather the Cobra gave them nothing to go on, because the guards spent hours doing headcounts and shaking down random cells.

Eventually the prison administration resorted to combing through their records in search of the Cobra's possible acquaintances, which was what led them to Tariq and details of the Graterford escape attempt. He too was moved to Home Block and like the Cobra refused to be intimidated into sharing any information with the authorities, forcing them to go about things the hard way: pouring over the records of hundreds of prisoners in search of a connection that would tie one of us to the Cobra. This process took so long that the staff had to take the prison off lockdown status and allow the inmates to resume their daily routine, so Nkosiyabo and I were actually able to get together at lunchtime and review our options. We both knew it was only a matter of time before they came for me, so I kept reiterating one thing to him: *Never stop trying to liberate yourself.*

Before the day was over six or seven guards entered my cell, handcuffed me, and escorted me over to the administration building. Those walks toward an unspecified location are long ones. For one thing we had to pass through dozens of locked doors, security enclosures, and fences, each one a reminder of the extent of my captivity, despite having come so close to freedom. And of course, the walks give you plenty of time to imagine the worst. For my part, I took the opportunity to remind myself of gang wars, confrontations with the Philadelphia police, beatings I'd taken in detention centers in the past, repeating in my mind that it had been bad before but I'd always pulled through. Finally we arrived at the door of a large conference room. There waiting for me was Lieutenant Polanski and an officer of the Pennsylvania State Police, which handled all crimes committed on prison grounds. I'd no sooner entered the room than Polanski leapt to his feet, grabbed me by the lapels of my uniform, and pinned me to a wall. He knew I was one of those sacks of shit in the cell with a mask on, he said; he knew everything, so why didn't I just come clean and give him the name of the fourth guy who was in there with us?

"We can do this the hard way or the easy way," he said. "So what'll it be, Shoatz?"

I looked him right in the eye and said, "We can do it any way you want."

He pushed me into a nearby chair and turned the proceedings over to the state policeman, who began to question me about the Cobra, Graterford, the incident in the cell, and a whole bunch of other things that I barely registered. When you know you're not going to answer, you become less and less interested in their questions. In that moment they held everything: files and files about my past, the keys to my handcuffs, the power to determine the rest of my life. I had only one thing, the choice to remain silent. Every time I refused to speak they got more and more riled up. For me, witnessing this was extremely gratifying, so I kept it up as long as I could.

Finally I said, "Officer, if you're gonna charge me with something, then you should go ahead and do that. If not, maybe you could let me get back to my cell."

Perhaps they had planned it all along, or perhaps that statement decided my fate, but within a few hours I had packed up my few personal possessions and was sitting in a van alongside several other chained and shackled prisoners all destined for the state prison at Huntingdon—a massive, menacing, medieval fortress about a hundred miles away.

CHAPTER 21

THE HONOR SYSTEM

They called it Breaking Camp—a reference to the "slave breakers" of the antebellum South who specialized in smashing the wills of unruly slaves. Huntingdon was where the state's most recalcitrant and implacable prisoners were sent to be "broken" out of certain undesirable behaviors by guards whose brutality toward prisoners was what I could call legendary. As far back as the 1950s, Old Heads on the Corner would tell us Young 'Uns stories about this place that stayed with me until the day I arrived at Huntingdon in the summer of 1976.

We were unloaded from the van and immediately paraded before a block of cells holding prisoners who were serving time in solitary confinement. A long line of guards wielding huge sticks kept up a constant stream of taunts, threats, and abuse as they oversaw the removal of our shackles, chains, and clothing. While the men in the Hole looked on, a handful of staff members examined every inch of our bodies. Over and over again the guards repeated that this wasn't an ordinary prison. Huntingdon was a special place, they said; *Ain't another quite like it in the whole of Pennsylvania.* But they didn't need to push the point. Most of us were already aware that things were done differently around here, mainly because of the actions and behavior of the prisoners in the Hole.

Usually there's a lot of talk between newcomers and the other inmates. The "intake" routine is our opportunity to greet familiar faces, exchange news, pass on information about someone's buddy at the facility you had just left, or learn which of your comrades were locked up in this joint. At Huntingdon, the guards had warned us that there'd be no talking. I had expected most people to flaunt this instruction just like they did in every other prison I'd been in, but to my surprise, not a single dude in the Hole opened his mouth the whole time we newcomers were subjected to the frisk search. What shocked me even more was that I actually recognized a number of prisoners on this block, almost all of whom had big reputations for being tough rebels, the kinds of inmates who were not easily intimidated or subdued. Witnessing them standing there in silence, or using a few desperate hand gestures to try to relay some message while the guards' backs were turned, was a sobering experience for me.

Later that evening I was given a small paper plateful of food but no utensils. When I asked for a spoon, the guard who'd delivered my meal gave me a look that said I was in trouble. He summoned three others and together they stormed my cell, screaming that I'd disrupted their routine, tearing the sheets and blankets off my bed, and generally causing chaos in my cell. After heaving my mattress onto the floor, they surrounded me with their truncheons and told me that if I ever dared to ask them for anything again, that would be *it*.

The intimidation continued for the rest of the week. I was summoned to the deputy warden's office a number of times and questioned about my past record. Sometimes these interrogations took place in the presence of another staff member or the captain of the guards. At first they pretended not to know anything about my escape attempts. Gradually they dropped a few comments about how Huntingdon had some of Pennsylvania's best marksmen stationed in its watchtowers. Finally, one of the warden's deputies came right out and said: "If you even think about trying to bust out of here, we'll kill you dead." Then he assigned a special guard to watch over me full-time and ordered my release into the general population.

The daily grind at Huntingdon took an enormous toll on its inmates' minds and bodies. Guards never even seemed to think twice about clubbing prisoners for the smallest of infractions—and sometimes for no reason at all, often in full view of the other inmates. Then there were the Glass Cages, an isolated section of the Hole comprising a few cells that were partially enclosed by walls of glass, which allowed the main control station to observe their occupants 24/7. These cells were also subjected to extreme temperature controls and could be made fiercely hot or cold depending on the mood of any given guard at any given time. At its highest setting the temperature got so hot that you could hardly bear to lie on the steel cot; at its lowest, you just froze through the night with nothing but a thin blanket for warmth. Huntingdon guards were also in the habit of severely goading prisoners with verbal or physical attacks, provoking them to do or say something out of line, just so they could then retaliate with a beating. I quickly came to see that this state of affairs was a game to them, a way to pass the time but also to act out their own frustration at being locked in here with us all day long. After all, for the duration of his shift a guard is essentially locked inside the prison, same us as.

Most of the men in here were so used to being overwhelmed and crushed that they had pretty much given up on anything other than going through the motions, following orders, making it through one day at a time. As far as recruiting supporters, it was an entirely inhospitable environment. On the other hand, I was beginning to regard it as an ideal place from which to launch a liberation attempt. For one thing, every prisoner was forced to exist in a constant state of high alert. I'd learned from my past escape attempts that many of our errors sprang from complacency or underestimating our adversary. There was no chance of that happening at Huntingdon. And for another thing, the guards were so sure of themselves, so convinced of their absolute power and our absolute subordination, that I believed we stood a good chance of flying under their radar if we just swallowed our pride, bore the daily humiliation, and complied with their demands. Then when the time was right we could execute a plan that would hopefully take our captors completely by surprise.

In my very first week I was placed on a kind of special observation status that dictated I return to my cell at six o'clock every evening. I was also made a Block Worker, meaning I was tasked with cleaning the block and sorting and passing out clean laundry, a cushy job compared to what I'd done in the past, and one that enabled me to move quite freely around the prison. It was during my rounds on this job that I discovered Mustafa was still locked up here following his transfer from Graterford's Death Row. As soon as we laid eyes on each other we both knew we were thinking the same thing: *How are we going to get out? And who are we going to recruit to help us?*

Selecting teammates for a liberation attempt is an immensely complex undertaking. A plan will succeed or fail depending on the ability of the chosen people to carry it out. Plus *all* relationships in a prison—not only between prisoners and guards, but among prisoners themselves and even the guards themselves—are fraught with a high level of peril. This is primarily due to the basic social arrangement in a prison, in which one group is charged with depriving another of every single one of their basic freedoms. One of my comrades once asked a Huntingdon guard what his rights were; the guard simply said, "You have the right to breathe." If you're fortunate enough to find even one person you can trust completely, then you will do everything in consultation with that person, which was exactly what Mustafa and I did.

It was he who brought Jordan Powell onto the team. I had never heard of the guy before, but Mustafa told me he was a Vietnam War veteran, highly trained in advanced combat and dedicated to the idea of liberating himself. I used my position as a Block Worker to swing by his cell and check him out. He was pretty much always in there practicing martial arts. Jordan always had a serious expression on his face, and even after we recruited him, he remained tight-lipped for a long time as he was accustomed to being a loner. Later he would open up a little bit and share some war stories with us. Yet what impressed me most was that even though we barely had a skeleton of a plan, and were not in a position to make any promises about the outcome, Jordan was completely down to follow our lead.

Then there was Harry Coleman. At first blush, you would immediately discount him as a candidate for a commando unit. He had a manner that I could only describe as effeminate and downright bookish. On the outside these might not be considered remarkable characteristics, but in a prison, offset against the macho swagger of hundreds of men, Harry stood out a mile. In fact, he was the type of prisoner who was usually preyed upon by rapists and sadists, but he seemed to be holding his own. Still, I would never even have entertained the possibility of recruiting him if he hadn't already been harboring similar plans of his own.

I first encountered Harry out of the blue one morning while I was standing in one of the school buildings, contemplating the prison wall down below. I was in the habit of seeking out observation points like this one, where I could spend my time methodically working through all the details involved in an escape plan, including the best possible exit routes. Harry walked up beside me and without any warning, without even making eye contact, stated that I could get a better look over the wall if I managed to gain access to a different school building located on the opposite side of the prison. I gave him a brief once over, then immediately left to follow up on his advice. I had to bamboozle my way past a few guards to gain entry to the school building he had mentioned—which I did by using my position as a Block Worker—and discovered that Harry was absolutely correct. The vantage point from this school building would allow me to observe the comings and goings outside the prison wall, as well as the movement of the guards around its perimeter on the inside. More importantly I had a bird's-eye view of two buildings that the administration referred to as Honor Blocks, which lay outside of Huntingdon's huge stone walls and were surrounded only by a barbed wire–topped chain-link fence.

Honor Blocks were the administration's greatest weapon in the daily psychological warfare they waged on prisoners, a place you went as a reward for good behavior, tantalizingly close to freedom. Inmates on the Honor Blocks had better food, higher wages, longer yard times, more books, extended visiting hours, nicer facilities, and most importantly, the chance of a shorter sentence. Their placement outside the "official" prison was part of their allure. To me, these Honor Blocks were rotten to the core, something worse than the plain-faced violence and misery of regular prison life: they were a broken promise, a tease and a lie. They were a place of false hope. And it didn't take me long to reach the conclusion that those blocks were where we would need to concentrate our efforts. So, in short, Harry had read my mind, and by doing so planted the cornerstone for the overall architecture of the plan. After Mustafa and I spent some time doing a "background check" on him, a process that involved delicate conversations with a number of our associates to ensure Harry was solid, I finally approached him in the exercise yard. Like Jordan he didn't say much, just accepted my invitation with a calm nod and a knowing smile.

Our next and last recruit was a guy named Craig "Yusuf" Earl-Washington, who had a voice so deep it was almost intimidating to talk to him. It was like he was speaking into a megaphone or a foghorn, so that whatever he said echoed for several seconds afterward. As far as physical appearances went, he and Mustafa could have been brothers. But their demeanors couldn't have been more different. Mustafa was a real tough guy but he managed to always emit a calmness around others that made it easy to be in his presence. Yusuf on the other hand was flinty, explosive, and quick to voice his objections, all of which made him come across as unreasonable and frightening. He never smiled either, and as a result he was constantly coming up against the guards, who considered him aggressive. For our part we understood that Yusuf's behavior was due entirely to his pent-up frustration and rage, which would serve the team well in what we knew would turn out to be a very physically demanding undertaking. Our challenge was to help him master his emotions so that he would stay focused on our collective goal. In another life, he might have been a poet. He had a lyrical mind and a philosophical side to him that, sadly, was never able to express itself inside the terrible environment we were in. Above all, Yusuf was a true soldier. He never aspired to a position of leadership. There was a steadfast loyalty in him that made him the best kind of team player—I don't think I ever met a man quite like him again.

Putting together a team wasn't the biggest obstacle. An even harder task was finding supporters who were willing to assist us without the payoff of joining our attempt. These were key prisoners with trusted positions or jobs, or access to equipment and gear that we planned to stockpile. On top of that we had to win the silence or cooperation of dudes who knew what we were up to and might compromise our plans in some way. Living in such close proximity for such long periods of time—and with so little to do but study those around you for reasons of personal safety and sometimes even survival—makes it difficult if not impossible to conceal your plans from other prisoners. We were for-tunate that, back then, most prisoners observed a strict convict code, which stipulated that everyone mind his own business, even while being aware of what was going on around him. Anyone who violated that code by cooperating with the guards was branded a snitch and was basically doomed. If someone was revealed to be a snitch, it wasn't unusual for this prisoner to be placed in solitary confinement for their own protection since the response of other prisoners to such a trans-gression was so severe.

Of course it wasn't enough for us to rely on this honor system. We had to be vigilant about perceived threats and neutralize them if neces-sary. One way to do this was by inviting possible traitors into our plans and feeding them false information. Still, guards were not in the habit of acting upon every "lead" that came their way; prisoners constantly had beef with one another and one way of settling scores was trying to get your adversary in trouble with the staff. So just as we had to carefully assess everyone around us, the guards too had to use their discretion in choosing which tips to follow and which to ignore. All of which created enough confusion that we could use it as cover for our own plans—as long as our core group remained solid, waterproof, and airtight. There was absolutely no room for suspicion, doubt, or mistrust among us.

I don't know about the other members of my team, but there were a couple of things that helped me stay on course. The first one occurred when I was transferred briefly back to Graterford, where my lawyer had arranged for some new hearings pertaining to my recent escape attempts and subsequent sentencing. By then I hadn't seen or heard from Asani in two years. In that period I'd reached some harsh conclusions regarding the shortcomings of my Muslim community, particularly those on the outside, all of which made me want to see her face-to-face and admit how wrong I'd been to cut her out of my life. She agreed to visit me, and I walked into the visiting room to see her sitting with one of my sisters, though I don't now recall which one. Just the sight of her affected me deeply because it brought back, in a flood, all the memories and affection I felt for her, which I had dammed up and kept at bay through sheer willpower. It all broke down in her presence, and I found myself rambling on about how I wouldn't be in prison forever and how much I still wanted a relationship with her. But by then she'd made other plans. She didn't say it in so many words during that visit, but shortly afterward I received a letter from my sister informing me that Asani had remarried.

Upon hearing that news, I experienced a shutdown like never before. I felt almost like something inside me had died. Added to this was the negative outcome of my hearings, with all my appeals struck down and more time piled on to my existing sentences. By the time I was transferred back to Huntingdon I was stone cold, my insides turned to solid ice. I became a machine, obsessed almost to the point of mania with our escape plan. Over and over again I told myself that this time I would get out or die trying.

But there was something else, too, that kept me fixated on my goal. It took me years to figure it out and when I finally did it was like something clicked in my mind, because I realized that all my liberation attempts were about something more than getting out of prison: at a much more fundamental level, they were about earning respect. I believe I can trace this desire back to the day when I watched the two cops on Douglas Street viciously beating my next-door neighbor. It wasn't just about witnessing a horrifying attack; it was also about noticing all the other Black people, men, women, and children, who just seemed paralyzed by the whole thing—unable to raise a hand or utter a word in defense of the victim, who himself was offering no resistance. Worst of all was the memory of my father standing over me, appearing to be just as petrified as I was. The whole episode filled me with a deep sense of shame for myself and everyone involved. Even though I was just a child at the time, I recognized it for what it was: a spectacle and a travesty that highlighted our lack of dignity. Ever since that day I've been looking to recover the dignity that was denied us in that moment. So you could say it was a combination of both factors—losing Asani for good and my almost lifelong quest for respect in the world—that kept me steadfast in a situation that was so imperiled many people would have described it as a suicide mission.

You might think I spent most of my time in the yard training my body, but the truth is I spent much more time in the prison library combing through material I thought would support the mindset required for such an undertaking. Prison libraries are notoriously barren places but I did find a couple of gems. Books like *The Great Escape* and *Colditz Story* were excellent accounts of Allied prisoners of war and their attempts to escape Nazi war camps during World War II. Much of it fit our situation exactly, the main difference being that the Allied POWs had a huge pool of recruits who had been trained to believe it was their duty to escape and to refuse to cooperate with their captors in any way—an outlook that was missing from all but a handful of men at Huntingdon. Both books were great page-turners and contained a wealth of ideas that could be adjusted to our circumstances, especially the tenacity of the characters who stayed the course even when their efforts were thwarted or their comrades recaptured or even killed. I also came across an extraordinary book entitled *No Surrender* about Japanese holdouts in the South Pacific islands following Japan's surrender. It detailed how a handful of Japanese soldiers spent years on jungle-covered islands resisting all attempts to force or lure them into coming into the open and surrendering, until they were finally persuaded to do so by loved ones who convinced them that ending their struggle would not stain their families' honor. I shared this book with my teammates with instructions to read it and pass it on, but years later I learned that one of our members, I forget which one, hoarded the book in his cell because of how much encouragement he derived from constantly rereading it! Mustafa located a Boy Scouts manual that contained a gold mine of tips on living out in the wilderness. We also shared with one another details of any movies or TV shows we'd seen in the past that might help us or psyche us up in some way, and we even managed to steal a couple of hunting magazines off the guards, which contained invaluable information on weapons maintenance and the surrounding environs.

Getting our hands on the required weaponry proved to be a huge challenge. Simple prison-made knives would not be enough to stop guards who were equipped with plexiglass shields, body armor, and helmets in addition to being trained to disarm prisoners of their shanks. We needed to up the ante to zip guns, but this required purchasing materials from dudes who worked in the maintenance shops—jobs that almost always went to white prisoners.

Now, in many ways Huntingdon was no different from other prisons. Although 65 percent of the inmates were Black, *all but one* of the guards was white. The only Black guard on the force was stationed in a watchtower, far from the general population. Aside from landing the best jobs, the white prisoners received no preferential treatment and were viewed by the staff as being just as "dangerous" and "ruthless" as Black prisoners, which allowed for a small degree of solidarity between the two racial groups. However, a Pennsylvania prison in the 1970s was still a highly segregated place and it was extremely rare for Black and white prisoners to be seen fraternizing with one another. Which meant that we needed to tread cautiously in our dealings with these white boys so as not to arouse any suspicion among the guards.

Over the course of several months we managed to purchase most of what we needed using the prevailing prison currency, cigarettes. Then, midway through our preparations, Mustafa's contact in the maintenance shops suddenly came to him with a message that he and his buddies knew we were planning to use these smuggled goods in an escape plan, and if we wanted their help procuring the remaining gear, we'd need to invite them to come along.

The guy's name was Buzzard, and he had a reputation for having some sway among a couple of powerful groups of white prisoners, so we couldn't just refuse his offer; plus we needed a few more crucial items smuggled out of the workshops and we didn't want to lose this key contact. Mustafa and I mulled this over at great length. If we said no we ran the risk of Buzzard alerting the guards to our actions, thereby inviting a lot of unnecessary scrutiny. On the other hand, we didn't know these white boys from a can of paint and the social arrangements here wouldn't allow many opportunities to vet them, which would put us in the precarious position of involving men we couldn't completely trust in a plan that required trust above all else. We didn't include our team in these deliberations; Jordan and Harry always deferred to our decisions anyway, and Yusuf would have been furious that we were even considering such a proposal. In the end Mustafa met Buzzard in the exercise yard and conveyed a one-word message: *Okay.*

These boys were sharp: they didn't miss a thing. At one point we had requested some small-diameter pipes that would serve as the barrels for our zip guns. Buzzard immediately demanded a meeting with

Mustafa to ask what they would be used for. Mustafa was forced to admit that we were building guns, a revelation that put both sides on high alert. Right away Mustafa could tell that Buzzard and his friends were uneasy about the Black team members being equipped with more firepower than them, because it meant that when it came to go time, we would be able to extend or adapt the basic plan in unknown ways. For our part we resented having to share this critical piece of information, and we steeled ourselves for some kind of confrontation.

At five o'clock the following morning, three guards woke me up, handcuffed me, and pulled me out onto the tier while they searched my cell. Looking down the row, I saw Mustafa in chains outside his cell. Something or someone had tipped the staff off. As I watched the guards tearing my stuff apart in the way that they do, ripping sheets off the bed, throwing books and toiletries onto the floor, I had eyes for only one thing: a small sandwich tray on my desk that contained a number of soft sugar candies. Earlier that week, Mustafa and I had received a delivery of bullets from one of our contacts on the streets and I'd hit on the idea of concealing them in plain sight by slicing open the candies, pressing the bullets into their centers, patching them back together, and recoating them in fresh sugar before placing them on the tray that all prisoners used for snacks and treats. Acquiring those bullets was no easy task. It had required many months of befriending and negotiating with a heavy hitter within Philadelphia's Black Mafia—a ferocious, ruthless, and resourceful organization that had grown so powerful in the years since I'd been in prison that they'd displaced the Italian Mafia—killing off or subduing anyone who'd opposed them—and now received protection money from just about every cartel, syndicate, or gang that wished to occupy Philly's streets. This group bore no resemblance to any formation I'd ever been part of. As far as I could tell, they had no purpose or politics beyond amassing wealth for themselves and their associates. If their members ended up in prison, they blackmailed the right people to win their freedom through the courts. The dude we approached was serving a long sentence for armed robbery, and the only reason Mustafa and I could even gain an audience with him was because by then our "rep" as revolutionaries dedicated to liberation placed us almost on par with these underworld operators. At the time, one's rep as a prisoner functioned like a credit score on the outside—you didn't need to show collateral, you could just sit on down at the negotiating table and get to business. So the fact that this dude had agreed to use his substantial network to smuggle bullets into the prison for us was no small shake, and I was on pins throughout the meticulous destruction of my cell. Thankfully, the guards completely overlooked the sweet confections! Out of the corner of my eye I could see the guards exit Mustafa's cell, also apparently empty-handed. A day later, Buzzard and a couple of other dudes who had done some smuggling for us were transferred to the Hole. Mustafa and I never said anything about it to each other, but we both knew those white boys had snitched on us, and had voluntarily gone into isolation for their own safety, to avoid any possible fallout.

We took all this in stride because we just couldn't afford to get sidetracked. Our next task was deciding on a location to stash all our stuff. Huntingdon was a huge old prison with hundreds of nooks and crannies, but the guards here were zealous and constantly conducting random inspections of the entire facility. Our only option was to enlist the support of established, approved prisoner organizations, which were given certain privileges like rooms in which to hold meetings or conduct activities. The groups ranged from spiritual organizations to sports teams to cultural enrichment programs and even educational initiatives, but for the most part they were all a sham. We called them "babysitters," whose function was to help the guards control the prisoner population by providing outlets for energy and frustration that might otherwise be channeled in more productive ways, such as escape attempts. Leaders of these groups were carefully selected and, thereafter, closely scrutinized to ensure that they acted first and foremost in the interest of the prison administration. If a leader went "astray" by trying to expand the scope of an organization to actually serve the prisoners' interests, or by advocating for the prisoners in any way, he would be promptly dismissed from his post and a new person appointed as his replacement. If that failed, the organization would be shut down altogether. On the other hand, there were a couple of genuine dudes in charge of a few initiatives who were walking the thin line of accomplishing really positive things for prisoners without unduly alarming the bureaucrats at the top of the pyramid. All we needed to do was locate these rare individuals and then approach them in a manner that would leave no room for debate about whether or not they would assist us.

Within a few months of studying all the organizations closely, Mustafa and I managed to single out one such individual—though I can't reveal the identity of the prisoner in question. All I will say is that he enjoyed near-universal respect among the inmates as a person who would never sell them out to the administration, the way other leaders were known to do. He also had a reputation for being fearless, which meant that we couldn't rely on force or threats. Instead, we confronted him one day in the exercise yard and unleashed a kind of verbal psychodrama on him, laying out our analysis of how these "prisoner support groups" were really just a smoke screen erected by our captors to distract us from our daily humiliation and dilute any possible resistance to our atrocious conditions of confinement. We essentially pinned him into a corner where in order to avoid looking like a charlatan, he'd have to either join our escape plan or allow us the use of his facilities. In the end he agreed to the latter, and wound up supporting us in ways we couldn't even have imagined.

For instance, he surprised us one day by having one of his followers make a special delivery to my cell. This particular prisoner was a huge weight lifter and authorized by the staff to carry some of his equipment to and from his cell in a large gym bag so that he could keep up his practice outside of regular exercise hours. On his way back from the gym one afternoon, he walked coolly into my cell and unzipped this bag to reveal a massive, heavy-duty truck jack, the one piece of hardware that was absolutely essential to our whole operation. I was dumbfounded, but after I'd got over my elation I realized I couldn't possibly risk it being discovered in a random cell search. To my surprise the dude didn't even ask any questions. He calmly zipped the bag back up and asked where it needed to go. He then proceeded to transport this enormous piece of equipment right through the heart of the prison to our "hiding place," which we'd been granted access to by the leader of the organization that conducted its business there. Along the way he encountered several guards who, after exchanging jokes with him about his weight lifting, unlocked various gates and allowed him to pass through them without asking a single question about what was in the bag. I lost count of the number of times Mustafa and I marveled at this maneuver—one of those unimaginable strokes of good fortune that, in my experience, strike only when your entire being is single-mindedly dedicated to a particular outcome. In this same manner, with varying degrees of danger and difficulty, we acquired pretty much everything else we needed—grappling hooks, reinforced fiberglass blankets, a rope, blackjacks, homemade military-style "survival" jackets whose pockets we stuffed with beef jerky, candy bars, and a mix of cornstarch, brown sugar, and crushed protein pills—until that moment when we could look at one another and just know that we were ready.

CHAPTER 22

THE FINAL FRONTIER

September 14, 1977, was the last time I saw Mustafa. We had known each other a little over a decade. Truth be told, I never once even considered this outcome. I just assumed I would have his friendship for decades more.

We had spent a year preparing for that day, a year of daily consultations and conspiracies. We'd developed an almost telepathic form of communication. We each knew how the other thought, we anticipated the same obstacles and often arrived at the same solutions. I had a high degree of respect for our other teammates, but no one could deny that Mustafa and I were the nucleus of the operation. Our final brain wave had been the realization that if we made it successfully over the prison walls and into the surrounding mountains and forests, we'd be hunted by teams of trained sniffer dogs. So the night before our attempt, we instructed the whole team to strip their cells and spray them with a strong-smelling insecticide we'd got our hands on. Afterward everyone would take showers and change into clean clothes and boots, which we would wear until our attempt the following day. We reasoned that this would eliminate or at least absolutely minimize any scent of our bodies in the cells, leaving the bloodhounds with little or nothing to go on.

We had to wait until six o'clock in the evening to set things in motion. That was the time of day when long lines of prisoners were being transferred from the outdoor exercise yard to their respective cellblocks. The plan was for Harry, Jordan, and Yusuf to create a disturbance at one end of the prison, thereby drawing various guards away from their regular posts and allowing Mustafa and me the chance to gather up all our gear and slip in among the prisoners heading for Block F—one of the two minimum-security Honor Blocks that lay outside the prison walls. We only needed to get to the entrance. Once there, we would already be close enough to the outside world to abandon stealth and use brute force to execute the next stage of our plan.

Part one went without a hitch. Keeping our heads down and our steps in pace with the hundreds of other prisoners in the queue, we made it to Block F. We didn't even try to bamboozle our way past the two sentries at the front desk. For one thing, Huntingdon guards were too sharp for that, and for another, we needed to subdue them completely before taking over the entire block. So on approaching the two-man barricade, Mustafa and I whipped out our shanks, and before they had time to react, we had them in armlocks with our knives to their throats. By then Yusuf, Jordan, and Harry had arrived on the scene, and they got busy binding the guards' hands and feet with tape while Mustafa and I raced through the block searching for any other staff who might be milling around that area. There were only two, and they also were swiftly held at knifepoint before being bound. Mustafa placed Jordan at the entrance to the Honor Block with instructions to let any remaining prisoners in but to allow no one to leave. Then I gathered up our massive truck jack and began to force one of the cell windows open, knowing we had only a few more moments in which to leverage the element of shock that had stunned the other prisoners into inaction and silence.

Most of them hastened to get out of our way—and stay out of our way. A couple of others began to assist us by ordering any overcurious or agitated inmates to "mind their own business." One dude shouted out, "Just keep doing whatever it was you were doing before these guys took on the block." Everything was happening so fast I barely registered any of this, but I do remember clearly how one prisoner tried to interfere with me while I worked the window. He was summarily chastised right on the spot by a whole chorus of inmates, which put a swift end to his meddling. After that we met no more resistance from our fellow prisoners; nor did any of them attempt to join us. Even as I worked desperately to wrench the window open, it occurred to me how broken they all were by the systematic terror they were forced to live with. And even the ones who still had some fire in them—like the dudes who had spoken up for us—were effectively neutralized by being on this damn Honor Block with its range of privileges and promises of release.

My efforts with the window were not bearing fruit. Leaving the jack on the floor I darted into a couple of empty cells and managed to tear their radiators from the walls, then use these as props to brace the jack against, but I still couldn't force open the window wide enough for us to shimmy through. While I was wrestling with this, the phone at the front desk was ringing repeatedly. We knew the Huntingdon routine well enough to figure that this was almost certainly the control center calling to inquire why the two guards on duty hadn't returned to the main prison to be reassigned to other posts for the night shift. So under threat of Mustafa's knife, and with clear instructions about what to say, one of the captured guards finally picked up the receiver and relayed an unconvincing message that everything was fine. Even before he hung up we knew it hadn't worked. The guard's stilted, terrified voice was sure to arouse enough suspicion on the other end of the line that the control center would at least dispatch a small team to investigate. We needed to be ready to receive them. I dropped what I was doing and joined the team by the entrance, where Mustafa had already laid out high-pressure fire hoses, which we would activate at his signal. With my body concealed behind a wall, I risked peering down the long corridor that connected the Honor Block with the main prison and saw a couple of guards approaching. I recognized one of them right away,

Sergeant Jansen, a man who knew me well. Before I could retract my head he'd made eye contact with me.

"Shoatz! What the hell do you think you're doing on this block—"

But before he could complete this sentence one of my teammates blasted the firehose at him. The crushing jet of water struck him directly in the face, knocking his glasses off and sending him stumbling while he screamed orders to his men: "Get 'em!" Then, instead of joining the charge toward us, Sergeant Jansen began to run in the opposite direction, presumably to summon more backup. Before I could set out in pursuit he had turned a corner that would put him in full sight of another guard station. It was time to put our backup plan into motion.

Holding one of the bound guards at knifepoint, I forced him to identify the keys that opened the gates to an enclosed yard that led to the gym. I tossed the keys to Mustafa, who led Jordan and Harry out into the yard while Yusuf and I remained behind as a rear guard on the cellblock. In that capacity we were able to neutralize one of Jansen's men, binding his hands and feet and dumping him alongside his colleagues. Through a cellblock window I could see that Mustafa, Jordan, and Harry had managed to scale the barbed wire–topped fence around the yard to the gym roof. That was the signal for me and Yusuf to follow. This was a tricky part to execute, as it meant abandoning the guards and trusting that the bonds would hold long enough to allow us also to make it to the safety of the roof and then down the other side. I was sprinting toward the gym wall when I suddenly discovered Yusuf wasn't by my side. I glanced over my shoulder and saw him wrestling with a different guard, who'd obviously been patrolling one of the catwalks around the Honor Block and been attracted by all the commotion there. I think I slowed down for a split second, but Yusuf hollered at me to keep going—in that deep, booming voice of his—and I obeyed, hauling myself up onto the gym roof alongside my comrades. I thought Yusuf would be able to neutralize the guard, or at least fight him off long enough to reach us. But he didn't. Instead he began to wrestle the guard away from the yard and back toward the cellblock, sacrificing his own freedom bid to give us the chance to get away.

Meanwhile Mustafa was frantically unraveling our rope and grappling hook system, feeding it down along the gym wall. We began to downclimb and this time, unlike at Graterford, the rope held long enough for all four of us to lower ourselves some thirty feet to the ground. This was where we had expected to meet and confront another guard patrol. But there was nothing and no one in sight. The final frontier was a twelve-foot fence also topped with barbed wire, about two hundred yards away from us. We ran toward it. I don't know what the others were thinking. I kept wondering when I'd feel a bullet in my back. We reached the fence. We clung to it like barnacles. All our training, hours of pushing and preparing our bodies, kicked in with a burst of adrenaline as we began to climb, racing ourselves to the top, dragging the fiberglass blanket up with us. Ten feet to freedom. Five, four, three. The whole fence shook and rattled but still no patrol came. Finally at the top, we draped the blanket over the barbed wire and then jumped or fell or collapsed to the other side, onto a tarred road I think was named Pike Street, though I didn't know for sure and I didn't care: we were out.

But being "out" of the facility didn't mean we were in the clear. This was a prison town—a gritty, dismal, lynch-mob town—and the moment I dropped to the ground I knew I faced as much or more peril here than I did on the inside. The first thing I noticed was a crowd of people gathering outside a rough, redneck-looking nightspot directly across from the prison. They were drenched in the flashing lights of an approaching police car. Almost simultaneously I realized the State Correctional Institution escape whistle was blasting into the night. For some reason I hadn't heard it before—maybe, in fight or flight mode, some of my senses had shut down or I'd just tuned out the sound, but now it was all I could hear, a shrill, insistent, piercing shriek that told me one thing: *Keep moving!* But when I tried to move I found myself trapped. My military vest, which contained all my food and outdoor survival gear, was snagged in the fence. I struggled to wrench myself free, but I was well and truly caught. I was forced to wriggle out of the vest altogether and leave it behind. On pure instinct I ran straight into the excited crowd that had congregated outside the pub, hoping they would provide a momentary shield between me and the occupant of the police car, who could otherwise just shoot me down. As I approached, the crowd parted, and if someone tried to stop me or grab at me, they failed. I darted between two buildings and found myself at yet another cross street, almost face-to-face with another police car. Clearly the reinforcements were being called in from all sides. I dove onto the ground and crawled on my belly toward a narrow gap beneath a rotten wooden building. But in escaping the eye of the cop, I'd caught the attention of a couple of neighborhood dogs who set up an incessant barking and yelping. One of them came running out of the house I was hiding under and, growling menacingly the whole time, approached my position until his snout and bared teeth were just a few feet from my face. I put my hand on the scabbard of my knife—the one thing that had made it with me to the outside. I didn't want to hurt the animal but I would need to drive it away if I hoped to escape detection. I began to ease myself out from under the building, talking soothingly to the dog the whole time. Still growling, it started backing away. By then the police car's flashing lights also seemed to be fading into the distance, which meant that the cop hadn't picked up on the dog's warning. Finally I came all the way out from under the damp wood. When I drew myself up to my full height, the dog took off and I ran in the opposite direction, zigzagging between poorly lit buildings that could have been homes or shops spaced about ten to twenty feet apart from one another. Even the streetlights were placed at wide distances from one another, so most of my movements were concealed in deep shadows cast by the looming woods on either side of the road.

I had no idea where my comrades were. Even more disturbing was that I had no clear idea of where *I* was. I had lost all sense of direction and I didn't recover it until I began stumbling down a steep embankment. I plunged so unexpectedly that I couldn't get a hold of my own body and I had to allow myself to fall to the earth, curled into a tight ball, and just roll all the way to the bottom.

I heard nothing but rushing water just below where I came to rest. In my mind I pulled up the maps of the area that we'd been studying for months, and with a cold feeling of dread I realized that this could only be the Juniata River, which runs right past the prison gates. I'd obviously gone in circles, retraced my own steps, and wound up exactly where I'd started. Glancing up I saw that one entire side of the hill I'd just tumbled down was bathed in moving lights that swept across and then back up the embankment: searchlights from police cars. Further toward the horizon were even brighter lights that didn't move, which I assumed to be the collected headlights of several vehicles stationed in one area. Despite the danger inherent in my next move, I knew I needed to verify this assumption; it was my only way to determine my precise location and, thereafter, the direction I'd subsequently travel in. So I began to haul myself back up the hill until I could look over the top. I had been exactly correct. I was back outside the prison, separated from it only by the parking lot, where at least two dozen vehicles were parked: state and local police, off-duty guards, prison search teams, and who knew who else.

I ran back down to the water and waded in. There was a strong undercurrent but I pressed on, going deeper until the water was up to my knees, and then set off in what I thought was a southerly direction. I don't know how long I walked before I noticed a bridge looming up ahead of me. Right away I knew it was the one that crossed the Juniata into the small town of Huntingdon, Pennsylvania. I could make out the silhouettes of about half a dozen people standing on it, peering down into the water or along the road that led back toward the prison. I quickly started to sidestep my way back to the embankment so I would be on sturdier footing if one of them tried to interfere with me, but my movements and the splashing water must have reached them in the stillness of the night because all at once they started shouting and pointing in my direction, and one of them took off running, presumably to alert the authorities.

I no longer had the luxury of trying to hide my footsteps and scent in the water. At a furious pace I clawed my way back up the embankment toward the road, ran across it, and squeezed into a thicket of trees on the other side. This was such a densely wooded area, with such thick undergrowth, that there was only one way to move through it quickly: one arm extended outward like a probe, the other curved in front of my face to protect my eyes. I didn't care about whatever damage the spikes, thorns, and branches did to any other part of my body.

I burst upon a break in the foliage and opened my eyes. Directly ahead of me was a vast cornfield, stalks standing over six feet high. I could just make out the faint sounds of large, speeding vehicles, which grew louder as I progressed at a rapid pace down one of the corn rows, grabbing several ears of corn as I went. When at last I came out on the other side, I found myself on the edge of a highway, which seemed to run parallel to a towering, undulating mountain range: the Appalachians. Only two highways passed this close to the prison: Route 22, which ran east to west, and 522, which ran north to south. I could say with a degree of certainty that this was 22. I also knew that my best chance of outrunning, outlasting, or outwitting my pursuers was to risk crossing the highway and head up into those mountains. I had to wait a long time for a decent lull in traffic, which took a great degree of restraint. Every couple of minutes I wrestled with myself, torn between the urges to keep moving as fast as possible and to lie low to minimize the chance of exposure. But eventually the moment came and I took it.

The closest mountain wasn't one of those that incline gently upward. It seemed to rise directly out of the earth and up into the sky; climbing it was one of the hardest things I've done. I had to grab hold of shrubs and sturdy saplings to haul myself up it inch by inch. I couldn't stop, not for a second. Everything depended on my getting up and over an outcrop of rocks before headlights flooded this section of the highway and gave away my position. I heard dogs barking in the distance, a terrifying sound that seemed to come closer the higher up I went. I could picture the tracking teams getting closer, charging across the cornfield I'd just passed through, tracing my scent across the highway and up the mountain. I lacerated my palms in my desperation to make progress. Each time my body shouted its resistance, I ignored it, until the dogs' barking had faded to a faint echo and I could collapse behind a cluster of jutting-out rocks, completely hidden from view, far enough away from the prison that I could catch my breath and taste the freedom.

PART THREE

CHAPTER 23

MAROONS

Maroons are refusers. They exist in a state of opposition to slavery. Throughout the centuries of conquest and exploitation that have marked our modern history, maroons have been the embodiments of autonomy and independence. Their history spans centuries and continents. Any place that has seen slavery has seen maroonage, but the stories of maroons have been mostly buried under books written by their captors and killers.

To the ignorant, maroons are pariahs in rags, starving primitives eking out an existence on the margins of empire. But to those of us who have studied maroons—the escaped Black slaves, indigenous people, and poor white peasants who refused to remain on the plantation—the term is synonymous with dignity and honor. Banding together in the dozens, in the hundreds, sometimes in the thousands, maroons forged alliances and formed liberated zones throughout the Americas and the Caribbean. These communities represented the highest form of civilization because they were comprised of free people. To us, maroons were not just icons, they were the very definition of royalty.

In September of 1977, there was a maroon running loose in the Appalachian Mountains of western Pennsylvania. Circumstances would force him to live rough, to lap water from puddles on the forest floor, to defecate in the open and eat live animals and wear his clothes to tatters, but every day that he remained at large, he was a king.

CHAPTER 24

SLAVE CATCHER TERRITORY

In the fall months, rural Pennsylvania is quite a place to behold. Foliage is abundant, every horizon and vista an explosion of yellows and reds and greens. Open fields stretch aimlessly toward the foot of the mountain range whose peaks and valleys swallow sunlight and toss it back on the landscape in a stunning array of colors. To a child, or a traveler just passing through, it appears peaceful, the ideal place for outdoor enthusiasts. But when my comrades and I were preparing for an extended period out in these mountains, we had to look past this façade and at the ugly reality beneath it. Despite its dense forests and rugged terrain, western Pennsylvania is not a runaway's paradise—it is, in fact, slave-catcher territory.

A Black body stands out like a sore thumb in Appalachia. Old coal towns are dejected places full of single-story dwellings surrounded by decaying porches whose residents don't take kindly to fugitives. It doesn't take much out here to turn villagers into vigilantes. The whole landscape is pocked with old farmhouses and abandoned mines, reminders that a once thriving economy has been replaced by a quiet, pervasive depression. Every home has a wasted pickup truck parked out front and a shotgun standing by the front door. There's not much out here to keep people occupied, or entertained. Anything amiss, anything out of the ordinary, will make itself felt like a rock plunged into a still lake.

On my first morning, I awoke at dawn. The stress and exertion of the night before had knocked me out cold, but the minute I opened my eyes I was back in do-or-die mode, determined to get my bearings and find a camouflaged hideaway before the sun had risen fully. I scrambled to the top of the mountain until I reached a vantage point from which I could look down on the town and the prison. I wouldn't have many more opportunities to come out into the open and get a bird's-eye view of my surroundings, so I tried to take it all in as a photographer would, freeze-framing the 360-degree vista in my mind.

My teammates and I had agreed that in the event of our separation we would meet up at Raystown Lake, twenty or thirty miles south of where I stood. We had talked at great length about what it would take to avoid capture in the meantime. Most importantly I'd warned the others against attempting to escape the area in a stolen vehicle. There were next to no Black people living out here, so being spotted during an attempted robbery was the equivalent of turning yourself in to the authorities. Plus I was pretty sure the state and local police would erect roadblocks at strategic points along both major highways that criss-crossed this part of the country, so even if we successfully acquired a set of hot wheels, we wouldn't get very far. The only safe way out was to take to the mountains until we could lose our pursuers, or until they abandoned their search. So I spent my first few days of freedom practicing everything I'd learned, from my employment in the forestry camp as a young boy right up to my training with the BUC.

Initially, my biggest concern was the dogs, so I spent a good amount of time laying a false trail by walking about half a mile into the woods and then backtracking until I reached a steep incline that led to a patch of dense undergrowth where I planned to build a hideout. I jumped down into the shrubbery and, trying not to disturb the natural formation of thorns and brambles, managed to squeeze into the very center of it. I stayed in there all day, dozing on and off until the sound of a two-way radio brought me out of slumber. I heard a man's voice quite nearby, then another saying something in response. They couldn't have been more than ten feet away, but I was so deep in the brambles that I couldn't make out their movements at all, which meant there was very little chance of them seeing me. Gradually the voices drifted away. I don't know whether it was the adrenaline or just the sheer exhaustion of planning and executing this escape, but soon after the men moved off I fell back into a deep sleep.

It was dusk when I awoke and decided it was probably safe to start my journey toward Raystown Lake. There was no moon that night, and the darkness was so impenetrable that at one point I had to stop and fashion a combination cane–walking stick to help guide me. I nibbled on the ears of corn as I went, walking steadily onward with no sense of time or distance until I became consumed by an overwhelming thirst. It had probably been over twenty-four hours since I'd had any liquids, and during that time I'd performed some extremely strenuous physical activity. That, combined with the bone-dry corn kernels, had just about dehydrated me altogether. I managed to ignore it for a few hours since there didn't appear to be a water source nearby. But the longer I walked, the more it tormented me. I had never experienced anything like this before, such a powerful need of something that it devoured all other thoughts. It took brutal effort to steel my mind against this urge and keep going. It wasn't until the early morning hours, as I stumbled down a steep hill onto a dirt road, that I noticed a greasy film of liquid pooled in the ruts made by a huge set of tires. I knelt down beside it, swept away the insects, oily lubricant, and grime from the surface, and cupped a few handfuls into my mouth. But it wasn't enough. A few hours later I came across a fairly deep stagnant pond. I waded in up to my thighs, lowered my head, and slaked my thirst—even though I knew I'd pay for it later. A little further down the trail was a small heap of trash from which I extracted an empty wine bottle and a pint whiskey bottle. I filled them both at the pool, then sat on the edge of the path to take off my boots. I was wearing two pairs of socks, and beneath them I'd wrapped each foot in elastic athletes' bandages. I slid each bottle into a sock, used chunks of bark as cork stoppers, and tied one of the bandages into a makeshift waist belt to carry them in.

I didn't get far before the sickness from that awful water hit me. There was no warning—just a series of stabbing pains in my stomach that had me rolling around on the ground, balled up in agony. When they eased up I tried crawling along the trail, but very soon a fresh spasm of pain overtook me and I was down again, writhing around. Every time I made even the slightest movement forward, those pains possessed me. By now it was getting close to sunrise and I needed to conceal myself, so I forced myself to stand and, bent double, proceeded along the dirt road until I discerned a kind of thicket I could crawl into.

I awoke four or five hours later in bright sunlight to find myself in the center of a beautiful cluster of hemlock trees. The ground beneath me was covered in a soft, thick mat of sweet-smelling hemlock needles. As idyllic as it was, I needed to get a move on and locate a more secure daytime spot where I would be well and truly concealed from any possible search parties. I walked on and on. A few times I spied open fields through breaks in the woods that seemed like the most direct route south, but I steeled myself to wait for nightfall before attempting to pass through such an exposed area. I stopped often to listen silently and intently for any sounds that might alert me to human activity, but for many hours I heard nothing.

I alternated between nibbling dry corn and taking tiny sips from my water bottles. Either whatever I'd consumed yesterday that made me sick had settled into the silt and debris at the bottom of the bottles or I'd built up some immunity to it—in any case, I didn't experience that pain again. When I couldn't walk anymore I crawled into a clump of foliage and fell asleep, then I awoke in the moonlight and continued my journey. All of a sudden the narrow path I was on opened up into a field with a couple of buildings at the far end of it. There were also trucks and moving vans parked outside. That could have been the end of the road for me—I was so overcome with the urge to hot wire one of those vehicles and get the hell out of those woods that I almost ran right across the field. With a tremendous effort I battled it down and instead made my way stealthily over to the buildings in search of anything that would help me brave the outdoors for as long as possible. After I'd got my hands on a heavy-duty moving blanket from one of the vans, I retreated back into the woods and lashed it to my back with the remaining elastic bandage. Once again I set off for Raystown Lake.

I lost track of how long I'd walked, and how far. For hours and hours I kept it up, stopping only when I skirted the edges of cornfields to pluck a few ears and add them to my "pack," on and on to the point of exhaustion, until it occurred to me, with a cold, prickling realization, that I was passing through familiar terrain. Of course in our survival training we'd read accounts of people who'd walked in circles for days on end, but I never thought it would happen to me. I'd taken care to make note of certain "landmarks"—distinctive trees or fields or other natural features—to ensure that I was always making southbound progress and not retracing my steps. Now I found myself back in almost the exact same spot I'd spent my very first night: hardly five miles away from the prison. For several moments I just stood there, flooded with shock and disappointment. Then I started to laugh, and once I started I couldn't stop. I laughed and laughed, at myself, at my circumstances, but maybe also from sheer relief and euphoria. Because without my even being aware of it, each hour that passed had built up in me a sense of accomplishment, a feeling of pride and pure joy that I had evaded capture, overcome any temptations that might have led me back into the hands of the state, and had absolutely everything I needed: food, water, sleeping gear, and my freedom. I hadn't felt that good in years, not since before I'd been captured in Philadelphia in 1972.

I could only guess at the kind of hysteria that followed our escape. I didn't know that Huntingdon's administration referred to our breakout as an "uprising" and hugely exaggerated our treatment of the guards as hostages, even though not a single one of them got hurt. I didn't know that a day after we flew the coop the FBI would be called in, and would approve federal charges against me for unlawful flight to avoid confinement. I didn't know that nearly a hundred state troopers and scores of off-duty guards would be summoned to the scene or that dozens of local residents would volunteer their services to the search operation. These were hardened white farmers who knew these mountains far better than I ever would, rugged hunters with exceptional aim and no qualms about shooting me on sight. Around me all was quiet, and all I could do was keep my head down and try to convince myself that my friends were doing the same.

I abandoned my plan to meet the others at the lake. Instead I decided to remain where I was, getting to know the area well enough that I might be able to outlast the search. Then, when I felt enough time had passed, I planned to leave the woods, commandeer a vehicle, and get as far away from Huntingdon as possible. But every day brought new challenges.

First it was the rains. Never before had I experienced the misery of being constantly soaking wet and cold, with no proper shelter and no way to change or alternate my clothing. At some point I had stumbled upon a construction site, from which I took a large piece of plastic sheeting. From then on, any time it rained I promptly removed all my clothes except my shoes, wrapped them in my sleeping bag, and then covered the whole lot with the plastic. I wasn't overly concerned with protecting my body from the rain as long as I had some dry clothes to change into afterward. So there I'd be, stark naked down to my boots, huddled under a tree or a clump of foliage, waiting for the showers to pass.

On a couple of occasions I returned to the mountain overlooking the prison so that I could peer down on the inmates in the outdoor exercise yard. This always gave me feeling akin to pity. Out here I was often cold and hungry, but I felt immeasurably better off than I did while on the inside. I imagined that perhaps the birds I used to witness perched on the prison wall observing our movements also found this segment of humanity pitiful.

A few times when I thought things might be settling down enough for me to make a move, I received a stark reminder that the entire area was still on red alert. One night, about a week after the escape, I risked crossing an open field in search of some corn. There was a house at the far end of it, and I actually saw its occupant come to the door and peer out in my general direction as though they had caught a glimpse of my movements in the moonlight. I dove down and was about to crawl away when my palm squashed something soft. It was a tomato. I had tasted nothing but dry corn for seven days and this fruit was like nectar to me. I devoured it, and then another and another, never taking my eyes from the house at the end of the field whose occupant had long since shut the door and moved away. I knew I should make a move as well, but I couldn't bring myself to abandon that tomato patch. Eventually a different person came to the door, again gazing out in my direction, and a few minutes later a police car drove up to the house. I froze completely, this time unable to move from fear. The paralysis kept hold of me while the policeman exited his car, exchanged some words with the person on the stoop, then returned to the vehicle and actually aimed his searchlight to almost the exact spot I was crouched in. I was on my belly, as low and motionless as I could be, and I guess those lights passed right over my body without picking out my silhouette. As soon as they faded, I eased my way back into the woods, mentally preparing myself for the heightened attention that would surely be directed toward this area.

The first thing I did was lay a false trail, then I backtracked until I reached an incline. I leapt down into a clump of undergrowth, opened up my pack, and removed a piece of plastic in which I'd been collecting dried deer droppings for just such an occasion. I tipped water over my boots and trouser legs all the way up to the knees, then carefully rubbed and worked the feces into the cloth and leather. It was a messy business, but I knew it was the only way to totally obliterate any scent that could otherwise be tracked from the tomato patch to wherever I chose to make my next hiding place. I refused to underestimate those dogs. For the next couple of days I kept a very low profile, remaining completely hidden during the daytime hours, barely even moving at night. After a few sunrises and sunsets had passed, I figured I'd once again thrown my pursuers off my track. But by now I was reaching the end of my endurance. These woods had sheltered me but they were also taking a toll on me and I knew I couldn't keep wandering through them aimlessly for much longer. It was time to make a move.

No sooner had I decided this than the opportunity presented itself. I was doing my reconnaissance one evening when, rounding the crest of a small hill, I noticed a single-story house that sat in a relatively isolated section of the woods at the end of a residential road. I got as close as I dared, then built a kind of nest out of the undergrowth on the hill where I planned to camp out and study the house's occupants for as long as necessary to discern their daily routine. I fashioned a tiny peephole through the brambles, trying not to disturb the natural foliage too much, from which I could just about make out the comings and goings from the house. However I ended up relying more on sounds than on sight to piece together a picture of this family.

Early every morning someone slammed the front door, got into a car, and drove away. Several hours later another, heavier-sounding vehicle pulled up at the front of the house—glimpses of color through the trees told me it was a school bus. A woman's voice exchanged pleasantries with a man, probably the driver, and someone was put on board before the bus drove away. The morning and early afternoon hours were quiet, interrupted only by the sounds and movements of someone attending to various domestic duties. The bus returned in the late afternoon, and after that I'd hear a child or children playing and riding some kind of bike or tricycle out front. Later still, closer to dusk, the car returned and its driver killed the engine and went inside. When darkness fell on my first night of observation, I descended the hill and ventured closer. That was when I spied a metal shed around the side of the house, the kind that's typically used to shelter tractor-style lawn mowers, the kind I could use to hide in. Now that I had come this close I was sorely tempted to peer in through one of the lit-up windows to familiarize myself with the home's interior layout, but I knew how foolish this would be, so I returned to my sentry post to keep watch. The next day passed in a similar fashion, and the next.

Once I had determined that the family followed a regular routine, I bit the bullet.

The day began the same as usual, with the car owner driving away early in the morning, but I waited until the school bus had left to sneak into the shed. Pretty soon, a woman came out the back door with a basket of laundry in her hands and headed for the basement steps. I followed her silently, eased my way inside, snuck up behind her, and clamped my hand over her mouth. She was frantic, but by speaking soothingly and assuring her that she wouldn't be harmed or hurt in any way, I managed to calm her down enough to ask if there was anyone else at home. No, she answered, no one. Keeping her hands pinned behind her back, I made her walk ahead of me up the stairs and into the house, where we searched every room until I was satisfied she'd told the truth—and until I got my hands on a 12-gauge shotgun and four shells. Everything took a long time. She was extremely agitated, obviously convinced that I was going to abuse her or even kill her, so I kept up a steady stream of comforting words about how I only wanted her help in getting out of this area and that if she cooperated with me I wouldn't touch a hair on her head.

Initially this did nothing to ease her anxiety, but the longer I remained in the house with her the more relaxed she became. Just as I felt I had gotten her into a state where she could answer a few questions, two cars pulled up outside. I was forced to clamp my hand over her mouth again while dragging her over to a window. She said the cars belonged to two loggers who parked at her place before heading for a worksite down the road.

"Don't lie to me," I told her. "I know there are search teams looking for those escaped prisoners. How many people are covering this area?"

"The search is over," she said. "It's been a couple of days now—they've given up looking for you. All the other men were captured some time ago."

My heart sank at these whispered words but I couldn't stop to process them. I was busy watching the two car owners disappearing down the road in the direction of a chained-off track that I'd noticed myself while scouting around the area. I realized now that it must lead to a logging site. The woman and I both breathed a little more easily after that but it didn't last long. I continued combing the house for weapons, supplies, anything I felt I could use. I was in the bedroom rifling through a closet when I saw it—a prison guard's uniform hanging among layers of ordinary clothes. And not just any guard's uniform—the man of the house was a Huntingdon prison guard! After a week of living in the wilderness I'd walked right into the lair of a man whose very livelihood depended on my capture and confinement. With that discovery the woman became almost hysterical. She was crying, pleading with me not to hurt her, talking complete nonsense, and practically tearing her hair out. It took all of my effort to bring her back into a functional state. I didn't try to say too much, just repeated two things over and over again: "I'm not here to hurt you or your family. I just need your help getting out. Okay? Do you understand?"

I made her come with me into the bathroom, which took a lot of coaxing and eventually a little force. I had no wish to terrorize her but I did need to move fast if I wanted to carry out my plan, the first stage of which involved changing my appearance as much as possible. But when I finally got her in there with me and turned to face the mirror above the sink, I understood why she was so agitated. I looked completely wild. My huge Afro was studded with bits of foliage and my beard was long and scraggly and unkempt. My eyes looked sunken and had a kind of madness to them that almost terrified even me. In fact, my whole face wore a taut, wary expression, like that of a hunted animal. For a few seconds I just stared at my reflection in shock, barely recognizing the person before me. Then I burst out laughing. I don't think this behavior made her feel any less frightened of me but at that moment I couldn't have cared less. I used an electric razor to clean my entire head and face, then changed into the guard's uniform and escorted her downstairs to the kitchen, where I made myself a snack, shooting a stream of questions at her the whole time.

She told me her name was Catherine Spencer. She and her husband, Henry, lived here with their two sons, both of whom were at school but would be returning soon. She also showed me a picture of Henry but I didn't recognize him. I explained over and over again that I meant her no harm, but I stressed that as long as I was in her company our fates were intertwined, so it was in her best interest to cooperate with me. This meant not alerting the authorities and when her husband came home, doing everything in her power to convince him that I hadn't mistreated her.

I had just finished my sandwich when the school bus pulled up outside. I directed Catherine to the front door and took up my position behind it. Only one boy entered the house. When she greeted him I caught the name Robbie. He couldn't have been more than six years old but right away my presence seemed to disturb him. Neither the prison uniform nor his mother's story that I was a colleague of his daddy's who was here to protect them until his father returned home put him at ease. My guess was that he'd never seen a Black person this close before. He clung to his mother, eyeing me suspiciously. But as soon as I started to tease him and play with him he warmed up to me, and before long the two us were like old friends. Later, while Catherine bathed him and made him a snack, I busied myself with sawing off the stock of the shotgun to make it more manageable in close places. I also found a hunting knife and scabbard, which I strapped to my waist. Around 2 p.m. the phone rang. After giving Catherine clear instructions not to utter a word of warning to whoever was on the line, I stood over her while she took the call. It was her elder son, asking if he could spend the rest of the afternoon at his grandpa's house. She was very composed, telling him, *Sure honey, you stay as long as you want.* We passed the rest of the afternoon in this unlikely tableau—an escaped prisoner, a prison guard's wife, and a little boy, all sitting around in the family's nice rural dwelling waiting for the man of the house to return home. I was armed but trying not to draw attention to this fact for Robbie's sake; his mother was terrified for her life but doing her best to appear normal so as not to alarm him. Robbie himself seemed both oblivious and highly attuned to the odd scenario, all of us slung between the perilous yet somehow mundane nature of the day.

But when I heard the guard's car approaching, all that changed. There was no more time for pleasantries. Using a piece of rope I'd found in the kitchen, I forced Catherine to lie on the couch and quickly bound her and Robbie together before placing a blanket on top of them. They were both crying but this time I couldn't stop to comfort them, I just cocked my shotgun and took up my position behind the front door.

I grabbed Henry Spencer as he entered, yelling at him to lie face down on the floor, and after getting him into a spread-eagle position, I searched him thoroughly before binding his hands and feet. The whole time his wife kept up a flow of frantic assurances that I hadn't hurt her, hadn't touched their son, and would let them all live if they just helped me out. I sat him on the couch beside his family. Being together like that seemed to comfort them all tremendously, so I was able to question Henry at some length, cross-checking his answers with his wife's version of events, all of which turned out to be true.

My comrades had been recaptured, the search had slackened off, and I actually stood a good chance of getting the hell out of here if the whole family was in the car and I remained concealed in the back. The best time to leave, Henry said, would be right then, midafternoon. So under the threat of my gun, I untied them and ushered them out to the car, husband and wife up front, me carrying my gear and their little boy.

To this day I have no idea what went through the Spencer family's minds as we took our road trip through Pennsylvania. All I know is that they must have taken my word about keeping them safe, because at no point did the husband or the wife attempt to summon help, or act against my instructions. I had directed the wife to take the wheel and head for Chambersburg, a route that required us to drive right past the prison gates, thus forcing me to crouch down on the floor of the vehicle for several seconds. I have to admit I was on edge that one of them might do something stupid like drive into the prison or try to signal to any number of guards stationed outside—but she was steady, and just headed south. I made her make several unnecessary detours, crossing the state line into Maryland, reentering Pennsylvania just below Uniontown, and finally heading in the direction of Pittsburgh for a while, even though that wasn't my intended destination. I was leaving those mountains far behind and heading for the home of a dude I'd met in prison whose family lived in a tiny town in southwestern Pennsylvania. Already I could taste the food I'd eat when I got there, could sense the pleasure of talking to someone besides myself or a hostage, could anticipate the sensation of actually being free and not confined in the vast, unfamiliar, and unfriendly wilderness.

About forty miles south of Pittsburgh, I had Catherine pull over in a wooded area where I planned to release the family and take the wheel myself. But by then the engine had overheated and for the life of me I couldn't get the vehicle to restart. For over an hour Henry, Catherine, and I tried to get the engine working, to no avail. Now there was some tricky calculus involved. Here I was with this family of hostages and no way to put between them and me enough distance for me to feel comfortable. On the other hand, if we were spotted, our little group would draw far too much attention, given that both Henry and I were clad in prison guard uniforms and it was unusual—if not downright unbelievable—for a Black man to be hobnobbing with a white family out in the boondocks of rural Pennsylvania in the middle of the night. Options were disappearing before my eyes until, through a process of quick elimination, I settled on binding the family tightly to a tree, abandoning the smoking car, and continuing as rapidly as possible on foot. I had given them my word that I wouldn't harm them, so I'd just have to trust my luck that by the time they freed themselves and ran for help, I'd be far enough away that my liberation wouldn't be compromised.

CHAPTER 25

HOW IN THE HELL IS THE SONOFABITCH DOING THIS?

At about two thirty in the morning on September 27, six-year-old Robbie Spencer managed to free himself from the makeshift bonds I'd used to secure him to a tree. I believe his parents talked him through the process, guessing correctly that a child would be able to slide his wrists out of the rope more easily than they could. Then, step by step, they would have instructed him on how to release them as well, because by 3 a.m. the entire Spencer family was knocking on the door of Betty Bolosky, a resident of Cokeburg in Washington County. Betty Bolosky was horrified by their tale of being kidnapped by an escaped convict because, as she would later tell the press, "You just don't expect that kind of thing to happen here. Folks round here don't even lock their front doors—that's the kind of community this is."

Over the next two weeks, hundreds of residents would echo her sentiments as Washington County was transformed from a sleepy little hamlet into the epicenter of a massive search operation. That very day fifty policemen, forty-five state troopers, teams of bloodhounds, and a handful of helicopters converged on the area. They combed the woods for a thirteen-mile radius, bushwhacking, clear-cutting, allowing their hounds to roam wherever their noses took them. Men stayed home from work and women drew their drapes, locked their windows, and barred their front doors. No one answered knocks after dark. Two entire school districts—the Beth Center District in Washington County and the Jefferson Morgan District in neighboring Greene County—canceled classes indefinitely, forcing nearly three thousand kids to stay home. Their parents were glad; they said they couldn't risk their children being attacked while they stood waiting for school buses on deserted rural roadsides. Days dragged on filled with rumors, sightings, and suspicions that swelled the ranks of the search parties and expanded the scope of their hunt. On October 8, a farmer in the Dry Tavern area of Greene County reported that someone had broken into one of his garden sheds and stolen some vegetables. That brought another ninety-man team into the vicinity, including nearly a dozen state troopers. This time they used German shepherds—the bloodhounds having failed to lead the police to their quarry—but these animals also came up short. Orchards grew heavy with fruit, families being too nervous to venture into fields to pick apples as they always did at this time of year. Dry Tavern became true to its name as even the local bars and clubs emptied of their regular patrons. Ex–coal miners carried straight razors and guns wherever they went, telling anyone who would listen that they weren't killers, no sir—"but if it came to him or us, then he'd have to go." Police watched the thermostats, hoping that the near-freezing nighttime temperatures would do what their expert canine teams couldn't and draw the escapee out of his lair. When questioned by the press they sounded confident that it was only a matter of time before the convict would be apprehended, but amongst themselves they expressed their doubts. In interviews they said things like, "It's not difficult to survive in the wilderness out here—there are berries and water for days!" But to one another they wondered: "How in the hell is the sonofabitch doing this?"

If I had had even an inkling of the extent of the frenzy my presence here would unleash, I would have done things very differently. For instance, I may not have ventured out of the woods toward an old steel mill, on the very evening I'd left the Spencer family tied to a tree, to make a call to my friend using a payphone I'd spotted in a factory lunchroom. I'd stashed all my gear in a hideaway deep in the woods, a few miles from where the car had broken down, after laying a false trail in the opposite direction as usual. I reasoned that if I couldn't make contact with this former prisoner I knew, who lived probably fifteen miles away, I'd go back to roughing it in the wilderness until the time was right to commandeer a vehicle. But the reaction of the workers in that mill made me realize that the police were already on my trail. They kept milling around me and whispering to one another while I fed coins into the payphone. The number rang but no one answered. Finally the men who'd been eyeing me suspiciously summoned a dude who appeared to be some kind of supervisor. He immediately got all up on me, asking what was I doing here and where was I trying to go and whether I needed some assistance. I had Henry Spencer's hunting knife concealed under the jacket of his guard uniform, but I was hugely outnumbered in this old factory, so after feeding them a pack of bullshit, I walked quickly out of the lunchroom, made my way back to the woods, and ran at breakneck speed to my hideout. I knew then that I had all but given away my location but it was too late to find a new one. I figured I just about had enough time to lay two more false trails before returning to the hideout to conceal myself completely, almost to the point of suffocation, inside the nest of thorns and brambles that both slashed and shielded me.

Less than forty-five minutes later, the search parties were on top of me. This time it felt much more intense, much closer and more insistent than the efforts around Huntingdon. It passed over and around me—I was, quite literally, in the eye of the hurricane.

First it was a helicopter buzzing overhead. Then it was dozens of men trampling through the undergrowth, sometimes mere feet from where I lay, their police radios periodically broadcasting messages while dogs barked in the distance. The helicopter was constantly crisscrossing the area: at one point it hovered so low that, glancing up through the brambles, I could actually make out the face of the pilot, right down to his mirrored aviator sunglasses! Someone in the passenger seat of the cockpit was scanning the forest floor with a pair of binoculars. I lay there with the shotgun across my chest. Earlier I had jacked a shell into the chamber, but I had no intention of using up any of my precious ammunition unless I was absolutely certain the pilot had detected my position precisely enough to direct the search teams to me. It stayed there all day, droning over my hideout like a huge, buzzing, deadly insect, occasionally drifting away only to return a few minutes later. But those brambles did their job; by evening the machine had risen higher and moved off completely.

On and off all day for hours on end the search continued. I lay so still for so long that eventually I actually dozed off, waking only when night had fallen. The moon was above me and all around was the deep silence of the woods that I was becoming so familiar with. Even though I knew it was probably safe to get up and move around I didn't. I lay there, my body stretched out luxuriously, reveling in the exhilaration of having outwitted my pursuers once again.

For three days I moved cautiously by night in the general direction of my friend's home, following a clear-cut path through the woods that had been laid to feed electricity to some high-voltage utility towers in the area, until I reached a small village. From a position underneath a small bridge, I could observe most of what was going on down on the main street. Maybe it was the result of having been in the wilds for so long, or perhaps I was losing a grip on my senses, but I became obsessed with that village. Some deep instinct told me to keep watch on it, to study every aspect of its shabby service stations, its drab storefronts, even an ice cream parlor where a bunch of young people had congregated. There had to be something here I could exploit, anything that would help me to bring about a change in my circumstances. Each day spent in the outdoors I was tossed between misery and euphoria. More than anything else I desired a plan, a concrete goal I could work toward that would give some meaning to my silent days and circuitous nights.

I watched until the village emptied out for the evening, checking the watch I'd taken from Henry Spencer to orient myself. It was nearly midnight by the time the last stragglers left the ice cream parlor, and by then I'd become possessed by an irrational, overpowering hunger. This wasn't a biological need that sprang from my body. In a purely physical sense I was entirely satiated by my daily consumption of water, dry corn, and occasional berries and crab apples. What I was experiencing was an entirely mental desire triggered and sustained by the weakest part of my brain, which had begun to crave some "regular" food. The sight of all these storefronts stocked with the kinds of goodies I hadn't indulged in for years had taken hold of me. I began to convince myself to make a dash across the bridge onto the main street and break into an establishment that had a mouthwatering display of sandwiches and cakes in the window. As I stood there wrestling with myself over this absurd scenario, a police car drove slowly down the street, turned a corner, and disappeared. The moment it was out of sight, I jumped up and sprinted across the bridge toward an alley that ran between the bakery and grocery store. I looked frantically for a way to scale the wall to the second story, where I might be able to gain access through a flimsy-looking window. But it was too high, impossible to reach without some kind of gear. Desperate, I began to hunt around for a rock or stone that I could use to break the main storefront window. I was down on my hands and knees in the alleyway feeling around for anything I could use when suddenly, I don't know how or why, I came to my senses. Here I was at the heart of a massive slave hunt, doing everything I could to retain my freedom, and I'd been about to gamble all my sacrifices for some bologna sandwiches and coffee cake.

Roundly chastising myself for my foolishness, I darted back across the road, back into the woods, back to my hideout, my blanket, my corn, my bottles of murky spring water. As I ran, and pretty much for the rest of the night, all I could think about was a chapter from the Holy Qu'ran about the prophet Moses struggling with the children of Israel after he had led them out of slavery and into the desert; how he was forced to condemn them for succumbing to the very same indulgences that I had just fallen prey to: a two-thousand-year-old story about human nature that will remain true as long as we give in to the temptations of our minds and the weaknesses of our flesh.

That experience steeled me against the wave of wind and rain that the following days brought. I was wetter and colder than I'd ever been in my life, but my will was solid. Whenever there was a letup in the rains, I dried my clothes and sleeping bag as best I could and gnawed on some soggy corn. When I noticed rust building up along the barrel of the shotgun I began to dedicate hours to scratching my scalp, then cleaning the oil from beneath my fingernails and applying it to the metal in slow, gentle strokes. I walked and slept, walked and slept.

I began experiencing delirium. People trying to sneak up on me; people standing right beside me. I'd open my eyes and see a person peering down on where I lay vulnerable and exposed. On a couple of occasions these hallucinations were so convincing that I grabbed my shotgun and aimed it at nothing and no one. I knew I couldn't go on like this much longer, but I also wasn't prepared to act irrationally. I continued to lie low, biding my time, conserving my strength. Then one day as I was trudging through the mud, I stepped on a large turtle. I bent down to examine it, half-buried in the earth. It was about ten inches long. I picked it up cautiously and used my knife to jab its throat before it could withdraw completely into its shell. With difficulty I hacked its shell open, and after removing some of its guts I ate that turtle raw. It was raining too hard to build a fire, and I couldn't abandon such a rich source of nourishment on that muddy hillside. It was a breaking point.

A couple of hours later I had collected a huge pile of dead tree parts and sodden branches and dragged them to the very edge of the forest. As darkness fell, I began running back and forth between the pile and the middle of the road, carrying armfuls of the stuff, dumping them down, returning for more, until I had erected a three-foot-high barrier on the deserted mountain pass. I had made up my mind: the very next vehicle that passed this way would be stopped, and forced to drive me far, far away from the mountains of rural Pennsylvania.

The moment I crouched down in the ditch at the lip of the woods, I saw dozens of flaws in my plan, the most obvious being how I would manage a situation in which two vehicles pulled up simultaneously on either side of the barrier. Before I could troubleshoot a solution, I heard an engine straining its way up the hill. It came to a halt at my barricade, then a door squeaked open. I was hidden so low I couldn't make out a single thing happening on the road, so I jacked a shell into my shotgun, leveled it to my shoulder, and scrambled out. Two young white men stood in the stream of light cast by the vehicle's headlamps.

"Get down on the ground!" I ordered. "Face down, on the road, now!"

I hadn't noticed a third guy in the driver's seat. Before his companions could obey my instructions, the driver threw the vehicle into reverse and began inching down the hill. I abandoned the pair, ran around to the driver's-side door of the moving vehicle, and rammed the snout of my gun into his face. At that very moment I heard first one and then another vehicle approaching the opposite side of the roadblock, both driving at a steady pace. Short of taking a hostage there was no way for me to regain control of the situation, and I was becoming frantic. Leaving everyone from the first car where they were, I raced around to the other side of the roadblock, flung open the door, and attempted to pull the driver out at gunpoint.

It was a Black guy, the first Black guy I'd seen since leaving the prison. While I was struggling with him, the driver of the second vehicle—a small Volkswagen—had managed to back up a few feet, swing his little car around in the narrow road, and speed back down the hill. In a complete panic I actually ran a few paces behind the Volkswagen before realizing what a futile chase that was. I returned to the car driven by the Black guy, leapt into the rear seat, and ordered him to crash through my roadblock. He was reluctant, but I had my gun against his neck and bit by bit he managed to bump and nudge the dead wood out of the way, finally driving over the remaining debris on his way down the hill. I ordered him to pick up his pace.

As we sped along the dark, winding road, I tried to get as much information as I could. He told me that the whole community knew about the search, and that most of the white residents of the town had joined the police's efforts. But, he said, there were a number of Black families in the area who had expressed a desire to help me, except that none of them had been able to locate my whereabouts. While he was talking I was barking out directions, telling him to head for a highway that led directly to Pittsburgh. Anytime I detected the lights of an approaching vehicle or any kind of populated area, I crouched down lower in the rear seat. We couldn't have been driving for more than five minutes before he began to slow down. The glow of flashing lights up ahead forced me to remain bent down on the floor, but I demanded a running report of what was happening outside. The dude said there was a state police roadblock up ahead—it was too large to drive through and the road was too narrow for him to turn his car around. By now we had slowed to a crawl. I jabbed the snout of that gun as hard as I could into the back seat and told him in no uncertain terms to floor the gas pedal and just bust on through that roadblock, but he was whimpering that the cops had their guns drawn on him as well. Then, without warning, while the car was still in motion, he flung open his door and lunged out, screaming, "I'm a hostage! I'm a hostage!"

Gunfire followed, brutal, incessant, determined gunfire. The car lurched to a halt against an embankment, and then someone was standing right by the window of the passenger seat above where I was still crouched on the floor, firing his weapon over and over again in the direction the driver of the vehicle had run. The shooter was standing so close I could actually see the fire erupting from the barrel of his weapon. I kept my head bent until the firing stopped and the next thing I heard was something tapping against the glass of the rear window. I turned around slowly to find a state trooper kneeling on the trunk, his revolver pointed directly at me. Before I could react, both passenger doors were flung open and a whole riot of voices was screaming at me to get down, show my hands, drop my weapon, put my face to the floor. Someone grabbed me by the neck, yanked me out, threw me on the roadside. A dozen pairs of hands roughly searched my body. I was dimly aware of lights flashing, some distant gunfire, a siren wailing nearby, and a steady stream of orders and instructions that I couldn't obey because so many people were piled on top of me. Someone clapped handcuffs on me. Someone else jerked me to my feet, kicked me forward and into a waiting police car. A state policeman sat beside me with his shotgun pressed up under my jaw. But even with me in chains and his weapon nearly choking me, he seemed extremely nervous; when I looked at him, he wouldn't meet my eyes. We drove in a caravan of police cars for what felt like miles until at last we pulled up outside a small, rural sub-station with a lynch mob waiting outside. They were jeering and cheering as a couple of policemen ushered me into the station. There were women and children among them. Their faces were lit up with that old fervor, that old, rabid delight that has traveled down the gene pool through generations from an earlier century: the raw, primitive satisfaction of the White Man witnessing a captured slave being returned to the plantation.

I had been free for twenty-seven days.

CHAPTER 26

BACK ON THE PLANTATION

I arrived at Western Penitentiary at 10 p.m. Also known as West Pen, or simply the Wall, this state correctional institution sat on the bank of the Ohio River just five miles west of downtown Pittsburgh. It was here that I received my hero's welcome.

The guards were obviously as rough and arrogant as ever, but as they marched me down Home Block, nothing they could say or do could curtail the outpouring of support from my comrades and even guys I didn't know. Home Block was huge, two tiers of forty cells each, which were mostly occupied by dudes from Philadelphia even though it was a Pittsburgh prison. They may not all have known me personally, but pretty much every prisoner in here was familiar with my situation. Disregarding the guards' instructions to *Pipe the fuck down* and *Shut the fuck up*, they yelled out to me one after the other after the other, giving me props for what I'd done.

I couldn't make out individual voices, so I called out, "Is Abdul Malik here?"

From way down on the tier he answered, "Yeah, yeah, I'm here, Harun. And Tariq's here."

So I said, "Where you at Tariq?"

And from the opposite tier came Tariq's voice: "Right here, man."

Nkosiyabo and Hakim also greeted me as the guards shoved me into a cell and knocked me around for a bit.

When they'd left I called out, "Damn Tariq...you know that shit that we was studying? That shit works, man!"

"Yeah, no kidding," Tariq called down the block. "Harun was running from them like a fucking *maroon!*"

Home Block echoed with a dozen guys voicing their agreement.

Then I asked, "How'd Mustafa make out, Tariq?"

A deep silence fell over both tiers, heavy as a rock. Finally Tariq asked, "You don't know?"

I said, "What's up, Tariq?"

"He didn't make it, man." Tariq's voice broke. I felt like I'd been hit by a thunderbolt. Nobody else said a word. For a while we just listened to Tariq cry. I guess all of us, in our respective cells, were observing a moment of silence for Mustafa. Tariq's sobs were magnified in that hollow, confined chamber, that tomb.

I waited a long while, and then said: "Yeah, well, you know what, Tariq? At least he ain't gotta go through this shit no more."

The official story was that Mustafa died of a "whiplash" injury, which allegedly occurred when he tripped over guard wires on the side of a highway. Police records say he severed the nerves in his spinal cord and died instantly. But none of us believed that story because we knew Mustafa was fit, agile, and athletic, not the kind of person to succumb to this type of rookie "accident." It was more likely, in our view, that he had been captured by either the state police or prison guards and subsequently beaten and killed. We had humiliated and outsmarted one of the most powerful, prideful, and violent groups of men in Pennsylvania, and Mustafa had paid the ultimate price for it. He was thirty years old.

Tariq later informed me that my sister Akila and one of Hamilton's brothers had actually come up to Huntingdon County with a private undertaker, but by then Mustafa's body had been put through all of the cutting up that usually accompanies a postmortem by the state coroner's office. When they finally got hold of his remains—or what remained of the remains—the private undertaker discovered a bruise and discoloration of the skin that pointed to a broken neck, which ran contrary to the police's official account. He said the only way to get closer to the truth would be for Mustafa's next of kin to order an independent autopsy, something no other party had the legal right to do. But the family were too upset over the whole affair to follow up on this advice. Instead, Mustafa was given a big funeral and respectfully buried. Of course none of us was allowed to attend. We mourned him privately, in the dead silence of our cells. I can't tell you what that was like: to lose Mustafa and to pretty much lose hope.

Shortly after my return, Home Block had become a very subdued place. For weeks the inmates had been following my progress on their staticky prison-issue radios. Tariq told me it was all they talked about. Night and day they'd speculated at length about my decisions, my movements, my fortunes. They might as well have been with me out there in the wilderness, he said; that's how much it lifted them up and carried them through each day. It made my recapture all the more crushing—my own disappointment magnified tenfold through the hopes of all these men who'd been rooting for me.

Before I had time to fully process my return or properly comprehend the news about Mustafa, my trial began. This was a long, drawn-out affair for which I was transported back and forth from Washington County. The first time I appeared in that rinky-dink courthouse in Beallsville, the small town where I was apprehended, dozens of residents from surrounding towns and villages turned up to gape and heckle at me. People brought their kids. One woman brought coffee and cake for the reporters. The judge set my bail at $110,000. I was pretty much silent during the hearing, mostly because I didn't have a whole lot to say. At one point I asked a district judge if I was entitled to an attorney. He took a short recess, came back, and said something to the effect of *That won't be necessary, Mr. Shoatz.* When I was leaving reporters surrounded me. They stuck cameras and microphones in my face.

"Tell them the slave was caught and he's going back to the plantation," I said. "That's all I am, just a runaway slave trying to get away."

They had a field day with that one. It appeared in every local newspaper. I don't know how many of them even understood what I meant. But I guess it made for a good headline.

While my trial was going on I began to make the acquaintance of a dude on Home Block named Xavier "Masamba" Wright. In the time I'd been on the run, Masamba had become something of a legend in the Pennsylvania prison circuit, even though he was originally from Chicago, for allegedly stabbing a white prisoner to death. Masamba pled innocent to the charge, but the whole incident created an aura around him that was almost palpable. This was partly due to the guards' graphic testimony—which unraveled years later when Masamba was acquitted of the murder—that they witnessed him stabbing the white prisoner repeatedly while they watched "helplessly" from their towers. An all-white jury sentenced him to death in 1976, and when I met him, he was awaiting a retrial in connection with those false allegations against him.

Masamba was a movie buff. He lived for big action, big moments, and it was as if there were always an audience watching it happen. He knew how to make an appearance—he walked into a room and people noticed him. I don't know what it was, a kind of charisma or energy that made him pop, like those characters in books or films that walk off the screen or off the page, larger than life. I think the thing he dreaded most was being ordinary. He couldn't tolerate boring people, or boredom in any form. Maybe that's why he never spoke of pain, even though he had endured a lot of it. I guess he just didn't think it worth commenting on. As far as he was concerned, what the body was capable of tolerating the mind had no business to question. And he loved to eat. Man! Loved good food in the way that can't be explained or understood by those who have not, at least once, starved.

Initially Masamba and I got to know each other in usual Home Block style—calling out from cell to cell, sharing ideas about books we were reading or what was happening in the movement. But a new development would soon make it possible for us to meet face-to-face and put in motion the wheels of an escape plan that would take us on a journey neither of us could have imagined down in the dungeons of Western Penitentiary.

This "development" came in the form of a cadre of young Black revolutionary sisters who had become active in the Black Liberation Movement in Pittsburgh. With most of the movement's leadership dead, incarcerated, or on the run, they had taken to visiting those brothers still committed to revolutionary ideals who were behind bars. One of these women, whom we called Farah, had developed a very close relationship with Abdul Malik. At his urging, she rounded up her sister-cadres and had each of them register as "official" visitors for me, Nkosiyabo, Tariq, and Masamba, so that we would all be allowed in the visiting room at the same time. It was the only way we could contrive a face-to-face meeting between all the brothers on Home Block.

The first time we managed this, shortly after my arrest, I walked into the visiting room to see this bevy of absolutely beautiful Black women sitting at a table waiting for us. They were all highly educated Muslim women, deeply committed to what was left of the liberation struggle, and young enough that, it seemed, they were willing to risk everything to achieve their goals. Besides Farah there was a woman who went by the nom de guerre Midnight and a pair of sisters named Yemoja and Zahara.

Now, these women were *for real*. Sometimes we couldn't quite believe that while the movement was falling apart, and our life and death sentences were pressing in on us, we had made contact with these audacious, steadfast, courageous individuals who seemed like they were ready for anything. Yemoja and I hit it off especially well, though her sister, Zahara, also impressed me with her razor-sharp mind and tenacious attitude. Like me, Yemoja was skilled at assessing people and situations: sizing up a person, scoping out a place, working out logistics or locating weak points in any plan. She had tremendous faith in the power of individuals to change history. I don't think she experienced fear in the way that most people do. She was more concerned with finding the line between what she was and wasn't willing to do. Once that had been determined, she made damn sure to stay in her lane.

Their visits brought us great comfort and solace, not only because of the news they carried to us from the outside world, but because they were the antidote to the purely male, cold, angular hardness of our life in prison. This small source of positive energy came at a critical time, because my life was about to take a most unpleasant turn.

Any time you plan an escape you must contend with the fact that if you are caught and returned to prison, you will have to face more than your usual dose of violence and mistreatment at the hands of the guards. Now not only had I outwitted one of the most notorious guard squads in the state, I had also evaded them for a whole month, and they were itching to get their hands on me. Anticipating this, my comrades and faithful sisters had already begun an earnest campaign of letter writing, mobilizing the local community and appealing to relevant authorities against my transfer to Huntingdon, which I believed would be tantamount to a death sentence. But it was 1977, a time when prison guards in Pennsylvania were an institution unto themselves, with strong unions and good-old-boy networks of well-placed muscle men in local and state governments. They didn't just pull strings, they could move mountains, so it didn't take long for me to find myself in a state police car on my way back to that big old jail.

I was taken straight to the Glass Cages, and there I was beaten more severely than ever before in my life. The only precaution those guards took was to spare my face, since they knew I would soon be appearing in court. Every other part of my body was fair game. They used clubs, boots, and fists and went at me until they were spent. The injuries I received in that cage, including severe damage to my testicles, remain with me to this day. In the days that followed they did everything possible to make my life a hellish nightmare: alternating the temperature in my cell between burning and freezing; showing up in platoons to threaten, intimidate, and terrorize me at all hours of the day and night; keeping bright lights on at all times; tampering with my meager servings of food; and once even serving me a sandwich with a cat's face and pawprint impressed upon it. I was handcuffed all the time. I wasn't allowed to make phone calls. I wasn't allowed to contact a lawyer.

Eventually, following a Herculean struggle with the prison administration, my sister Akila and my old comrade Mitch Edwards managed to arrange a brief visit, to which they brought along a young white lawyer named Jerry Leibovitz. Jerry was something of a firebrand. He had worked at a prison himself, before leaving to practice law, and was now earning a reputation as a strong critic of the entire incarceration system. The staff and even some of the higher-up bureaucrats both feared and despised him. When he saw my condition and heard my account of what was happening, he joined with my family and friends to launch a massive campaign on my behalf. They bombarded the media with press releases, and Jerry assembled a blistering array of legal documents that he fired off to various public officials, sympathetic human rights organizations, and even old, established religious groups who held some sway in these parts.

Within twenty-four hours I began to see the fruits of their labors. The threats and harassment dried up completely. A couple of the guards even started calling me "Mr. Shoatz." A few days later I found myself in court for a hearing where a district judge approved my transfer back to Western Penitentiary. It was during that hearing that I laid eyes on my wife, Betty, and my son Russell III, who by that time was a little boy of ten. I hadn't seen him in over seven years. Yemoja sat on the other side of the courtroom, which was filled down to the last seat with my loyal supporters.

Back at Western, things didn't improve a whole lot. I was still in solitary confinement and the superintendent, Lieutenant Edward, had raised the level of terror throughout the entire prison in order to dampen the spirit of rebellion that my liberation attempt seemed to have brought on. At least two or three times every week, he and five or six of his guards would invade a prisoner's cell to beat or intimidate him. They came dressed in helmets, flak jackets, and heavy-duty jumpsuits, carrying long black sticks, plastic shields, and mace. They would congregate in the door of the cell, then mace the prisoner mercilessly before piling in, hidden behind their shields. Hollering and cussing at the prisoner in raw filth, they'd beat him, cuff him, and drag him—sometimes unconscious and always in full view of the rest of us—down the tier and into an isolated basement cell. Later they'd reassemble on the tier still in their riot gear and march in formation past every cell on the block, attempting to provoke a response that would justify another cell invasion or attack.

It was next to impossible to ignore them, especially if one knew the prisoner being subjected to that kind of unnecessary abuse. Even those of us who had been around long enough to know that speaking back or standing up was futile sometimes gave in and paid for it later. Often they'd single me out, telling me that their pals at Huntingdon had asked them to "take care of me the first chance they got." I existed in a constant state of anxiety, always keyed up, taut and tense and prepared for anything. On one hand, I knew the guards had to exercise caution in their dealings with me since I had become a kind of statewide celebrity and the eye of the media was still trained on the prison. I received regular visits from my family, from politically minded supporters who'd heard about the escape, and a stream of journalists seeking firsthand accounts of my time in the mountains. Still, I knew those guards would stop at nothing to do me some serious harm whenever and however they could, which caused me to develop a deep paranoia that they would attempt to poison my food. I began to refuse all meals that came from the kitchens, switching almost overnight to a strict diet of commissary snacks and vending machine items: chips, cookies, cakes, and highly processed sandwiches that could be obtained in the visiting room. Because we didn't earn decent wages, there was a limit to what I could purchase at the commissary, so Nkosiyabo tried to help supplement my new regime by sending me foodstuffs from his own tray or using his own meager earnings to buy me packaged snacks.

Since we weren't allowed to pass things from cell to cell we developed a system called "fishing," to be used at 10 p.m. every night, when the guard shift was changing. It entailed fashioning fishing lines from thin strips of cloth torn from our bedsheets. We would "cast" these down the tier by attaching a lump of soggy toilet paper to one end of the line. Since we had to aim blindly, by sticking our arms out through our food slots, tossing the line down the tier, and hoping for the best, the receiver had to be ready with a rolled-up magazine or newspaper to draw the line nearer if it landed too far from his cell. In the middle of the line was a pillowcase that served as a pouch for the goods. All the while the other prisoners on the block were alert to the guards' movements and would pass on signals or call out coded messages if they detected anyone approaching while a fishing operation was in progress. Still, even with the help of my comrades my health was deteriorating rapidly, and my mind was slipping along with it.

I guess the prison noticed this because a few months after getting on my crazy diet, they began to monitor me closely, and refer to me as a Psychiatric Observation Prisoner—someone whose behavior indicated that he might have to be put on psychiatric medication. These measures did not, of course, spring from any kind of concern for my welfare, since the guards' terror tactics continued unabated—it was done entirely to cover the administration's back in the case of a potential future lawsuit. During one of my hearings I was so wound up that I attacked Jerry Leibovitz in the courtroom, lunging at him from across the table when he wouldn't follow my instructions to pursue a particular line of questioning with one of the witnesses. A bunch of guards slammed me to the floor, and once I was restrained they hustled me out into a small holding cell. From then on I wasn't allowed to attend my own trial, but was forced to sit in a separate chamber, chained to a chair, where I could listen to the proceedings on a wireless radio. Anytime the judge needed something clarified, he brought the entire session into this holding cell.

Everything was pointing to a collapse of some kind, but besides tightening my bonds and increasing surveillance on me, the prison was unwilling to do anything positive or productive to deal with my mental degradation. For a whole year I lived in such an extreme state of uncertainty and fear that when my sentencing date arrived, in October of 1978, my nerves were pretty near fried.

An all-white jury in Cumberland County Court found me guilty of assault, escape, robbery, and kidnapping, which carried a combined maximum penalty of fifty-two years. The state had wanted me convicted of aggressive assault, which would have added another life sentence to the one I was already serving, but the jury felt there was too much conflicting testimony. For instance, although the guards claimed I attempted to knife them during the Huntingdon escape, this account was contradicted by three separate inmates whom the state called as witnesses. And Henry Spencer, the prison guard I'd kidnapped, refused to testify against me. In fact, both he and his wife remained tight-lipped throughout my trial despite numerous efforts on the part of newspaper men and politicians to coax out of them a dramatic retelling of their hours spent as my hostages. They refused to say anything at all about the incident beyond one statement to the press immediately following my capture: "He kept his word that he wouldn't hurt us."

To this day I've thought about their silence. And I'm willing to guess it's because they couldn't quite believe that this brutal, blood-thirsty escaped convict, whom the papers referred to as Killer Shoatz, didn't touch a hair on their heads! I spoke to them and treated them as respectfully as my circumstances would allow. But the public wasn't interested in that view of me, so really, what more could they say?

Seven women and five men deliberated on my case for several hours. Most of the male jurors were retired professionals, and most of the women were housewives. One guy was a plasterer; one lady was a bookkeeper. They were all good, wholesome, small-town people, full of good old-fashioned small-town bigotry. When they returned with their verdict, two policemen carried my chair into the courtroom. Later, as I was being escorted out into the sheriff's van, a huge mob descended upon me, a mix of reporters, onlookers, supporters, and photographers, but I remember only one thing clearly: my sister Akila running alongside the police car as it picked up speed, her eyes locked on mine.

I didn't betray a shred of emotion. I didn't utter a single word.

A few weeks later I found myself on a six-seat plane, cuffed and shackled and under armed guard, heading for Scranton, Pennsylvania. I was met at the airport by cops, sheriffs, and deputies and driven twenty-three miles to Waymart, to the Farview State Hospital for the Criminally Insane.

CHAPTER 27

CRIMINALLY INSANE

If Huntingdon was where they broke you, Farview was where you went to die.

It was the state's only facility entirely dedicated to housing adult males who were deemed to suffer from severe mental disturbances. The word *criminal* in its title was something of a misnomer, since the vast majority of Farview's residents had never been accused or convicted of any crime—rather they had been admitted to this so-called hospital by family, friends, or local authorities who believed them to be so deranged and dangerous that they could no longer function in society. Though its inmates were referred to as patients, Farview was a prison, plain and simple, where the guards masqueraded as mental health workers. These men practiced such a violent and sadistic form of discipline and control that by the time I arrived there in 1978, the facility was almost completely shut down due to an investigation into the deaths of numerous residents over a twenty-year period. Farview's enormous complex could easily accommodate anywhere from 2,500 to 3,500 people, but that population had been whittled down to just two or three hundred—the rest having supposedly been reintegrated into society.

Farview was notorious for something called the Shoe Leather Treatment, which was routinely meted out to unruly or uncooperative patients. It involved ten or eleven male "nurses" surrounding the patient and kicking him into submission—in other words, into unconsciousness. The patient would then be dragged across the floor and stripped naked before being tossed into a locked room. Because most patients were constantly in such a catatonic state, the nurses got away not only with extreme levels of violence but also rituals of humiliation and degradation. They relied on the fact that these men had no one on the outside who cared enough to listen to their accounts of the abuse that took place—and even if they did speak up, their compromised mental state pretty much assured that their word would never be taken seriously. So most of what went on at Farview was a well-kept secret between the nurses and their charges.

Since coming under investigation, however, the hospital's administrators had brought in a whole cadre of doctors and nurses whose job it was to supplement the Shoe Leather Treatment with something they called "chemotherapy." This regimen entailed doling out a huge variety of psychotropic medications that essentially drugged the patients into a coma. At the time the effects of these drugs were relatively unknown, so the whole thing was really a massive clinical trial using human subjects as lab rats.

Probably the only good thing about Farview was that since the combination of staff violence and medications had turned most residents into zombies, the levels of institutional security practiced here were far more lax than any other "correctional" facility I have ever been in. I discovered this on my very first day there. Given my record of past escapes, not to mention my behavior throughout my trial, I had expected to be chained and manacled 24/7 or, failing that, to be strapped to a bed in a padded room until I could convince the staff that I was not "a danger to myself or others." But when I arrived I was relieved of my shackles, interviewed in a most civil manner by one of the medical staff, and led to a clean, brightly lit room where I spent no more than two hours before being released into what they called a "dayroom"—a common area where the patients milled around, passing the hours between meals, without handcuffs and with only minimal supervision in the form of a nurse in a glass-enclosed "observation" room. It was, in short, the best treatment I'd received since being recaptured in Beallsville.

It just goes to show that the most effective forms of control aren't always the most openly hostile ones. As I would learn during the remainder of my time at Farview, and over the many long decades that have followed, messing with a person's mind can be a much more brutal act than confining or torturing their body.

During my first few weeks at the institution, I observed my fellow inmates with pity. The open ward where we spent most of our days was a lethargic soup of comatose men who stared blankly at the walls, babbled quietly to themselves, or flopped about on the benches that lined the common room. Some of them even carried around cushions and pillows that they used to fashion makeshift beds on the benches. Compared to the facilities I'd been in, where most of the guys were at peak physical fitness—having nothing else to do most of the day except work out—this was a pathetic sight to behold. I couldn't wrap my head around a human being losing control of their senses to such a debilitating extent. But less than a week after arriving I was no different from any of them.

Every evening around eight o'clock I was forced to take a hundred-milligram dose of a drug called Thorazine. It was never handed to me—I literally had to stand there, open-mouthed, while a nurse tipped the pill into my throat. She then instructed me to wash it down with a cup of orange juice. The Thorazine was so powerful that I would be knocked out almost immediately after swallowing it. I had to drag myself up the stairs to my dormitory, where I slept the sleep of the dead. If the staff hadn't forced me out of bed every morning, I would gladly have skipped breakfast. I would not regain my full equilibrium until close to 1 p.m. With a massive effort I got myself down to the exercise yard, where I would stumble around the jogging track for an hour, or until I had managed to sweat the drug out of my system—but by then I had only a few hours of lucidity before I was once again force-fed the medication. The whole routine was unlike anything I had encountered or endured in regular prisons, and it quickly became crystal clear to me that I was in much more danger here than I had been at any other facility.

I got my hands on some medical texts to read up on the dosages, uses, and side effects of the cocktail of drugs being administered to the patients. Most of them were not fully understood, and there was little conclusive evidence about their long-term effects beyond an overall acknowledgment among the scientific community that sustained use would cause permanent impairment of the functioning of one's brain, nervous system, and body tissues.

It all came to a head for me one night when, after dragging myself to the bathroom, I passed out at the urinal. When I regained consciousness, a number of nurses were standing over me and one of them said, "Put that thing back in his pajamas." Even that couldn't prompt me to pull myself together. I was paralyzed, flat on my back staring at the ceiling, until I heard the medication cart trundling into the bathroom. The next thing I knew, a nurse was kneeling beside me, peering into my eyes, examining my body, and then I was in a wheelchair being rushed to the infirmary, where my stomach was pumped out. Later, I learned the staff had "accidentally" given me an overdose. I was kept in intensive care for two days.

From that point onward, I made up my mind not to swallow a single more pill. I devised a system whereby I could take the dose into my mouth and hold it there long enough to walk away and spit it out. Without those chemicals coursing through my mind and body, I began to regain my consciousness and as usual returned to the same question: How was I going to get out?

Right away, two things happened that answered this question for me. First, Masamba was transferred to Farview. He was trying to overturn the death sentence he'd received for the murder of the white prisoner, but the judge who was retrying the case first wanted to ascertain whether he was competent to stand trial. Hearings were scheduled to start in March of 1980, a year from the date of his transfer, which would give the state ample time to determine whether or not he was of sound mind. For Masamba, the months that stood between him and this retrial represented a kind of "last chance" to liberate himself once and for all, since he was convinced that any judge or jury in these parts would uphold the death sentence against him. He brought that sense of urgency with him to the institution, so that in addition to my relief at being around someone I could actually confide in, his arrival rekindled my own commitment to liberation and gave us a firm timeline for our plan. For us it was a simple matter of getting free. But if anyone else had heard us, they'd have probably thought we were nuts. Probably have thought: *You'd have to be criminally insane!*

The second thing that kept me on track was my budding relationship with Yemoja. She had quickly become more than a companion. I discovered that she had a brilliant mind and a determined will of steel, and we had begun to run up huge long-distance phone bills trying to stay in touch. When Masamba was transferred to Farview, she began to visit both of us, and soon she and her sister, Zahara, became instrumental in our plan, which took shape over a two-year period, between the summer of 1978 and the spring of 1980. Other supporters came and went, some peeling quietly away, others dropping like hot potatoes when they realized the audacity of what we intended to do. As Zahara once remarked: "Soon as the rubber meets the road, everyone sits quiet as a church mouse peeing on cotton."

And so it came down to the four of us—Masamba and me, and Yemoja and Zahara, who at the time had a six-year-old son named Jamil. This little boy would accompany his mother and aunt on their visits to Farview and eventually proved to be an invaluable asset to our team.

Farview was designed in the early 1900s to be—in the architect's own words—"a prison without walls." It was built on a nearly one-thousand-acre piece of land, donated to the Commonwealth of Pennsylvania by the Delaware and Hudson Railway, at one of the highest points of elevation in the state. It was named for the spectacular view of the surrounding Moosic Mountains and countryside below. Initially comprising a cluster of oblong brick buildings that encircled an indoor courtyard, the "hospital" soon became only a small part of an operation that included a forty-three-acre farm, dairies, and factories for producing goods like bricks and soaps, where inmates were put to work through a system known as "industrial therapy" or "industrial peonage." There were also workshops for crafting, knitting, carpentry, weaving, laundering, and baking. In the 1920s it added several hundred acres of orchards and vineyards, and at the peak of its operation Farview owned herds of bulls, cows, and deer, several flocks of chickens and sheep, and dozens of pigs. By the time Masamba and I arrived there, many of these facilities had been shut down. All that really remained of the original plan for the hospital was a sense that very little security was required to keep inmates within bounds. Beyond the hospital wards were acres and acres of unfenced, unguarded, and unattended farmland and farm buildings, which led directly into the rugged mountains of Pennsylvania.

So Yemoja and Zahara began a period of reconnaissance of the extensive hospital grounds and the mountainous community surrounding it. Every couple of months they drove up from Pittsburgh, scoping out hiking paths and mountain roads along the way. During their visits in the big, open common room, Zahara would instruct her son to run around playfully so that, under the guise of chasing him down, she could get a good look at the corridors and passageways that led in and out of the visiting area, as well as familiarize herself with the nurses' stations that stood between us and freedom.

Yemoja and Zahara were hardcore. They were part of a coterie back in Pittsburgh that was holding the tattered ends of a movement together. Their small, tight group tracked down jailed revolutionaries across the state and visited them, heard them out on a number of issues, and transmitted their messages to a wide audience via their Saturday night radio program. They attended our trials, met the lawyers, read the books, and assessed all the ways we might get free. We didn't know the half of what they did, but we guessed at it and trusted them.

They were cut from a very different cloth than us, most of them having attended prestigious colleges and universities, but they were disillusioned by the formal education system. Unlike so many of those who had been active in the sixties whose devotion had been watered down by years of intense police repression, these women still had fire in their bellies. And unlike a lot of the women I'd come to know through the movement, including Asani, I got the feeling they were not averse to the idea of armed struggle.

It wasn't until I met Yemoja and Zahara that I really began to understand women's collective power. With Betty I'd been so jealous of her relationship with her mother and sister that I never stopped to consider what a force they were. Asani exercised her power over me to demand respectful treatment as a comrade and a partner—but that was where I drew the line. When she and the other female members of the BUC tried to form a power block against the men's guerrilla tactics, we shot them down. When they tried to convince us to stay afloat in our communities, we went underground and dragged them down with us. Now here were these two sisters laying out the blueprint of a hair-brained scheme, and Masamba and I were happy to sit back and say: *Yes, Ma'am! You're the boss!* We didn't necessarily consider the risks we were setting them up for unreasonable because we still viewed our actions within the larger context of the Black Liberation Movement.

It was right around this time that another sister in the movement made history. On November 2, 1979, a woman named Assata Shakur escaped from the Clinton Correctional Facility for Women in New Jersey.

Prior to being imprisoned, she had been active in the Black Liberation Movement in New York and New Jersey and had come under intense police surveillance and FBI scrutiny. She was convicted of killing a state trooper during a shootout on the New Jersey Turnpike in 1973 under a state law that did not require proof that she actually fired the shots that resulted in the officer's death. Hundreds of supporters protested against her conviction and incarceration on the grounds that she had faced an unfair trial, and again against the harsh conditions she faced while inside the women's prison. While she was serving a life sentence, a group of BLA members known as the Family planned and executed her escape. They allegedly carried heavy weapons including .45-caliber pistols and sticks of dynamite into the prison visiting room, but not a single person was killed or injured during the operation. It was rumored that Assata lived underground in Pittsburgh for several years before making her way to Cuba via the Bahamas, where she received political asylum in 1984.

The entire incident was a massive blow to state and federal authorities. A nationwide manhunt ended in failure, despite the FBI adding Assata to its list of most-wanted terrorists and putting a million-dollar bounty on her head. Far from assisting government agents in their search, thousands of New York City residents hung posters in their windows that read *Assata is welcome here*. In response the NYPD violently raided homes and apartment buildings, earning them even more bad press and ill will among residents. Thousands marched in support of Assata in the streets. Phenomenal amounts of money were poured into managing, containing, and covering up pieces of the story, but the message was clear: public opinion both in the US and internationally was overwhelmingly on the side of the Black Liberation Movement, its freedom fighters, and its political prisoners. In the few, rare statements Assata made following her liberation, she insisted on identifying herself as a "20th century escaped slave" and labeling Cuba as a one of the largest, most resistant, and most courageous maroon communities in the world.

When Masamba and I heard about Assata's exploits, we also fixed our eyes and our hearts on Cuba. We had no idea how or whether we'd make it, but that was our destination.

Our plan required absolute precision, an almost military attention to detail, and the highest level of commitment. In the past, I had placed my trust in my fellow prisoners, generally people who shared my revolutionary ideals, religious convictions, and personal integrity. I had never attempted an escape that involved people outside the institution in which I was incarcerated. Relying on Yemoja and Zahara introduced new perils because they had less to gain and far more to lose than Masamba or I.

In my mind they were an unstoppable force. Since my time with them was so limited, I spent hours imagining them meticulously laying the groundwork for us, doing what we were unable to on the inside. I imagined them acquiring a safe house, somewhere outside of Pittsburgh, where they could stockpile the weapons we required for liberation. I imagined what they'd do if the authorities raided this venue, how they might conceal the weapons up in the rafters of the old, crumbling house. I pictured them on Friday nights, at a pub, with their cadre of sisters talking through the logistics, using their network of women activists to acquire a small arsenal of winter survival gear: food and warm clothing, first aid kits and medicines, and ammunition and tools. I pictured them doing what I'd do in their situation: drawing maps by hand, and then drawing them again until the topographies were drawn in their minds. While snow piled up in the hospital grounds and the surrounding mountains, I imagined them acquiring a sled that we could use to haul our gear up and down the steep terrain. Perhaps they were hand-sewing the requisite clothing to wear on the day of the attempt: a combination body harness and skirt with large, concealed pockets that could be used to carry weapons into the facility. If it were me, I'd also be conducting dry runs to ascertain how best to avoid, neutralize, or minimize triggering Farview's security systems on the actual day. I imagined them parked outside the facility every night, timing the searchlights that swept over the surrounding countryside, so they would know precisely when to move and when to take cover.

In Farview's nearly hundred years of existence, its staff had grown complacent and confident that the inmates here were too debilitated to attempt anything as daring as we were about to undertake. The nurses seemed to have more faith in their mind-altering drugs than regular prison guards had in their locked doors and guns and riot gear. So they were taken completely by surprise when, on March 4, 1980, a young Black woman helped bust two patients out of their facility in broad daylight.

On that particular day, a Jesuit nun accompanied Yemoja to the visiting room. Perhaps she thought the presence of a member of the clergy would set the staff at ease, and also boost her own confidence as she walked into the facility. This nun had no knowledge of our plans. She had agreed to come along purely out of goodwill, Yemoja having told her that Masamba and I didn't receive many visitors and would appreciate some company. They were ushered into the dayroom, where Yemoja greeted me as usual with an embrace, a gesture that wasn't allowed in most other correctional facilities.

"You got 'em?" I whispered in her ear.

"Yes."

Masamba and I sat at one of the tables with the nun while Yemoja went to the bathroom. It was a test of endurance to not constantly turn around and steal glances at the nurses stationed in their booths at either end of the visiting room, knowing that just a few feet away Yemoja was lifting up her skirts, undoing her harnesses, and reassembling a range of firearms that had been dismantled in order for her to conceal them on her person on the way in. All around us the patients babbled and snoozed and generally behaved as they usually did. Having the nun to talk to was a good distraction, something concrete to focus on that would keep our adrenaline at manageable levels until it was time for action.

Yemoja returned a few minutes later. Again she embraced me, only this time we used it as cover for me to remove a revolver from her waist belt. The minute the gun was securely in my hands I wheeled around and shouted at everyone to get up against the wall. Beside me, Yemoja was sliding the shotgun out of a body sling, loading a thirty-shot clip into it, and passing it over to Masamba. The nun screamed as I ushered her over to the wall where most of the patients and their visitors had already lined up, their faces turned away from the action, their arms in the air. I yanked the phone off its hook on the wall and left the receiver dangling. While I had all the patients at gunpoint I commanded the nurses to leave their booths and take up similar positions. Then, directing Masamba to take over, I pulled Yemoja over to the visiting-room door in a tight embrace to block off the view of what was going on inside from three hospital attendants who were charging down the corridor. When they were close enough, I revealed my gun and ordered them inside.

Yemoja covered the door and Masamba covered the patients, their visitors, and the nurses while I got down to business with Steve Farman, the supervising officer: I ordered him to escort us outside, and along the way give instructions to a guard stationed in a booth at a kind of intersection between converging corridors to open the necessary gates and allow us to pass through undisturbed. For a brief moment Steve actually tried to explain that he wasn't allowed to assist any inmate attempting to escape! Masamba had been pretty quiet up to this point, but Steve's words made him completely lose it. Turning his gun away from the inmates, he aimed it right at Steve, screaming at me that this guy was stalling for time and could cost us the entire operation. Seeing Masamba become agitated like that prompted me to pull back the hammer on my own revolver, take careful aim with both hands, and repeat my instructions slowly and clearly. This time Steve had no trouble understanding that we meant business! Within a few seconds he was escorting Yemoja out of the visiting room and down the corridor toward the front gate. I followed ten feet behind and Masamba brought up the rear, his shotgun trained on a straggling line of patients, visitors, and nurses whom he planned to lock into one of the unused dayrooms on the ground floor before rejoining our team.

Things were happening fast. Before we reached the intersection Masamba peeled away from our procession, ordering his hostages to take up spread-eagle positions on the floor in one of the vacant rooms. Meanwhile Yemoja continued to coolly walk toward the guard booth while I got behind a wall, my gun trained on Steve Farman, whose presence prompted the attendant on duty to open the gate, no questions asked, only commenting casually that Yemoja was leaving earlier than usual. As soon as I heard the gate lock shifting I ran around the corner, sprinted up to the gate, and forced it open, knocking the guard off balance as I did so. Once I'd collared him, Yemoja patted him down frantically, searching for the keys on his belt holder that would unlock our way to liberation. He didn't struggle. I believe the whole situation was so far outside anything he would have imagined or prepared for that he was partially stunned into submission. The sight of my revolver took care of the rest.

While Yemoja was locating the keys, I spied a nurse fleeing into a room adjoining the one Masamba had the hostages in and locking the door behind her. I yelled for Masamba to leave everyone where they were. As he came tearing down the corridor Yemoja managed to extract the keys from the holder and unlock the penultimate gate. I took the guard as my hostage as Masamba skidded to a stop beside me, and then all four of us were running toward Yemoja's car.

She jumped into the driver's seat, Masamba climbed in beside her, and I took my hostage into the rear. As Yemoja engaged the engine, I forced the guard down onto the floor beside me and Masamba also managed to conceal his enormous body on the floor of the passenger seat. Yemoja drove straight for the main gates, toward the final guard booth standing between us and freedom. She lowered her window as she neared the booth but at the same time veered the car at a strange angle so it would be harder for the attendant to see what was going on inside. To detract attention from her odd behavior, she made some utterly mundane comment to him about why she was leaving early. I couldn't see out of the window but this tactic seemed to work, because the next thing I heard was the gate opening, and then Yemoja was picking up speed, racing down the wide, sweeping driveway and out onto the curving mountainous road.

In the back seat I was struggling to bind and gag the guard, using my teeth to tear strips from a roll of masking tape. Weeks of severe winter storms had turned the roads to ice, and our car slipped and slid along for about ten minutes before Yemoja pulled to a stop in a heavily wooded area. Awaiting us here was a different getaway vehicle driven by a friend of Yemoja's, so we left the guard taped up in our car, squeezed into the new set of wheels, and sped away. I knew it wouldn't take the guard long to work his way out of the bind I'd put him in. It was the dead of winter and if I had restrained him more securely there was a good chance he would have frozen to death on the side of the road, so I'd kept the tape fairly lose around his wrists. We worked out that we had less than an hour before he freed himself and alerted the authorities—hardly enough time to clear the state before the police started setting up roadblocks everywhere.

Yemoja had anticipated all of this beforehand and stashed our gear a few miles from the prison, buried under forest debris on the roadside at the head of a mountain trail. I felt much better once the escape car had dropped us at the trailhead and driven away. From my last liberation experience I knew that the wilderness, however harsh the terrain, however menacing the prospect, was my friend. Roads and vehicles were infinitely more dangerous—wide, open spaces where you gave yourself away. So I hyped my companions up while we dragged on layers of heavy outdoor clothing and snow boots, loaded up a high-powered rifle, switched on our scanner radio, and began our trek into the woods. Though most of the intel we received from the radio was shot through with static, we heard enough to know that our ruse had been successful: every police dispatch seemed to be directing units to either set up roadblocks or be on the alert for two cars whose descriptions matched the vehicles we'd used. For the time being at least, their eye was drawn well away from the freezing mountainside where three revolutionaries were dragging a sled of survival supplies through two feet of snow, beaming with joy.

CHAPTER 28

HUNTED AND FROZEN

Masamba and I were the ones tasting freedom for the first time in two years—but it was Yemoja who kept us going in those early days with her infectious enthusiasm, fierce excitement, and unwavering resilience.

As we took turns muscling the sled up and down hills and embankments, she kept repeating one thing over and over: "Who would have ever thought we could pull this off?" Her attitude was contagious. Masamba was in any case reeling from the fact that he'd escaped the jaws of the state right on the eve of his trial. As for me, in addition to the rush of being free and the prospect of securing asylum somewhere outside of the country, I was pumped up by the fact that I'd helped this phenomenal young woman realize just what she was capable of. The current between Yemoja and me was electric, to the point that Masamba began to joke that if we couldn't keep our hands off each other we would never make it to our destination.

Our plan was to head southeast, staying off-grid for at least a month before even attempting to show ourselves in a populated area. We knew, both from my own case and from various other high-profile breakouts, that sustaining a search over a long period of time cost the government an astronomical sum of money, which weighed heavily in their decision about when to abandon their efforts. If we could outlast them, if we could endure a couple of weeks of physical misery, we stood a good chance of making our way to a small town where Yemoja could call for help—she had already lined up a number of friends and supporters who would be on alert for our signal, whenever it came, and had offered to meet us anywhere and take us anywhere. But within just a few hours of fleeing Farview, we were confronted with the reality of just how tough winter wilderness survival can be.

To start with, there was little to no foliage to hide behind. Vegetation was sparse, most trees were dead. This meant that we would have to rely on dips, valleys, and defiles to shelter us at night and to conceal us if we got wind of an approaching threat. Secondly, there was the matter of our tracks. It was impossible to move without cutting a straight, visible path through the deep snow, which meant we had to travel at night and then one person had to return to our starting point the next morning and walk backward, using a broom to erase any sign of our footprints as they retraced their steps back to the others.

Far more importantly, we had to devise ways to stay warm. It wasn't enough to bundle up in coats and hats—at night the temperatures out here fell below freezing—and since we couldn't risk lighting fires, we needed to find alternative methods. On the very first night, as we lay fully clothed in sleeping bags that we'd unfurled at the base of a narrow gorge, while obsessively running through channels on our scanner radio listening for anything that might tip us off to the search parties moving in our direction, Yemoja began to complain of unbearable pain in her toes. It was easily -10°F, possibly lower, and there was no doubt in my mind that the pain in her feet was at least partially brought on by the cold. I also suspected her boots might be too tight, but we couldn't chance taking them off and exposing her body to the wind. Instead I had her stand up and exercise with me. We did jumping jacks. We ran on the spot. I worked her vigorously for twenty minutes without stopping until her blood circulation began to improve and warmth trickled down to her extremities. She was able to sleep through the night, but by the following morning, Masamba's fingers had begun to swell.

We had to manage several things simultaneously. Someone had to return to our starting position with the broom and erase our tracks. Someone else had to gather fallen twigs and branches that we could use to build a kind of ambush bunker about fifty to a hundred feet above our defile from which we could launch an attack if we heard anyone approaching. One person would have to man this bunker at all times, and if it came to it, that person would need to hold any hostile parties at bay long enough for the others to pack our belongings and get a head start away from that area. Lastly, one of us needed to sort through, reorganize, and repack our supplies before we could move on to our next hideout. There was a lot of stuff on that sled, and we needed to shed some of it and lighten our load in order to conserve as much energy as possible. So while Masamba trekked backward with the broom, I built the bunker, leaving Yemoja to deal with our supplies—with strict instructions to get rid of a bright red parka that had somehow made its way into our stack of warm clothing. I was convinced this particular article would give away our position even if someone only glimpsed it from a great distance away. Whatever we weren't taking, we would leave buried in the snow.

By the time night fell, three fingers on Masamba's left hand were so badly engorged from frostbite that he couldn't get them through the trigger guard on his rifle. Yemoja had spent most of the day treating them with the meager supplies in our first aid kit and improvising bandages that might keep the worst of the cold at bay, but with each hour that passed we were coming closer to the realization that we would either have to accept the sacrifice of Masamba's hand or descend the mountains to seek proper medical care. At Masamba's insistence we decided to sleep on it and come to a final decision the following morning.

The freezing cold roused us early. We ate only because we had to, and because we knew that even a small, protein-heavy snack would help buttress our bodies against the cold. Leaving the other two in the defile, I made my way to the bunker, took up my position, and fell into deep thought. Masamba wasn't doing any better. None of us had exchanged a word about it, but we all knew from looking at his fingers that we needed to exit the mountains that day. It was a terrible blow, but the situation wasn't hopeless. If we were cautious and smart, we could incorporate this wrinkle into our existing plans. In my mind I was scanning maps of the area that we'd studied before the breakout, trying to plot the best, safest route out that would hopefully avoid police traps and checkpoints. We'd have to risk stealing a vehicle in order to get Masamba to some kind of clinic far enough away from Farview that he wouldn't be recognized. And after that—well, we'd take it from there.

Suddenly I caught a flash of red moving between the trees. I squinted into the snow, but whatever it was had vanished. Then I saw it again, fifty feet in front of me and slightly up an incline, in the same direction we'd come two days ago. I knew Yemoja or Masamba had planned to return to our starting point to double-check that we hadn't left a single track in the snow—but I was livid. I had specifically warned Yemoja against wearing that red parka, and the sight of it now just confirmed my hunch that it was a dead giveaway in this barren white landscape. I watched her approaching. She skirted a line of trees, moving slowly and cautiously. Then, instead of descending the hill in the direction of our bunker and base camp, she began to edge around it in a lateral direction that would take her farther away and around our position—as though she was trying to approach us from behind. There was something very strange about her movements, like she was uncertain of what lay ahead or which way to go. That's when I realized that the person I was watching wasn't Yemoja. It was a man—a hunter—in a bright red coat, and he was carrying a rifle.

I plunged deep down into the snow, knowing that I had few options but to let him get as close as possible and then try to capture him. But the longer I watched him, the clearer it became that he wouldn't be taken unawares. He was walking more purposefully now, following a definite path toward us; he had clearly discovered our tracks. He came closer and closer. Because he was on an incline, there was every chance that he would see me if he glanced up even briefly from the trail he was following so intently.

When he got within thirty yards of my position I jumped up and screamed at him to freeze. Momentarily stunned by my voice, he stopped dead, but a second later he had raised his own rifle to a firing position. In a total panic I let lose a burst of fire from my submachine gun but my aim was off. The huntsman had his back to me now and was running frantically back up the incline. Again I fired, squeezing the trigger for a good five seconds and unleashing a virtual hail of bullets, all of which missed their mark. Frantic, I started chasing him, but since he was on higher ground than me it wasn't easy closing the distance between us. He must have realized this, because he suddenly turned and began to run sideways, making it even harder for me to give chase while advancing up the side of the mountain. While I was scrambling around in the snow and ice, he turned, lifted his rifle, and tried to take aim at me. I braced myself against a tree, determined to put a stop to him this time. I fired every single round left in that thirty-shot clip. I made that hunter dance, jumping and ducking and twisting away from my gunfire, but once again, to my complete and crushing disappointment, I failed to hit my target.

While I was loading a fresh clip into the machine gun he took off running again, but before he could get much further I heard the bark of a high-powered rifle somewhere behind me—Masamba or Yemoja, firing from our base camp. I flung myself down into the snow to avoid being in their line of fire, even though I had just realized that all of these precautions were too late. Not only was the huntsman out of sight, but I had just glimpsed a house in the distance where a figure was standing outside a back door, peering down the mountainside. I don't know if they saw me, but a moment later the door slammed shut, meaning whoever it was would soon be calling the authorities and this entire area would shortly be swarming with police.

Abandoning all caution I got to my feet and raced back to our base camp inside the gorge. Yemoja was strapping fresh bandages onto Masamba's useless fingers, so I got busy flinging a few items into an emergency pack we'd prepared ahead of time. We would have to leave behind everything but the weapons and one or two other absolute necessities. Based on my Huntingdon experience, I guessed we had less than thirty minutes to clear that area completely, and given that there were three of us instead of just one, we probably wouldn't be able to conceal ourselves in the snow until the search passed on. We needed to get to the top of the mountain, over and down the other side, and commandeer a vehicle: quite literally, our worst-case scenario unfolding right before our eyes. But as we slogged up the mountainside, Yemoja carrying the rifle, Masamba the shotgun, and I the submachine gun, I kept telling myself that though we were in a dangerous position, we were still fighting maroons with a fighting chance.

We hadn't been hiking for more than fifteen minutes when we heard the heavy rotor of a helicopter headed our way. Yemoja yelled at us to get down on the snow, then she threw white sheets over me and Masamba and another one over herself. The copter swept back and forth, directly overhead but clearly unable to detect our position. I worried briefly that our sheets might flap and rustle in the wind from the blades, but all three of us held tight to the corners of those white sheets until the helicopter lifted higher, drifted further, and finally moved to a location far enough away that we could reveal ourselves and keep moving.

The clock was ticking, all three of us aware that we no longer had the luxury of simply moving forward. Very soon the manhunt would be upon us. We needed to find a solid defensive position, erect a bunker, and prepare ourselves for a confrontation of some kind. I thought back to my days with the BUC when our protocol had always revolved around self-defense: outlast the enemy; buy some time; and maybe, just maybe, you could get away, if not unscathed, then at least alive.

As had happened so many times during my escape from Huntingdon, we discovered that the land itself wanted us to win. We had been searching for only about ten minutes before we discovered an outcrop of rocks clinging to the mountainside. One large boulder stood at the front of this stony cluster, almost like a giant shield around which we could erect a decent military-style bunker out of dead wood. This task required all of us to draw on our deepest reserves of strength because it entailed running up and down and back and forth, carrying wood and brambles, with no letup, constantly aware that with each minute that passed our captors were closing in.

Yemoja worked like a beast. Masamba acted like the excruciating pain from his frozen and distended fingers didn't even matter. Above us the helicopter continued to buzz and grumble, never quite approaching our position but never leaving the general vicinity. Gradually, police sirens made themselves heard down below. Then came the crackle and static from radios or walkie-talkies, distant at first but drawing ever nearer. If any of us was agitated, we didn't let the others see it. For a couple of minutes after completing work on our fortress we just sat silently—almost calmly—side by side. At last I crouched down behind the big rock and raised a pair of binoculars to my eyes. I immediately picked out about half a dozen state police officers bearing rifles and shotguns hot on our trail. I relayed this to Yemoja and Masamba. Wordlessly, we prepared for battle.

When they spotted the rocky outcrop they began to spread out in a skirmish line. One dude—possibly some kind of chief or sergeant—was motioning wildly for his men to try to circle round us in order to approach from the rear flank, where we'd be most vulnerable. I gave the signal and all three of us opened fire at once.

Almost immediately my submachine gun jammed, but with Yemoja and Masamba leveling a steady stream of gunfire at the police, I could take a minute to switch weapons. Meanwhile all the officers were diving down into the snow, returning fire. Their rounds registered on the rocks all around us, but we were well protected. Unfortunately there was now no way for us to avoid detection by the helicopter, which came roaring directly above us. I turned my high-powered 30.06 rifle into the air and fired repeatedly. The pilot got the message loud and clear—quicker than I thought he would. Within seconds the helicopter had retreated so far it was nothing more than a speck in the sky. All was chaos. The police's automatic weapons were doing so much damage to the surrounding trees that chunks of wood were flying in all directions and a kind of fine, powdery sawdust was raining down on our heads and into the bunker. Because our weapons and ammunition were limited, we spent a disproportionate amount of time with our backs to the huge rock, crouched in a defensive position, only occasionally attempting to return their fire. It wasn't just about outlasting their volley—a much harder task was maintaining our equilibrium in the middle of a gun battle. The sound and fury of so much weaponry, especially when one is outnumbered, is a deeply stressful thing to endure; it can fry your nerves, dissolve your will. But there was nothing we could do. We couldn't budge from our position. The only thing that brought us some solace was the fact that the officers seemed highly reluctant to advance. After a full half an hour of attacking us they were no closer to our bunker than they'd been when the battle commenced.

It was around then that someone on the police side ordered a lull in the shooting. After the riot of noise, the sudden silence fell like a blanket upon the mountain, smothering everything. Then a man's voice called to us through a bullhorn, strident and clear:

"Lay down your weapons! This is your last chance to surrender. Come out with your hands up!"

I don't know what prompted me to do it—perhaps we'd anticipated such a situation and discussed this kind of contingency, or maybe it just came to me in the moment. Either way, my reply was very clear: we wouldn't come out unless they sent a newspaper reporter to act as a go-between. The cop laughed into his bullhorn.

"That's not gonna happen," he said. "Now I'm gonna ask you one more time: drop your weapons and come out with your hands in the air, and no one's gonna get hurt." His bullhorn picked up and magnified the mocking laughter and derision of other officers in the group. Then a different voice spoke into the megaphone, informing me that our situation was hopeless and our best bet would be to take their best offer. Not one word out of their mouths sounded genuine. In fact I was convinced that the entire conversation was a ruse, something to distract us from their actions. Right then, Masamba spotted a small party advancing on our right flank—they'd used the lull in gunfire to sneak up on us. All three of us immediately turned our attention and our weapons onto this little faction and pretty soon drove them back to where they came from. But this exchange opened up a whole new attack. We were being attacked from multiple angles. Obviously frustrated by our refusal to surrender, someone gave the signal for the cops to send us another volley, and this one lasted even longer than the first, the scream of gunfire eating away at me until it felt like it was gnawing on my very bones.

Then, again, a pause. This time the man who spoke addressed me and Masamba by name.

"Shoatz...Wright...I want you to listen closely. Now, I'm not here to hurt either of you. I'm with the Federal Bureau of Investigation and I've been sent to make sure everyone gets out of this in one piece. But I'm going to need you both to cooperate, alright? I can get you both out of here safely if you do exactly as I say. So put down your weapons and raise your hands, and I will make damn sure that none of these officers touches a hair on your head. Do you understand?"

This time it was Masamba who answered, asking for a lawyer. He yelled that there was nothing stopping the cops from gunning us down on sight and we wanted someone neutral brought on, someone who could guarantee our protection.

"I'm afraid I can't do that, Mr. Wright," the detective said into the bullhorn.

"Then no deal," Masamba yelled, before firing a couple of rounds in their general direction.

It was around then that I noticed a complete change in Yemoja's behavior. Until that moment she had been shoulder to shoulder with us, never displaying even a crack in her armor. But throughout the negotiations she'd fallen silent, and now when I looked into her face I saw an expression of deep contemplation, and perhaps even a shadow of fear.

"What if I surrendered?" she asked.

Both Masamba and I were of the opinion that if any of us came out from behind those rocks, our body would instantly be riddled with bullets—and we told her so. By then, however, I think her mind was made up. That was the kind of person she was. She would not have even broached the subject before arriving at the conclusion. This dawned on Masamba and me simultaneously, and after a few moments of ragged silence between us, he called out to the authorities to hold their fire because the woman in our party was about to comply with their demands. As she prepared to stand, I had to turn away: I simply couldn't shake the vision of her body being torn to shreds by their bullets.

But they kept their word. Yemoja raised herself out from behind the rocks, hands in the air, and before they'd even taken her into captivity, the officers were yelling for me and Masamba to follow suit. With Yemoja in an exposed position like that, we could hardly refuse, so against my will, against the tide of blood coursing through my veins, against everything I had stood for and suffered for and bled for, I gave myself into the hands of the state, allowed them to lash those wretched handcuffs around my wrists, to roughly probe my body, and to march me down the mountainside, a captive once more.

Only this time, it was forever.

PART FOUR

CHAPTER 29

DOWN IN THE DUNGEON

I defended myself in court. I didn't trust anyone else to present the facts of my case honestly and accurately. The trial was held in Lackawanna County, Pennsylvania, and was heard by an all-white, small-town jury. My opposing counsel was a highly ambitious lawyer. I recall this guy being on the scene from the moment I was arrested, determined to make a name for himself on the back of my capture. Together with dozens of police personnel who were badly shaken by their encounter with Masamba, Yemoja, and me, he gave dramatic press conferences with blow-by-blow accounts of the two-hour shootout that resulted in our surrender. As far as I could surmise, he never lingered long on the fact that no one was killed or even injured during that battle. He chose instead to focus on what a harrowing experience it had been for these cops, who had at their disposal all the firepower they could ask for, the unmitigated support of the state, the moral high ground from which to launch their attack, and resources, ammunition, and weaponry that we could only dream of. To hear how terrified they'd been, and how relieved to have escaped alive, was my only consolation in a period of otherwise severe, overwhelming, almost suffocating disappointment.

It didn't matter that everything was slanted against me in that courtroom. I was already serving back-to-back life sentences. No matter how things went here, I knew I would be returned to prison, knew I faced several lifetimes of torture, humiliation, and misery. I didn't deceive myself that any outcome in Lackawanna would change my basic circumstances. Even so, I felt I was entitled to a few hours on the floor to make one very simple argument: that I was not a common criminal, a cold-blooded killer, or a carefree escape artist. I was a political prisoner, and should be judged accordingly.

To do this I had to go all the way back to my days with the Black Unity Council and the Black Liberation Army. I summoned as witnesses Philadelphia cops who were only too willing to tell the jurors all about my past record as a revolutionary activist—though of course they didn't use this term. I also called upon FBI agents to give accounts of my membership with the Black Panther Party, and to detail the extent of their manhunt during my two years underground. They didn't realize that their testimony played right into my strategy of presenting myself as a politically motivated individual, who had been officially affiliated with a group that had declared itself at war with the US government. Using the Freedom of Information Act, I obtained an excellent set of documents detailing how the FBI's former director, J. Edgar Hoover, had targeted me for suppression as an "enemy combatant" involved in "urban guerrilla warfare." I then linked all of that to a little-used Pennsylvania state law that allowed one to claim "justification in escaping prison" if one could show that his or her life had been imperiled in that institution. This argument needed no embellishments or exaggerations—a simple rundown of daily prison life, along with a few added details of my treatment at both Western and Huntingdon following my escape, sufficed to paint a picture of the constant danger I faced.

I called both Yemoja and Masamba to the stand, and although Masamba was facing a death sentence of his own, and Yemoja also risked losing much from her continued support of me, they both testified favorably in my defense, attesting to the hardships I'd faced in prison and my commitment to political goals that would justify my liberation attempts.

Throughout it all I could see the opposing counsel becoming more and more agitated. I think it was because over the course of several days, the jury seemed to be coming around to my story. Their demeanor, their attention to my arguments, some of their reactions to testimony from my witnesses all pointed to a softening that I had never seen in any other jury before. When it came time for my closing arguments I held nothing back. This was my moment to walk in the footsteps of my great ancestor Joseph Cinqué, who led a mutiny onboard the *Amistad* slave ship in 1839 and was subsequently acquitted by the US Supreme Court after representing himself at trial. By that point in my life, I was a highly learned individual, having dedicated many, many years to careful study of history and politics, so I never stumbled over my words and had hundreds of dates and details at my fingertips. By the time I sat down and my opposing counsel rose to make his final remarks, he looked positively panicked.

In the end, of course, the jury ruled against me, convicted me on multiple counts pertaining to my escape, and asked the judge to hand me yet another life sentence. After defending himself in the same court, Masamba received the same penalty, and both of us were moved to the state prison at Dallas, where we staged the last big battle of our lives.

The basement cellblock that served as Dallas's Hole was referred to as the Dungeon—because that's exactly what it was. Dallas was an old prison and this underground tomb had long since been condemned by state prison officials, but unbeknownst to them the guards periodically utilized it for intractable prisoners. We were placed on a special status known as the Harrisburg Lockup, which meant that we would not be released into the general population unless the top prison officials who sat in the state capital at Harrisburg specifically directed it. It involved such a harsh regime that the only prisoners who were actually put on that status were those who had killed guards or were effective jailhouse lawyers, whom the guards loathed above all others; radical Muslim religious leaders; or skilled escape artists who were considered the highest possible flight risk. It was common knowledge in the prisoner circuit that the only way out of the Harrisburg Lockup was a huge, outside-the-walls offensive that forced the courts to intervene. Otherwise either you served out your sentence or you died down there in the Dungeon.

Masamba and I learned this the hard way—after sustaining a fifty-five-day hunger strike to try to earn our release into the general population.

During our first few weeks down there, we were fed small meals on paper plates and allowed out of our cells only for two hours, one at a time, to exercise on the tier and then shower. The solitude was total, with even the guards being stationed not outside our cells but on the floor above. Masamba and I were separated by about nine or ten cells, which made conversation and "fishing"—our system of passing a line from cell to cell in order to send or receive goods from one another—nearly impossible. And anyway, we had nothing in our possession to exchange. We were allowed no books, no newspapers, no radios or televisions. The absence of any distractions, any intellectual stimulants, was particularly taxing in the weeks immediately following our recapture. Having come so close to freedom only to have it snatched from underneath us was devastating. In the past I had often wondered what exactly made people break down and cry, since this wasn't really an urge I had ever given in to. But after our rearrest on the mountain slopes I frequently found myself on the verge of tears. That level of emotional stress combined with endless hours of isolation opened my eyes to a new world of discouragement. As Tariq once pointed out on Death Row: "That's what we got, that's all we fucking got, man: all the fucking time in the world."

For several weeks, Masamba and I refused all meals, consuming only sugar water. At first the guards took no notice. Then, as our bodies started to show signs of deterioration, they tried their old trick of shuffling us around: I was moved to the Hole at Lackawanna County Jail, and Masamba was sent back to Farview. But the hospital staff refused to keep him there for more than a couple of days, on the grounds that he was not suffering from any mental health conditions. After a few more failed attempts to dump us in one institution or another, we were brought right back to Dallas, by which time six or seven of the other seventeen prisoners held in the Dungeon had joined our strike.

We went strong for a month, thirty whole days, which dragged into forty, into fifty. We were losing weight rapidly but nothing else seemed to be happening. The guards showed no signs of agitation or concern. They weren't even bothering us with threats or orders to call off our protest. This was because we were so isolated, so cut off from the world, that our strike had no resonance outside the prison walls.

For any protest action to be effective it must be sustained on all sides. A man starving himself to death is meaningless unless someone sees it happen: unless a photographer puts it in the newspapers or a preacher shouts about it from the pulpit. We needed press, political activists, politicians, peaceniks, anyone who could tell the world. We had none of it. By day fifty-five I was down to 119 pounds and the administration had not moved an inch on our demand to be released into the general population. We were killing ourselves and no one was watching. Who could we appeal to? We didn't have access to pens or paper, let alone lawyers or organizations that might have supported our cause. Our base on the outside was shattered—my family had already walked through hell and back in support of my actions, and the movement was spent. It had taken the government years to pull off this feat. They'd played every dirty game in the book: they'd sent drugs and detectives into our communities, dangled plea bargains and professional advancement opportunities before dedicated revolutionaries. They'd sealed the borders, seized our weapons, frozen bank accounts, and discredited our leaders.

The year was 1981. Emaciated, on the edge of madness, Masamba and I called off our strike.

Ever since our trial in Lackawanna County we had been held under a regime that included having our cells ransacked every day. We'd be either shackled to the windows for the duration of these raids or else manacled and locked up in one of the shower stalls. We'd return to find our meager living quarters trashed, our few personal belongings strewn everywhere.

In addition, every thirty days we were forced to face a three-person panel known as a Program Review Committee, or PRC, which would determine if we qualified for release into the general population. It didn't take us long to figure out that these "meetings" were designed entirely to further crush our spirits and remind us that we were in for the long haul. Legally speaking, the committee was obliged to base their decision entirely on our behavior in the Hole, but every time we sat before them they brought up details of our old records and past escapes as a means of justifying our continued confinement in the Dungeon.

So you could say that by the time the riot occurred, we were pretty much at the end of our rope.

It all started with a guard attack on a young dude named Switch, who, like us, was constantly being harassed with intrusive cell searches. He was a big guy, about six feet three inches tall, weighing around 220 pounds, and very athletic, so he didn't always take the guards' abuse lying down. Everyone who knew him knew that it was only a matter of time before he got into a full-blown confrontation with the staff. One afternoon I was jolted out of a nap by the sounds that put all prisoners on red alert: sticks and fists hitting flesh, concrete, and steel, mixed with the grunts, hollering, and cursing that say in no uncertain terms that one of ours is being attacked, and any one of us could be next. Jumping up off my bunk, I thrust a mirror between the bars and observed four or five guards jostling one another for space outside a cell down the tier. A couple minutes later they dragged Switch out and hustled him off in the direction of a basement cell where no one would be able to see or hear what happened and where, a few months ago, another prisoner had been found dead, allegedly after hanging himself. Two of the staff members in the posse were supervisors who wore white shirts—those shirts were covered in blood.

By then most of the other seventeen prisoners on the block were also standing at their doors with mirrors in their hands, and a number of us were shouting, hollering, and cursing at the guards, trying to divert some of their attention away from Switch and onto us. As he disappeared from sight some of the prisoners screamed at the guards, daring them to come back and open up all our cells so that we could all "mix it up," meaning join the fray. Other prisoners were detailing what exactly they would do to the guards' families once they were released from this hellhole.

This type of scene was not uncommon. Everyone was so highly strung from being locked up for twenty-two or twenty-three hours each day that people were constantly either collapsing into a catatonic state or falling victim to these uncontrolled outbursts of anger that we referred to as "going off."

As always, I wanted to direct all this energy into an organized effort of some kind that, instead of earning us random punishments, might help bring about a fundamental change in our living conditions. With a huge effort I managed to calm everyone down enough that we could agree on a collective demand: that Switch be removed from the basement and given immediate medical attention, or else we would "tear the block up." We called first for an audience with the block sergeant, then with the shift commander, and finally with a captain who had been involved in the raid. When no one responded, we got down to business.

I tore a bed sheet into strips and used them to make a thick turban to cover my head and most of my face. With the remaining strips and a towel I fashioned a protective cup for my penis and testicles. I put all my important documents, like legal paperwork, in a box under my bunk for safekeeping. I smeared hair grease and soap all over the floor. Finally I took out my most prized possession, a very small razor blade, and secured it between two plastic toothbrush handles. I lashed this makeshift knife onto my right arm using a shoelace. I was ready.

At my signal, all the prisoners set about stuffing up their toilet bowls with their prison blankets, then repeatedly flushing them until water overflowed the bowls and ran out of our cells and down the block. Some of the younger guys who'd managed to acquire matches were setting small fires using clothing and paperwork as kindling, or else hurling their possessions out of their cells onto the tier. At my second signal everyone stopped what they were doing in order to beat on the bars of their cages, verbally taunting and tempting the guards to come get us. We knew we were in for a rough time, but there was enough pent-up rage on that cellblock to withstand whatever was coming.

Someone at the end of the block yelled, "Goon Squad's here!" and then they were upon us.

The Goon Squad was led by one of the warden's deputies, a mass of brainless muscle whom we all referred to as Knucklehead. He had no intellectual capabilities that we could discern. What he did have was a strong stomach for blood. He led his men directly to cell number four, where a dreadlocked prisoner named Willie was constantly being abused by guards under suspicion of his association with MOVE, a highly radical Black liberation group from Philadelphia who had come under intense surveillance and scrutiny in the eighties. When Willie refused Knucklehead's order to present his wrists for handcuffing, the squad placed a protective shield across his bars and assaulted him with an entire industrial-sized spray can of mace. Then they lowered their eye shields and invaded his cell, first one group of five and then—when those five men proved unable to subdue Willie—a second, even larger posse. My mirror showed me very little of what was actually going on in the cell, but the sounds of bodies, clubs, and plastic shields crashing into one another and the walls told me that Willie, who was in excellent physical condition, was putting up a hell of a struggle. But ten against one can only end in submission, and I watched as they dragged his unconscious body out of his cell and down the tier, still kicking, beating, assaulting, and abusing him, even though he was practically lifeless.

They made their way systematically down the block until they reached my cell. I stood well back against the rear wall, a wet towel draped over my face in preparation for the mace. I endured it for a couple of seconds then fell to my knees, pretending to be incapacitated, but really I was peering out from behind my towel while they slid open my cell door and piled inside, a wall of flak jackets, riot shields, helmets, and clubs. They were lashing out with their sticks, using their shields to pin me against the wall, but I was doing substantial damage with my knife, throwing my elbows in such a way that I was slicing open their exposed arms, hands, and legs any chance I got. I was on the floor and they were on top of me, but that razor blade served me well. Even while sustaining stunning blows to every part of my body, I was managing to draw blood from a number of the Goon Squad members. After all, for them, quelling a prison riot was just one aspect of a thankless job. For us it was a struggle for life.

Eventually one of them managed to wrench the toothbrush holder off my arm. That was it. He showed no mercy as he lacerated every inch of me he could reach, lashing through the thick fabric of my jumpsuit and finally nearly severing the index finger of my left hand. I didn't stop struggling even after they'd put me in cuffs and were dragging me along the tier. I was still full of energy and I was determined to tire them out before they got me down into the basement. They pulled off all my clothes and flung me into a cell, buck naked, before charging back upstairs for more.

Although I was bleeding from more injuries than I could count, and one of my fingers was hanging off my hand, I felt great! I couldn't stop pacing up and down my cell, hollering words of encouragement to Willie, Switch, Masamba, and whoever else was brought down to join me. I felt no pain. I felt nothing but the exhilaration of having fought back. We had tapped into the kind of adrenaline that doesn't last just hours but days. We couldn't and wouldn't be subdued. Even though we were confined, we sustained the war for nearly a week, verbally abusing the guards every chance we got, and one time even flinging cups of our own urine on them.

No one knew. This epic drama played itself out in secret. No one sings of battles waged underground. The details are muffled in the darkness and dust and dismal isolation of a world below the world. Up above us they wrote over the riot with their gilded fountain pens. America's fantasy of the Black man as an unruly beast fit only for a cage has been crafted to perfection in courtrooms by learned men who spun our stories of survival into gruesome accounts of senseless violence.

We were hauled up before a local magistrate and tried on fresh charges, including on the particularly damaging count of "assault by a life prisoner," which added decades more jail time to our sentences. By then hearing these verdicts was nothing new to us. Masamba and I parted ways in good spirits, assuming that somewhere down the road we would see each other again.

We didn't know then what the authorities had in store. We never guessed they were cooking up a foul plan that would not only change our lives forever, but alter the very landscape of incarceration in the United States.

CHAPTER 30

THE LIFERS ASSOCIATION

B y 1983, every prisoner who knew me, or knew of me, addressed me as Maroon. That name—my name—had become synonymous with escape. This of course brought me notoriety among the guards, but it also brought a certain status among the other prisoners. I guess you could say I had become something of a celebrity in the Pennsylvania prison circuit. This was largely due to the press coverage of both my escape from Huntingdon and my and Masamba's breakout from Farview. Dozens of hungry reporters had chased the story, painting me as an escape artist with almost superhuman capabilities. Guards and prison officials fed this "myth" of Russell Shoatz as a dangerous convict capable of almost anything. For instance I learned that following my successful escape from Huntingdon, a huge platoon of police was stationed around Western Penitentiary for fear that I would stage a riot there in order to break out my comrades, such as Tariq and Abdul Malik. No one seemed to question the logic of how one man, operating entirely alone in the Pennsylvania wilderness, could travel the nearly two hundred miles between Huntingdon and Western and single-handedly break two prisoners out of a heavily guarded facility! But all that hyperbole was a double-edged sword: On one hand it enabled the state to justify spending huge amounts of money hunting me down, and it later helped convince jurors and judges to lock me up and throw away the key. On the flip side, it made me a legend.

When I arrived back at Western after standing trial for the Dallas riot, I'd expected to slip back into my old routine: scoping out the joint for familiar faces, making contact with my people on the outside, and keeping up the struggle as best I could. Instead I found myself meeting and greeting a long queue of inmates, most of whom were strangers but who seemed to be familiar with every detail of my life—as well as some embellishments and exaggerations along the way! Because I had not one but *two* successful liberation attempts under my belt, their attitude toward me went from respect to reverence. Long Timers sought me out to ask my views on a number of matters, and Short Timers wanted the bragging rights of having met me, just to convey to their associates on the outside. I began to feel a heavy burden of responsibility toward all these men, not only to live up to their image of me but to channel their excitement into more productive avenues. So as soon as the Program Review Committee approved my release from the Restricted Housing Unit into the general population, I got to work.

Right off the bat I had an unwilling ally in this matter. His name was Errol "Ibrahim" Banks-Holmes, a dude I had known in my Morganza days. At the time he was also serving a life sentence at Western on some bogus charges related to a robbery he didn't commit. He had also, through a process of intense self-education, become a very effective jailhouse lawyer. Like me he read voraciously and was a wealth of information on a number of subjects. But although he was a politically conscious individual who had converted to Islam, he had recently grown disillusioned with the other prisoners and was of the opinion that they had become so "institutionalized" it was worthless to even try to move and shake them in the direction of liberation. He ascribed this to the changing times, arguing that the gulf between the seventies and the eighties was so big a man could disappear into it. He once described it to me this way:

In the seventies we read books. In the eighties guys are watching TV. In the seventies we practiced martial arts. In the eighties they're listening to rap music tapes. In the seventies we talked about socialism and capitalism, but nowadays guys only want to talk about culture and racism. In the seventies we planned escapes, but in the eighties guys started joining football and basketball teams run by the prison administration. In the seventies we organized work stoppages to win privileges like school release, conjugal visitations, and public speaking engagements, but in the eighties guys are bringing weapons to these programs and getting them shut down. In the seventies, the prisons were full of politically conscious prisoners who would take a beating for each other—hell, we would even take a bullet for each other. These days the only thing you can get your fellow prisoners to stand up for is the head count.

Even though I didn't necessarily disagree with him, I couldn't let his analysis of the situation interfere with my plans. As far as I was concerned, people like Errol Ibrahim and I had a duty toward the other men in here to pass on our learning and do absolutely everything in our power to help them win their freedom while doing the same for ourselves. Still, I couldn't deny that the changing climate would make it difficult if not impossible to carry out what I will call "old-school" liberation attempts. The authorities were busy investing massive amounts of resources in new and improved facilities that followed the same trajectory as the technological advancements taking place at that time: instead of trying to secure the walls, they were erecting electric fences; instead of adding more riot squads, they were installing closed-circuit surveillance systems. I knew that if we wanted to get free, or bring about changes in our miserable living conditions, we'd have to find new and creative ways to go about it.

This was a completely new mindset for me. For decades I had been steeped in the militant view of myself as a soldier. I was a slave to the notion that armed struggle against the oppressor was the best—indeed the *only*—viable option for Africans in America. As such, I viewed myself, and many other Black prisoners, as prisoners of war who were honor bound to escape the enemy's clutches, just as many British and American troops escaped Nazi prison camps during World War II. As a POW I was also morally opposed to any attempt to "negotiate" with my oppressor, to recognize their courts, or to cooperate with their legal processes in any way. But with continued study, especially during my time in the Restricted Housing Unit at Western following the Farview escape, came new insights.

In particular I started closely following the Solidarity trade union movement in Poland, which had begun in 1980. At the height of its influence, that trade union had several million members, accounting for about a third of Poland's working population, and they were engaged in an all-out struggle against the communist government. That was the first time I really began to recognize the power of peaceful revolutionary change. I had not forgotten the strides made by Martin Luther King and the Civil Rights Movement, but I had been too caught up in the armed struggle to truly digest or study their nonviolent tactics. In retrospect, I realized that our hunger strike in the Hole at Dallas had closely mirrored the "civil disobedience" approach of both Solidarity and the Civil Rights Movement—though at the time I had preferred to equate our actions with those of the Irish Republican Army in Northern Ireland, again because that particular struggle was more in line with my belief that an armed uprising was the only way forward. Solidarity changed all that. From the eighties onward I made a definite shift toward a more "aboveground" approach to the problem of our collective incarceration, and it started with me trying to organize the Lifers.

What the courts call a "natural life sentence" is, for a prisoner, "death by incarceration." It stands to reason, therefore, that a man serving one or more of these sentences is largely devoid of hope. At Western there were hundreds of people serving either life or such long sentences without the possibility of parole that they were resigned to dying behind bars. The lethargy, idleness, and disillusionment of these inmates permeated the entire prison, and I was convinced that uniting them in a successful campaign would bring about massive changes in the prison culture at Western. To do this I needed legal advice from guys like Errol Ibrahim who, despite his initial reluctance, quickly became a leading member of the movement.

So, we did our research and took it to the people. At the time, Western's prison population was over 56 percent Black, yet there had never been a Black president of the prison-approved Lifers Association. Not only that, but we also discovered, and presented compelling evidence of the fact, that this association routinely funneled a large portion of its membership "dues" to the Police Benevolent Association, the union representing pigs and prison guards! Significant amounts of this money also found their way to charitable organizations run by guards' wives on the outside. As a result there was no formal body representing the true interests of Lifers and Long Timers and our "dues" were lining the pockets of our jailers.

Errol Ibrahim and I rallied the men hard—no easy task considering that many of these dudes had started or joined various rackets inside the prison. They did so either to win some clout that would help them endure decades upon decades inside, or to satisfy and sustain any number of cravings, desires, and addictions that develop in a prison, from cigarettes to smut. Ultimately, we convinced a number of other inmates to join us in a mass lobbying campaign to actually change state laws to allow Lifers to become eligible for parole. We made the case that most men in the joint were there as a result of centuries of oppression starting from slavery, which had resulted in higher rates of sickness, poverty, and illiteracy in Black communities. What the authorities referred to as "crime" was actually a continuation of the legacy of Black oppression in White America, enabling the government to round up and incarcerate thousands upon thousands of African Americans and force them to labor in shackles, just as they had done on the Southern plantations for centuries. We argued that this unfair system entitled people to a second chance in the form of parole or early release. We also rallied prisoners around the promise that if we could take control of the Lifers Association, we would use our funds to hire lawyers to represent Lifers before the Pardon and Commutation Board and donate our limited funds exclusively to charities and organizations that cared for abused women and children. We began writing letters to canvas support on the outside. We wanted to bring a wave of pressure strong enough to crash over the prison walls.

In the summer of 1983 the association held its annual election and I was voted in as president—unanimously. The prison's response was swift. That same evening all the newly elected officers of the Lifers Association, including the two vice presidents, secretary, treasurer, and sergeant at arms, were summoned to a meeting by the warden. In his office, in the presence of several staff members and two of his deputies, the warden instructed my fellow office-bearers to hold a new election immediately, adding that he "would not tolerate nor recognize Russell Shoatz as the president." Riled up by Errol Ibrahim, who was the appointed legal counsel for the organization, my cabinet along with the general membership refused to follow the warden's order. They argued that I had been appointed through an official, democratic process that they couldn't violate.

A few days later I found myself back in the Hole, but the administration didn't stop there. All the office-bearers, including Errol Ibrahim, were transferred to other prisons, and the entire Lifers Association was shut down. Errol Ibrahim filed suit in the US District Court for the Western District of Pennsylvania, arguing that the administration's response violated our First Amendment rights, but of course the court ruled against us. Meanwhile the warden at Western had me placed on indefinite administrative custody in the Restricted Housing Unit on the grounds that I posed a grave threat to prison security.

It took me a while to digest this overblown reaction on the part of the prison administration. In all the years I'd been incarcerated I'd grown accustomed to being flung into solitary confinement in response to incidents of a physical nature—riots, escape attempts, defending myself against guard brutality, hunger strikes, and other events in that vein. This was the first time I'd been retaliated against for actions that were completely aboveground, in fact, for playing completely by the rules! It shocked me, briefly, to realize that the authorities viewed our nonviolent "civil disobedience" tactics the same way they saw our armed insurrections, and punished them both the same.

This didn't deter me from my mission to agitate and organize the other inmates. If anything, I doubled down. In the past I had taken advantage of the endless prison time to educate myself. Now I changed tracks and embarked on a mass public prison education campaign involving every single prisoner in the Hole at Western. I did this through a series of "seminars," the idea for which came from a prisoner named Leslie Harris, the smartest guy I have ever known personally. He and I had done some stints together in the Holes at Dallas and Western, during which time he was the only prisoner I knew of who had access to a TV and a radio. He didn't squander these tools—instead he used them to amass a wealth of knowledge on a range of subjects. I came to regard him as my own private encyclopedia—anytime I had a doubt or query about something, I'd call him to his cell door and pose questions for which he always had not only answers but a whole bunch of related information. Our spirited debates and conversations taught me that intellectual stimulation can really help to hold on to one's sanity. Leslie believed that group seminars were a great way to relieve the stresses of solitary confinement, but he died in the Hole before he had a chance to properly test this theory.

So when they put me back in the Hole at Western I began to implement the template that Leslie had suggested, gathering as many other prisoners as I could.

This, of course, was anathema to the authorities. A place built on misery can't stand exhilaration. Poison shies away from its antidote. As enthusiastically as I developed my curriculum and program, so too did the jailers sharpen their knives against me.

CHAPTER 31

FREE

H ave you heard of a *quilombo*? Or a *mocambo*? Or a *palenque*?

They refer to the liberated zones, the communities built by maroons far away from the plantations. They are societies of free people. They are places where escaped Black slaves joined hands with Indigenous people and poor whites in a truce against a civilization built on human misery.

They existed all over the world. Palmares in Brazil. The Great Dismal Swamp in Florida. In Haiti, Jamaica, Surinam, Colombia, French Guiana, Mexico, the Bahamas, Texas, Oklahoma. They go by many names: the Garifuna, the Accompong, the Seminoles, the Boni, the Matawi. Point to any place on a map where there was slavery, and your finger will touch a place that is, or once was, a quilombo.

To be in a quilombo is to be prepared. Maroonage is not a single event, it is a way of life. Maroons don't simply *get* free—they have to *stay* free. And even then their work is not done. They must return, and keep returning, to free others. This is the hardest task of all because sometimes slaves are whipped and scalded so badly they become blind to their own bondage. We have to see our chains before we can break them.

The slave masters and slave catchers never stop hunting them, so maroons have to sharpen their ears and eyes and spears. They have to become the highest grade of humanity in order to outwit, outlast, and outfight the armies of their oppressors. This means that no matter where they go, they are always in the eye of the hurricane. To be a maroon is to be a hunted individual in the heart of the empire.

In the 1980s, we built a quilombo inside the Pennsylvania Department of Corrections. We were convicted, caged, and chained, yet we found a way to get free.

CHAPTER 32

QUILOMBO

There's a whole world out there, within reach of our fingertips, but it's the business of our oppressors to make our respective struggles appear isolated, disconnected, and doomed. I wanted to change that, starting with a handful of prisoners locked up for life in a state penitentiary in rural Pennsylvania.

Ever since the Black Unity Council got involved with the Panthers in 1969, I had seen all of my actions as being in solidarity with the oppressed masses globally. I had known of Third-World liberation movements prior to that, but the Black Panther Party helped to elevate both my consciousness and my commitment to recognizing just how much the United States and its imperial project have hindered effective international solidarity between freedom fighters. The Panthers also always stressed the need to unite people who in many ways constituted internal colonies within the United States, including Puerto Ricans, Mexican and Hispanic peoples, and Native Americans. Were it not for the FBI's brutal counterinsurgency program—which killed, jailed, or exiled the most dynamic movement leaders—many of these domestic populations might have achieved victory by standing together for a united set of demands.

By the time I started the seminars in 1983, I possessed a mine of information on this subject, but I was reluctant to simply spew this knowledge at the other participants. So I devised a system whereby everyone who wished to be a part of the program got a chance to either suggest or "present" material on various Third-World liberation struggles, as well as on the geography, history, and culture of those places. In the beginning we spent a lot of time covering the national liberation movements on the African continent, in Palestine, in Vietnam, and in South and Central America, as well as resistance movements in Western nations like Ireland, Italy, and Germany. My goal was to provoke the seminar participants to "think globally while acting locally"—to realize that they were linked to thousands of other people in a chain of exploitation that had also laid the groundwork for their own oppression and incarceration.

Getting all the study aids into the hands of the seminarians proved to be a huge challenge. Most prison libraries are dreadful places, poorly stocked and generally catering to the lowest literary tastes. What makes it past the censorship board is largely limited to pulp. However, I was in touch with a number of publications on the outside that would mail us their material free of charge—*Workers World*, *The Guardian*, and *Prairie Fire* being just a few of the newspapers and magazines we subscribed to. Additionally both the East and West Coast Black Panther Party chapters—or what was left of them—obliged by sending us whatever material they could muster. At the time it didn't occur to me that some of the participants might not be able to read or write, and that whatever contributions they made came purely as a result of listening to the discussion or talking to other participants in between the sessions.

Once in possession of the literature, we had to figure out ways to pass it around. And since we obviously didn't have the ability to make copies, we needed to allocate enough time for each person to receive and review the readings before sharing them with the next participant. So every piece of material was either "fished" or "driven" from cell to cell. This was a major undertaking that required the following process:

First you had to buy a tube of toothpaste from the commissary. You squeezed out the contents and mixed the toothpaste with soap to make a paste that, when it hardened, became a glue-like substance. Next you sawed off the nozzle of the tube using the edge of the metal sink as a knife. Then you used your prison-issue pen to punch a hole at the top of the tube. Into this hole you inserted a "fishing line" made from braided threads that had been removed from your blanket, towel, bed-sheet, jumpsuit—whatever you could lay your hands on, because this line needed to be between twenty and forty feet long. Once the line was securely tied, you coated the tube in the sticky paste and then, if you lived on the top tier, you maneuvered it out of your cell and slid it over the tier until it dangled in front of the cell door of someone on the bottom tier. That person then grabbed your line and attached the contraband—in this case, our reading materials—to the sticky paste, and then you simply hauled your line back into your cell. They say necessity is the mother of invention, and in those days we had no choice but to get creative! But we all had a good attitude about it because, pretty soon, those seminars became the thing we lived for.

Every Tuesday and Thursday from noon until 3 p.m., the Hole became an electrified classroom. Not every prisoner in the Restricted Housing Unit was an official seminarian but our discussions were so enthusiastic and enlightening that even those who weren't part of our group respected the hours set aside for our lessons and offered no disturbances or interruptions. We followed a strict protocol whereby everyone got a chance to present material before we opened the floor for questions and debate. Since we couldn't see one another, and had to rely on only our voices, it was essential that everyone respected one another—you couldn't simply yell over someone you disagreed with. You had your time to speak but were expected to yield the floor to your opponents as well. Considering our circumstances, it all ran amazingly smoothly. In time, we became a community whose commitment to one another went beyond our collective learning. For instance, we began a group exercise program where we would do the same routines at the same time in our respective cells, calling out encouragement to one another. We pooled the little money we had—what we either earned from prison jobs or received from our families—and made sure everyone received something from the commissary every week. We added contests where participants could win candy bars or other special treats by answering questions about each week's material.

Some of the topics were a natural fit: most guys knew at least something of Vietnam and Palestine owing to the ubiquitous news coverage of those struggles. A lot of the guys were enamored of the cause of the Palestinians, although more for the machismo aspect of their daring actions such as hijacking planes, than for the practical and tactical aspects of their protracted struggle for self-determination. Most of our group's members had come of age at the height of the war in Vietnam, in addition to which our seminars often included firsthand accounts from both Black and white military veterans who had personally fought against the Vietcong. I must state here that nobody felt or expressed any sympathy for these veterans. They were politely given a chance to tell their stories, but most participants viewed them as guys who'd been suckered into risking their lives in Vietnam, only to return to the US to become entrapped in foul situations that led them to prison.

Other subjects proved more of a challenge. For instance, none of the seminar participants knew anything about the Irish Republican Army (IRA) and its offshoots in Northern Ireland. Most of our members were Black, and when I first introduced the topic I could almost *see* them—through the concrete and steel that separated us—drifting off. Moreover many of them had experienced their share of beef with Irish Americans in the segregated cities of Philadelphia and Pittsburgh, and couldn't understand why I was so adamant about studying a European country. But I had structured the program in a way that tolerated no racialized diversions, since we were a multiracial group, and in the end they figured that I always had good reasons for introducing any subject. After that it was a simple matter of letting the history speak for itself, and pretty soon guys who'd once warred on the streets with Irish

Americans found themselves relating very differently to an essentially colonized people. They became outraged by Britain's domination of that country culminating in a famine in the nineteenth century that killed millions of Irish people and forced a mass migration to the US, where they faced even more discrimination as "white niggers." Our debates on the IRA became as intensive and explosive as our seminars on Vietnam! More importantly, the lingering hostility between Black and Irish prisoners in the Hole gave way to a united search for solutions to racial tensions within the prison, including programs to address their shared grievances. These advances made it easier for me to introduce units on other anti-imperialist formations in Europe, like the Red Brigades in Italy and the Baader-Meinhof/Red Army Faction in West Germany.

On the African continent we covered the people's wars led by the African Party for the Independence of Guinea and Cape Verde (PAIGC); the Popular Movement for the Liberation of Angola (MPLA); the Front for the Liberation of Mozambique (FREMLO); the Zimbabwe African National Union (ZANU) and the Zimbabwe African People's Union (ZAPU), the two liberation movements in Rhodesia, now Zimbabwe; and the war in Ethiopia resulting in the breakaway of Eritrea, which was at the time the longest continuous armed struggle on that continent. We also reached out to US-based groups like the African Liberation Support Committee, which was deeply involved in sending material aid to conflict-affected African nations, especially to South Africa during the anti-apartheid movement. Since we didn't have money, we donated our time, writing letters to our comrades and families on the streets urging them to do their part in the effort.

Never, throughout all my years of curating these sessions, did I consider myself the "teacher" and the other participants as "students." We were engaged in a collective "self-education" project and I learned as much as anyone else. A particularly enlightening moment for me came when someone from the outside—I can't remember who—sent me a book called *Dalit: Black Untouchables of India* detailing the long and gruesome history of India's caste system, which is essentially a racialized hierarchy that has resulted in terrible brutality toward the lowest castes, or Dalits. I had no idea about this community, whose people not only had black skin but also identified with oppressed Black people around the world, equating their subjugation at the hands of upper-caste Hindu communities with various systems of apartheid around the world, including in the United States. This eye-opening book prompted us to study the region further, and I was able to receive a subscription from a publication called *Dalit Voice*, which touched on numerous political issues in South Asia.

This magazine in turn led us to the little-publicized civil war on the island of Sri Lanka, where a group called the Liberation Tigers of Tamil Eelam were engaged in an armed struggle for national liberation. This conflict was fascinating to us, mostly because of the LTTE's pioneering use of suicide commandos, and women suicide bombers in particular. It was the first time we had heard of such an innovation in warfare, and it took us by storm. The LTTE, and to some extent the IRA, acted as a kind of living laboratory for us on how a minority community takes up arms against a much stronger, majority-ruled regime. All of the seminarians were obsessed with this particular point of theory, and we spent many hours discussing the lessons these distant groups had to offer us in our liberation struggle.

Through our seminars, we also followed a strict policy of offering help and physical solidarity to one another—if anyone in our collective had a problem with the prison staff, we would be there for them even if it meant physically fighting off the guards.

The authorities despised us for it. We had turned a situation designed to punish, torture, and intimidate us into one of empowerment and upliftment, and it frustrated and infuriated them. First they tried to disrupt us. Every time a session was in progress guards would either bang on their metal lockers so loud we couldn't hear one another, or bring in prisoners with anger management problems or other mental health issues in the hope that their tantrums and meltdowns and babbling would make any kind of discussion among the seminarians impossible. We met these vile tactics with patience and perseverance until the guards gave up. In fact, a couple of the guards eventually became so interested in our discussions that they would come to my or other participants' cells to comment on what they had heard or to offer a supporting or opposing point of view! After all, for eight hours at a stretch they were also stuck in the dismal Hole, so it made sense that they too were desperate for things to occupy their minds. That was the thing about quilombos—they were almost always multiracial societies.

Having failed to get their minions to crush our program, the administration tried shuffling me back and forth between Dallas and Western—always under the pretext of some bogus rule infraction, like "unauthorized group activity." Each time I was transferred I simply took my template with me and implemented it in whatever Hole I happened to be in. The cells in the Holes at both institutions were tiny, seven feet by seven feet at Western and seven by eight at Dallas; the main difference was that the cells at Dallas had barred doors, which made it easier to simply pass reading material on to your neighbor, whereas everything at Western had to be either fished or driven from cell to cell. Each place presented unique challenges but nothing we couldn't overcome. Whenever Errol Ibrahim and I found ourselves in the same Restricted Housing Unit we shared the job of "curating" the study groups since he was an equally avid reader and had a lot to offer on a number of subjects.

It wasn't just us, either—all around the country prisoners were finding ways to band together, to make demands, to somehow offset the wretchedness of incarceration. I don't know how many other prisoners started programs that were similar to ours; all I know is rebellion was fomenting in new and different ways.

Then, in the fall of 1989, the inmates at the State Correctional Institution at Camp Hill went on a three-day riot and burned the prison to the ground. Once the smoke cleared, it gave Pennsylvania prison authorities carte blanche to reorganize the state's entire prison system along even more draconian lines. Their first order of business was to funnel the most "troublesome" inmates into the federal prison system, and that was how I and about twenty other seminarians ended up being transferred around the country on the grounds that we had somehow participated in or incited the riot at Camp Hill—even though we were locked up in a completely different institution over a hundred miles away!

On November 17, 1989, I was placed in the Hole at the federal penitentiary in Leavenworth, Kansas. I don't know what became of the others. Fortunately my lawyers were quickly able to prove that my transfer was based on completely bogus charges, so I was released into the general population. I spent two years in Leavenworth without a single infraction, yet when I was finally transferred back to Pennsylvania in June of 1991, I was flung back into the Restricted Housing Unit at Western.

I remained there until 1995, the year the Pennsylvania Department of Corrections unveiled their greatest weapon against us.

CHAPTER 33

WAR ON THE MIND

This is how the story ends. It is not an account of daring escapes or winter wilderness survival or dramatic shootouts. It's about hanging on. Fighting your captors any way you can. Each day you endure intact and ticking is a victory. This is the quiet, concluding chapter of my life, penned from a place you cannot fathom unless you've been here.

Some people say the Pennsylvania Department of Corrections built the Control Unit at the State Correctional Institution at Greene just for me. I don't know if this is true. What I do know is this: I was locked in one of its loathsome cells for nearly two decades. I know it better than I know any other place on earth. To my knowledge, no other man ever spent as much time in the Hole at Greene as I did, so if they built it for me, they got their money's worth.

Greene is a maximum-security prison, or supermax. It was constructed in 1993 in a rural pocket of southwestern Pennsylvania close to the border with West Virginia. During my nearly two decades in its Control Unit, I spent twenty-three hours a day inside a cage measuring thirteen by seven feet. I was not allowed to touch, or be touched by, another human being. My cell had no bars—instead it had a solid, rubber-sealed door that ensured I not only saw no one, but also spoke to no one. There was a strict "no talking" rule, brilliantly enforced through a high-tech surveillance system that allowed guards to tune in to each prisoner's cell via an intercom. This meant that any efforts to communicate with other prisoners through the tiny air ducts in our cells were quickly neutralized. When leaving my cell for any reason whatsoever—be it to shower or exercise in isolated cubicles or spend my allocated time in the library "cage"—I was forced to extend my arms through a slot in the door so that a guard could shackle me before releasing me. The lights were kept on 24/7. When I received visitors, I was first made to wear handcuffs that connected to a belt around my waist, as well as leg irons, before shuffling into a small room where I spoke to my family or friends via a telephone from behind a bulletproof sheet of glass. My chains were kept on throughout these meetings, and the conversations were monitored by the guards. Outside of these occasional visits from my supporters, who had to travel hundreds of miles to spend a few hours with me, my isolation from the world was total and complete. A single year in the Control Unit at Greene was worse than five years in any other Hole I've ever been in.

Ask any prison official why I spent so much time at Greene, and they will give you a bunch of boilerplate lies: *flight risk*; *escape artist*; *violent and dangerous*; *a threat to prison security*. Ask any prisoner, and they won't hesitate to give you the real reason: *seminars*.

On paper, Greene's Control Unit is reserved for men who've committed heinous crimes, men like the young neo-Nazi convicted in the gruesome Freeman family murders, who was incarcerated there for several years. I'm sure there are a couple of other hardened criminals who've passed through Greene's Control Unit, but in reality, it is the place where the Pennsylvania prison administration sends its most politically conscious prisoners, men who are determined to educate, agitate, and organize their fellow inmates to secure basic rights in an otherwise legally and ethically barren system.

It is a testament to the power of my seminars that the authorities went to such lengths to kill them. It has also made me realize that I was mistaken in the belief that what our enemies fear most are guns: they are far more terrified of our minds. Educated and organized, we pose a grave threat to the status quo. The torture technicians who developed the paradigm used to construct and operate these Control Units understood that. They realized that they had to not only separate and incapacitate prisoners with leadership qualities—prisoners like me, Ko Ko, Errol Ibrahim, and so many others—but also try to break those individuals' minds and bodies or keep them isolated until they were dead. This was a form of violence with which I was unfamiliar, the kind that leaves no scars, a purely psychological "war on the mind" rivaling the kinds of torture used on prisoners at the notorious Cherry Hill Penitentiary in Philadelphia back in the 1800s, before that institution was shut down.

The goal, plain and simple, is to drive inmates mad.

If I hadn't spent decades training my mind and body to withstand terrible hardships, they might have succeeded in doing just that. If not for my years as a soldier and a fugitive I would not have possessed the skills required to withstand the pressure of such a prolonged period of isolation. I could have become one of those men who cut their lives short. Humans are not built to live in cages. At our core we are deeply social creatures. Anything more than thirty days in isolation is considered by the highest authorities to constitute "cruel and unusual punishment"—though I would argue that even a few hours in such conditions are taxing on the spirit.

I was fifty years old when I entered the Control Unit at Greene. If I hadn't been Maroon, I might not have made it.

Here's what an average day at Greene looked like for me: arise from bed between four and four thirty in the morning. Begin by making my ablutions and then performing salat (prayers), which I continue to do at prescribed times throughout the day—although as the years passed and my physical condition deteriorated, I became unable to assume certain positions, forcing me to make my salat seated upright on my bed. That done, I fix a bowl of instant oatmeal and pop a baby aspirin prescribed for the poor blood circulation in my legs. I pull on compression stockings and turn on the TV to world news.

Then I pull out the big gun, the thing that kept me sane for seventeen years in the Hole—my endorphins. For years, both as a BUC member and later as a prisoner, I had practiced a strict physical regimen without ever fully understanding the biochemical processes involved in the body's production and release of endorphins during exercise. Tapping into the full potential of this natural drug has saved me from a lifetime of dependence on pharmaceuticals: it's my painkiller, my antidepressant, my sleeping pill, and my multivitamin. It's the only thing that is totally mine to produce and consume in abundance. My jailers can't regulate my supply or my intake; in fact, they can do nothing to deprive me of the positive effects of my own endorphins short of outright killing me! I always start with fifteen minutes of "bread baskets," which are exercises for my midsection. As soon as I work up a little sweat I down a glass of water and move immediately on to a forty-five-minute round of shadowboxing mixed with martial arts. I do fifteen-minute reps, with short water breaks in between, holding an eighteen-ounce book in each hand. There isn't a day when I don't push myself, trying different routines and combinations each time. When I'm done I have a quick washup at the sink in my cell before taking a fifteen-minute sitz bath in a warm water–filled basin. I started doing this after one of the prison doctors diagnosed me with prostate cancer a decade after arriving at Greene. A subsequent biopsy conducted at an outside hospital suggested that my symptoms—leg and pelvic pain—were more likely caused by an enlarged prostate. Probably as a result of all the beatings at the hands of guards in various institutions. Either way, I found that the sitz bath relaxed the area and relieved the worst of the pain, so it became part of my daily routine.

By this point in the day, the depression that hit me when I woke up has abated somewhat, and I'm usually feeling pretty good. Six fifteen calls for me to give the guard my letters to mail as well as sign up for the outdoor exercise yard before sitting down to breakfast. Since I was first incarcerated in the seventies, prison food has deteriorated by about 80 percent. It used to be that the penitentiaries ran their own large farms and dairies, so at least part of what was served up on the trays was fresh and edible. In the nineties it all turned to junk and I've had to use a lot of willpower to stop myself from becoming addicted to the stuff. I used to have a sweet tooth, but seeing how some of my comrades developed medical conditions related to poor nutrition, and their subsequent neglect by the prison system, caused me to kick this habit hard. I did this by systematically gathering up any pastries or sweets that arrived on my food tray and dumping them in my toilet. What all this adds up to is that my diet at Greene consisted primarily of what I could purchase from the commissary, supplemented with a few items that I salvaged from the trays. So breakfast is Raisin Bran cereal mixed with a handful of unsalted nuts; lunch will involve a portion of boiled vegetables with unsalted crackers and peanut butter; and dinner is usually a piece of broiled meat and whatever else I can stomach from the trays, all washed down with a glass of Tang. I always feel terrible that I can't share my commissary purchases with other prisoners in the Hole, like we did at Western and Dallas, but the setup here makes it impossible.

Next, if it's a yard day, I'll get some outdoor exercise time. I may see one or two guys that I know, but they will probably be so far away that we won't be able to do more than wave at one another. Back in my cell I'll do some writing, or I'll pace up and down while reading a book, paper, or magazine. However, I have to be careful not to blaze through my reading matter too quickly—Greene has a strict ten-book rule, which means that if I finish them too fast, I have to suffer a long period without any new material until I can return one lot of books and receive another. At one point I could tune in to NPR or the BBC on my in-cell radio, but lost both channels when I was relocated to a remote cell some years after arriving at Greene. Next on the agenda is lunch, followed by my midday salat, and yoga. Though I got quite deep into yoga for a while, I've been forced to make a lot of modifications to my practice due to chronic pain in my legs. After going through a series of poses, I'll watch a little TV to keep up with pop culture and get an idea of the forces shaping people's minds on the street. Around this time I need a nap, since I'm unable to sleep more than four or five hours at a stretch during the night. This could be due to my advancing age, or perhaps the fact that the lights in the Control Unit are kept on 24/7. Or maybe because I'm always on alert here for random cell searches, which are usually accompanied by the guards screaming at me and confiscating my possessions on the grounds of their being "contraband." Either way, I'll knock off for about an hour, or until it's nearly dinnertime. Thus the day passes. Thus the days pass. After the last meal appears through the food slot a guard brings me my mail. I sit down and read my letters, making notes so I can answer them at leisure later that evening or the following morning. I pace, I pray. I generally read until midnight. I offer a final salat for the night before climbing into bed.

Does it sound like the dismal routine of a man defeated?

What if I told you that all the time, I was also making a shank?

Prison shanks are one of the most powerful weapons in the world because they are crafted out of sheer desperation. A well-made shank requires patience, ingenuity, cunning, resourcefulness, and fury. Nothing else could turn a toothbrush, or a pencil, into a sword.

You cannot simulate the conditions required for the production of shanks. They cannot be manufactured on the streets or anywhere in the free world. A true shank is the work of a prisoner. It is a tiny pinprick of light glinting in the depths of hell. Before you sit down to fashion a shank you must first recognize that you have nothing. Only then can you begin the work of sharpening.

That cell in the Hole at Greene made me fine-tune every thought in my mind to razor sharpness. When they take everything from you, you have no choice but to see things as they are. You cannot lie to yourself anymore. I have always been a diligent student: whether it was assessing the shortcomings of the Black Liberation Movement or questioning the teachings of my Islamic leaders, I had long developed a habit of getting down to the basics. Solitary confinement forced me to turn that quality into a weapon.

Down in that torture chamber I began to pen the story of my life. Without the distraction of seminars, my old comrades, or even my family I had no one but myself to talk things through with. I became my own teacher but not in the way you might think: Not an old man lecturing to a younger version of himself. It was more like paring away accumulated layers of bullshit, polishing old ideas, and sewing on fresh ones. Carving something anew: Maroon.

My first experience of solitary confinement was at Morganza when I was sixteen years old. During that time I scratched one message onto the wall:

The Fair One Shall Prevail.

It was a philosophy born from experience but also from ignorance. As a child, I had deluded myself into thinking there was such a thing as a fair fight—because the only people I was fighting were other Black boys! I trusted in my fists to win the respect of my peers. I thought there was such a thing as earning your place in the world.

As I developed a political consciousness in my early twenties and turned away from fratricidal gang wars, I subscribed to a different motto:

The Gun Shall Prevail.

This, I now know, was an equally misguided understanding of the world. I was steeped in the notions of the Black Liberation Movement, namely *vanguardism*. According to this belief, advanced by RAM and later adopted by the Panthers, there is only one formation capable of leading the people in a mass uprising and, later, armed struggle. I had to watch with my own eyes, and experience with my own loss of freedom, how doomed this kind of thinking was. After studying vanguard parties and movements for years, I have now reached the conclusion that they *always, inevitably* fall into the trap of recreating the same oppressive structures of the very system they are trying to dismantle! They do this by subordinating the masses of working people to the will of The Party—whatever party this may be—and its leadership, until the so-called revolutionary vanguard is indistinguishable from the old, entrenched political elite.

It's taken me many years to gain clarity on these matters, and to scratch a different message onto the wall of my cell at Greene:

The Hydra Shall Prevail.

According to Greek mythology, the Hydra was a many-headed serpent whose heads would each be replaced by two more when struck off. It's also the longest constellation in the sky but with no particularly bright star. More importantly, it was the name used by Dutch settlers to describe the maroons of Surinam, whose decentralized organizational structure confounded white plantation owners for centuries! The Hydra refers to an ancient fighting formation devised and perfected over the years by maroons all over the Western hemisphere, a method of guerrilla warfare that does not rely on one party, one leader, or one front. It is an unpredictable beast that multiplies when attacked. The Hydra stands in opposition to the dragon, a creature of great size, strength, and cunning, but that can be defeated with a single blow to its heart or central nervous system. The dragon represents a standing army organized on rigid, hierarchical lines—whether in the service of a king, an empire, a republic, or even a revolutionary movement!

The Black Panthers had tried to become the Dragon. We had appointed front men and looked to them to drive our collective struggle rather than guiding it from below. This left us open to sabotage by state forces who guessed—correctly—that if they decimated or discredited our leaders, they could plunge the whole movement into disarray. We did not mobilize our greatest asset, our people. I don't mean our people organized into armed militias or underground cells, but in our original fighting formations, as families and communities. We had praised our ancestors but failed to mimic them. We had not studied the maroons. We tried to bend ourselves into the shape of our oppressors rather than rising to our true form as the Hydra.

On a parallel track, I reached a second, far more disturbing conclusion. This one also required me to backtrack over my life and confront the most unsavory aspect of myself: my attitude toward women. All my life I had been surrounded by women of great strength and character:

the Big Cheese and my mother; my sister Akila; my wife, Betty; Asani, who was my great companion and soulmate; and the sisters Yemoja and Zahara. Yet I had failed to treat them with the respect and reverence they deserved. Why was this?

To answer this question I had to revise my entire understanding of the origins of oppression in the world. All my life I'd been obsessed with the White Man. White teachers, white gangs, white cops, white mobs, white guards. I traced the fall of humanity to the transatlantic slave trade, which redrew the contours of the world in a gruesome pattern of whiplash wounds upon the backs of Black men and women. But as I read and debated with myself down in the Hole at Greene, as I sharpened my mindshank, I began to see that the wellspring of oppression lay much further back in history. Six thousand years back, as a matter of fact. And it had nothing to do with the supremacy of one race over another, but in the subjugation of women by men. Not racism but patriarchy: that most ancient system of coercion and control that is still dominant in the world today.

It is not enough to say that this system is slanted against women. It is more accurate to say that its very survival is dependent on women's eternal subjugation to men. It is upheld through the normalization of sexual violence in everyday life, the enforced exclusion of women from the highest ranks of economic and political life, and—most crucially—the rendering of women's labor invisible, and thus unpaid. A majority of women in the world live under this trifecta of oppression: sexual slavery, economic apartheid, and male-dominated political fascism. It hit me that this was as true of women in a remote corner of sub-Saharan Africa as it was for women in Philadelphia in the 1960s, including the ones I called my wife, my sisters, my comrades, or my lover.

All of a sudden I found myself freed from years of self-deception. I saw, in terribly clear light, how much I'd been steeped in the culture of patriarchy. How my despicable actions toward the women in my life could not be brushed aside as those of a "frustrated" or "misguided" young man but were patriarchal violence, plain and simple. I had been a low-down, dirty womanizer, and though I had thrown off many of its trappings when I joined the movement, I carried that kernel of patriarchy in my heart. It was this that allowed me, and so many other men, to degrade, dismiss, divorce, dishonor, and disrespect the women in our lives, all under the supposed banner of making "sacrifices" for our struggle.

I wish I could have seen this sooner. I had to go all the way back to the beginning to understand—back to my early childhood. No, even earlier. Back to my birth, which is to say, back to the place where I should have known love.

There are all kinds of love: love of the Source of Universal Power (Allah, God, or the other names that our species designates for this all-powerful entity); a mother's love, our first source of comfort, which we continue to seek all of our days; love of family (however defined), the special love of offspring, their offspring, and so on; love of a partner, which is reinforced by sex; loves that are platonic, deep, but absent of any sexual, physical intimacy; the love of *creating*, with our minds, hands, and actions; loves that are so far beyond our understanding that they might better be described as "addictions"; and finally self-love, which is better understood as self-confidence, self-worth, and the belief that one can cope with life's twists and turns.

I believe a lot of my skewed thinking was initially caused by a lack of mother's love. By a lack of tenderness. My mother was never cruel to me. And I can't say I was ever mistreated or willfully wronged by any member of my family. But my childhood and young adult years were marked by a kind of quiet neglect, an absence of affection or attention. I was a mouth to feed in a household stretched to its limits. The only times my mother sought me out were when I was rumbling with the Corner. Once she even put on her hat and coat, marched into the playground where I was fighting a bunch of dudes from the Moon Gang, and dragged me back home! These isolated gestures were disciplinary measures taken to keep me in line. There was nothing even remotely resembling fondness, let alone love.

I was so deeply involved in gangs and going to jail until I was eighteen, I never had a girlfriend until I met Betty in late 1962. It was during the fall of that year, and I was trying to settle down a little. She was open to being "my girl," and with me not having any experiences in that area, I immediately transferred all of my desires for a mother's love onto her shoulders. And even though I was very self-centered in wanting to do things that Betty didn't like—hanging out with my Corner boys, for example—I still looked to her to satisfy my deepest longings for love.

Thus I fell deeply in love with her.

I believe, however, that Betty could not or would not display any deep love in return, if she felt such toward me. We lived in the same house, slept together, ate together, went to family affairs together—but we never even talked to each other! I know now that neither of us had much to say beyond household matters. That was long before I cared anything about the movement, and thus being able to lie in each other's arms reading and discussing topics connected to that compelling matter was absent. Nor were Betty and I ever friends.

Feeling that I was not getting that mother's love from Betty, who by then had become my wife, I became a terrible womanizer. In fact, by the fall of 1966 I was a full-blown tramp. I still had a strong sense of being Betty's husband and the father of both Theresa and Sharon, who were born in 1964 and 1965, as well as being a man who "provides" for his family. I had "fell out of love," as it's said, with Betty, yet I clung to our marriage despite everything I did with women outside of it. Maybe that was because my father and mother were my models and they had been together all of my then twenty-three years. Or maybe I was hoping that one day Betty would show me the kind of love I had wanted all my life.

Things drifted along like that until the contradictions between Betty and me blew up after I smacked her during a terrible argument. She subsequently had me arrested for that. I was furious at her for a long time. I could not see, then, that she was utterly justified in seeking help from the police after I hit her. All I could think about was my own humiliation at the hands of those racist police. Later I rented an apartment and fell into a debilitating cycle of drinking and trying to be a hustler. In truth I was trying to fully reorder my life, but each day I was slipping more into madness. I was mentally and emotionally in such a way that I could have ended up even killing Betty, although I now know the real problems were inside of me. I needed a new direction that did not include Betty, except as the mother of my children.

That was when I met Asani.

Right away things were different with her. For one thing, we laughed and talked together as much as we made love. There were other little things too, like the fact that she always greeted me with a kiss. I had never known simple affection like that before, the kind of mother's love I had always yearned for. The tenderness I felt, for her and with her, shook me to my core—it called up extreme reactions to minor incidents, like the time I was prepared to shoot her husband if he laid a hand on her, or when I nearly killed my own Corner boy, Ace, for stepping out of bounds with her sister.

I began to do some real soul-searching, and while lying alone in bed in my apartment one night, I finally understood that I was behaving this way because I was truly in love with her. I had never acted that way over or about any other woman in my life, not my wife or any of the others I was seeing on the side. Being able to recognize and savor that insight was blissful. But it also set off alarm bells because it conjured up visions of her exercising great power over me. To put it very bluntly, I was scared of her. Love can make an individual fearful of losing the person they derive that love from. Such a state of existence can make one do irrational and downright ugly things! In my case I decided to hide how deep my love for her was.

I did this, at a huge cost to both of us, throughout our relationship, including the years we spent in the movement dedicating our lives to the Black struggle while raising our children. This was a colossal mistake. This was how patriarchy destroyed not just our individual families but a whole movement. We, the men, were enamored of what we called the Che Guevara methods of warfare. We did not see the twisted masculinity at the heart of it because we had taught ourselves to respond to love with defensiveness, stoicism, and hardness. We had trained ourselves to ignore the women in our lives and dismiss their opposition to armed struggle. We never heard their concerns as wisdom, we called it nagging. Maybe if we had heeded them, we could have found a way to keep our people together instead of accepting the old gang mentality that death and jail were our only options. Maybe we could have loved our women like they deserved to be loved.

It wasn't only the Panthers who were responsible for this kind of flawed thinking. Many other political and even religious formations fell into the same trap.

I experienced this myself when I joined the Muslim community in Graterford in the early seventies, shortly after my arrest. I already was a spiritual person. Even during the darkest periods of my life I would always get on my knees and offer a prayer to the Creator. But I still had reservations about becoming a Muslim, because I feared that the way most Muslims I met practiced Islam seemed to me to be involved in escapist denial—meaning they put undue emphasis on religious rituals in the hope and belief that such behavior would outweigh their responsibility to struggle against the injustices that surrounded their existence. When I finally converted, I was bombarded with a withering list of supposedly "Islamic" moral restrictions, many of which I now know are an elaborate set of customs that have been refined and passed along as "divine" but are in reality simply control mechanisms, designed to subjugate women. Since I considered myself a "good brother" I planned to also be a righteous Muslim. Thus I sat at the feet of all the learned "emirs" and "imams" who visited Graterford from Philly, New York City, Washington, DC, and the Middle East, then went forth to try to do as they had instructed.

I and the other Muslim converts at Graterford were repeatedly told that we should divorce ourselves from or cease contact with our wives or girlfriends in the street. A whole host of supposedly religiously based reasons were quoted to support that idea. All of which I can nowadays demolish, but as a new convert I was on a "hear and obey" level. Inside I was in turmoil about severing ties with Asani, but I reasoned that if Allah, as I was told, required such a sacrifice, then I would do it and pray that the Creator would provide a way to remove the obstacles that stood between us. I was still stuck in the Che Guevara–style stoicism that dictated that we must discount any suffering we undergo in order to reach our goal, which was now, for me, in Muslim garb. And so the next time Asani came to visit me, I simply refused to see her, and sent a message that she should go on her way. This took an emotional toll on me that I can scarcely describe except to say that for seventeen years my heart ached for her.

I was a damned fool. A few years later, I came to see the error of my ways. Almost everyone I had viewed as a righteous religious leader had been shown to be charlatans, escapists, pimps, or cowards—to me, anyway. The way they practiced Islam showed that they were looking for another fad or lifestyle to evade the all-too-painful reality of being both Black and oppressed in this country. But by then it was too late.

Many years later, when we had resumed contact, Asani told me to be sure to see the movie *The Color Purple*. She had seen it, she said, and cried throughout. My situation was such that it took me a few years to see it. When I did, I too felt a lot of sympathy for the female characters and disgust toward the males portrayed. But being stuck-on stupid, it took me quite a few years to recognize that I *was* one of those male characters. That was a terrible blow to my ego, since I was still thinking of myself as one of the "righteous brothers" and this was a terrible contradiction. But what really got to me was the insight that Asani had been crying because of things that I and others had done to her that were being portrayed in that movie.

At the time there was a debate about the author of the book that the screenplay was based on. It was said that the author was "bashing Black men," something I discounted because I had known too many Black men who fit those roles, although I didn't recognize myself as one right away. Later I was crushed to have to admit to myself that I too had acted like that sorry-ass character Mister portrayed by Danny Glover. Worse than the violence—which I was guilty of, on occasion—was hiding my love for the women in my life, the same way that Mister hid Miss Celie's love letters from her sister. And for the same essential reason: to keep them from recognizing just how much power they had in our relationship; to dim their self-worth; to be better able to control them; to keep them from discovering that I was scared of them. Scared that the love that I had would lessen my ability to dominate our affairs and thus make me less able to pursue my own selfish dreams.

I'm ashamed to be writing all of this.

But it also brings me some relief. I owe it to the women in my life whom I've wronged to return something that belonged to them, something I've denied them for too long. Like how Mister finally came to his senses and reunited Miss Celie with her sister, I can at least give this back, this sorry explanation of my mixed-up, broken-up love.

Perhaps the last thing I will scratch on the wall with my shank is this: *The Woman Shall Prevail.*

You don't create a shank just for the heck of it. It is built to be used, and sooner or later you must pull it out and do battle. As fast and furiously as my ideas crystallized, I dispatched my writings into the world, and waited.

I turned sixty.

I turned seventy.

I developed cataracts in my eyes. I started using a cane. More than one prison official told me I would die in the Hole at Greene. Every year I went up before the Program Review Committee to determine whether or not I could be released into the general prison population. The PRC is supposed to base their decision *solely* on a prisoner's current record, but although I had no rule violations and no infractions, year after year they denied my release, citing past escapes when really they feared I would organize the prisoners, build quilombos. Multiple courts struck down my lawsuits petitioning for relief from this misery. Higher-ups in the Department of Corrections said in no uncertain terms that I would be released into general population only "over their dead bodies."

I call bullshit to all that. Because on February 20, 2014, at the age of seventy-one, I escaped from the Hole.

CHAPTER 34

DRAGON

There's one thing every prisoner wants to get his hands on: contraband. That's because almost every item a human being might associate with comfort or pleasure is banned in prison. One of the longest lists of impermissible items in any prison is the list of banned books. Prison administrations will tell you they mostly screen books for violence or sexually explicit material. False. I've been locked up long enough to know that pornography and pulp often make it past the censors. Slim paperbacks and smutty magazines have a way of slipping through the bars. It's a different kind of book that gets jammed at the entrance, books that are heavy with history or bulging with truth.

Black books.

Here are just some that have been banned over the years:

The Souls of Black Folk by W. E. B. Du Bois
Blood in My Eye by George Jackson
Soul on Ice by Eldridge Cleaver
The Bluest Eye by Toni Morrison
Narrative of the Life of Frederick Douglass

The Autobiography of Malcolm X
Twelve Years a Slave by Solomon Northup

In 2014, the Pennsylvania Department of Corrections added a title to the list:

Maroon the Implacable: The Collected Writings of Russell Maroon Shoatz.

That book was my shank. It was how I dug my long tunnel to freedom from the Hole.

It was a Chinese American revolutionary musician named Fred Ho who convinced me to utilize my shank to its full effect. We had been corresponding for years through snail mail. He'd been reading my prison writings, which had appeared in a number of magazines and newsletters, and had been engaging me in rigorous debates about patriarchy, vanguardism, and maroonage.

In 2012 he flew out to Greene to visit me. He had recently been given a death sentence in the form of a terminal colon cancer diagnosis, an illness he had been battling for years and which had turned metastatic. When we "met" face-to-face, in a little booth divided by bulletproof glass and speaking through a wall payphone tapped by a prison guard in a neighboring booth, he in a brightly colored silk suit and I shackled and chained, it was a meeting of the minds of two men who were staring death in the face.

Fred was convening a formation of artists and organizers in New York City called Scientific Soul Sessions. This collective was fusing elements of the Black Arts Movement of the 1960s with a new kind of revolutionary consciousness. They had rejected Eurocentric ideas of socialism and were digging up an older form of communism, the one practiced by Indigenous people and maroons for centuries before Karl Marx! They had identified the biggest flaw in the old colonial-capitalist matrix, namely its total reliance on ecological destruction, and in its place they were advancing the notion of ecosocialism, a worldview that put the earth, not humans, at the center of all struggles for justice. He said their work echoed with the same ideas and theories I'd been dispatching into the world for several years. They were living my writings.

He had come to deliver a simple message: he was going to get me out of solitary confinement. He would dedicate his last remaining years to this cause. He had envisioned from start to finish a huge international campaign to "Free Maroon," which was to be his last stand, the final battle before cancer claimed him. The campaign would be a testing ground for my own theories about the maroons. It was an opportunity to unleash the Hydra.

For any campaign to be successful you have to know your enemy. I had spent a lifetime in Pennsylvania prisons. I was intimately familiar with the entire apparatus, not only the individual facilities that claimed years of my life but its whole philosophy, its reason for being. They would have you believe that prisons are mere holding cells, temporary accommodation for the "dregs of society." Really they are death camps, a Final Solution. The goal is not to rehabilitate and release inmates but to claim them, heart and soul. Like capitalism, prisons rely on endless accumulation, not of wealth but of people. Those of us on the inside know that prisons are intended to keep all "free" people in a permanent state of terror, which is what all sturdy empires are built upon. The longer we are here, wretched thousands of us in prison suits and chains, the more soundly White America sleeps, and the better behaved her children.

The Pennsylvania Department of Corrections is just one cog in this vast carceral system. It's an old institution whose racist roots go deep. The guards are well paid and the administrators are tough. In much of rural Pennsylvania, prisons form the very backbone of an otherwise barren economy, providing employment to thousands of people. Streets and suburbs surrounding correctional institutions boast names like Justice Way and Progress Drive, reminding all the residents and workers that they're out here doing the Lord's good work. They do not simply bow to demands. To pry something or someone from the maw of the Pennsylvania Department of Corrections would require tremendous power.

I made this clear to Fred. I did not believe his goal was possible. I suggested other names—other cases of incarcerated Black Panthers who I felt were more endangered or who stood a better chance than I did of actually getting out.

But Fred was not one of those guys who just accepts a no and walks away. Like me he had touched the limits of life. During particularly difficult bouts of chemotherapy he had drifted in and out of death, which makes you see things clearly. All his life he'd been involved in revolutionary organizing, and he'd grown disenchanted with what he called the US left—the remnants of socialist, Marxist, and communist parties that had disintegrated into infighting; student movements that had been co-opted by university administrations; and what he called the NGO-ization of once radical working-class struggles, a process that had taken people off the streets and put them instead on a payroll. He felt an urgent call to re-fire a revolutionary consciousness in America.

He saw the glint of my shank and he urged me to wield it.

So we got to work.

Every oppressed people have a Hydra slumbering in their midst. On the surface it might appear that they are going about their business, but dig a little in the soil, sprinkle some water, and allow a bit of sunlight to filter down into the tunnels, and you will see something sprouting. People of conscience awake. Feet that have forgotten how to march take the streets again.

When we founded the Black Unity Council in the sixties I had a huge network of supporters in Philadelphia, from my Corner to my family and everything in between: pastors, neighbors, coworkers. When I went underground, this network expanded to include politically conscious individuals around the country, scores of people who sheltered and supported me. During my time in prison this circle expanded still further to include members of my religious community, as well as prisoners throughout the state of Pennsylvania and all of our supporters on the outside. That base sustained me through years of courtroom trials and appeals. It came to my aid when I was being tortured by jailers. It lifted up my name even when my name was a burden to bear, when my name was associated with sedition, lawlessness, and murder.

Sometimes I wasn't even aware of the efforts undertaken on my behalf, or the hardships borne by others as a result of my actions. Years later my sister Akila shared fragments of this struggle: How FBI agents hounded my mother and my sisters for my whereabouts during the underground phase. How Betty was once reduced to living in a shelter with our children since I had not been able to provide for them while on the run or imprisoned. When I learned all this while locked up in the Hole at Greene, I came to the conclusion that I had no right to demand or even expect any more support from the outside than I had already laid claim to.

But that's the thing about maroons. They have a way of stirring something in people's hearts, the yearning of every soul to be free.

I awoke the Hydra. I urged my new supporters to join hands with my lawyers, who for years had been filing Freedom of Information requests for my case files and various other documentation pertaining to my arrest, trial, and incarceration. A handful of dedicated activists tracked down my prison writings, which had been floating around in dusty archives or far-flung corners of the Internet. Three of my seven children—Theresa, Sharon, and Russell III—who had been fighting a steady battle on my behalf for most of their adult lives, redoubled their efforts to win my release. They funneled all my supporters through their ranks, which were comprised primarily of artists and organizations.

In the seventies and eighties we'd needed truck jacks and ropes to break out. Fred relied more on his baritone saxophone! Scientific Soul Sessions aimed high and burrowed deep—they put on concerts to raise funds for my legal team while also making inroads into Philly to contact my family members and old Corner boys. They ignited elements of my network that had lain dormant for some time. My sister Akila, who was also struggling with cancer, filled a bus with women from her religious community and they drove down to New York City to attend fundraising events on my behalf. People I never thought I'd see again, people forced to keep low profiles after their involvement with my escapes, stood up and said: "We're still here." One of these people was Zahara, Yemoja's sister, who became, for a time, my principal storyteller.

The campaign began to amass hundreds of signatures on a petition demanding my release from solitary confinement. A big law firm agreed to take on my case pro bono, and we filed a federal lawsuit against the entire Pennsylvania Department of Corrections for holding me in isolation for twenty-two consecutive years. We charged that such cruel and unusual punishment violated the Eighth Amendment to the US Constitution, and that I'd been deprived of due process rights.

The United Nations got involved—their representative on torture singled out my case before the entire world body of nations, saying that solitary confinement of the kind I'd endured constituted a violation of international law.

We published my book, *Maroon the Implacable*, and it went on tour around the United States along with Theresa, my daughter and staunchest spokesperson. Fortunately, the book was banned across Pennsylvania prisons, which increased its popularity tenfold. Ask any educated prisoner and he will tell you: a banned book is a coveted book!

The demands on the prison administration increased. The movement made life uncomfortable; an itch and then a thorn in their side. My supporters flooded the prison with letters, jammed the fax machine, and clogged up their phone lines. The name Maroon began to appear in unlikely places, in churches in Harlem, bookstores in Washington, DC, cafes in Austin, universities in Minneapolis. Nobel laureates made appeals on my behalf, and hip-hop artists dropped my name.

I will not lay out here exactly how all of this unfolded. The Hydra is a mysterious creature and she conceals secrets in each of her heads! What I write here is a matter of public record, available for any interested parties to peruse at their leisure. All I will say is that the Department of Corrections did not know what had hit it, because like an animal backed into a corner, it became both aggressive and cunning.

In the dead of night, on March 28, 2013, I was woken by guards. They told me to pack my belongings.

Why?

Just shut up and get your things together, Shoatz.

That's how it works in prison—no explanations, only orders. I didn't have much. It didn't take long to put what I needed into a box. I was handcuffed and escorted out of that terrible cage I'd lived in for seventeen years.

They put me on a prison van. All I could tell by peering through the bars into the black night was that we were heading east. We drove and drove, passing nothing, for three hundred miles. I thought about my father on his long-distance truck drives. I thought about slave ships and the Underground Railroad. I thought about my mother and Mustafa. On and on through the state of Pennsylvania, the state where Kevin "Ko Ko" Turner made history. Where the Whackers at Morganza chased runaways through the cornfields. A rural landscape dotted with clean white courthouses where dirty white judges served up life sentences like milkshakes in a diner. A prison van ferrying a convict passed the Appalachian Mountains where once he'd been free.

At dawn we reached our destination: the State Correctional Institution at Mahanoy, a lower-security facility close to Philadelphia.

Do you want to know how it felt, being in a new place after so many years in a steel cell? Shall I describe it to you?

What can I say? There's not much difference between one hole and another.

For several weeks I remained in solitary confinement at Mahanoy. I received no communication from the authorities as to who had ordered my transfer or why.

I received a stream of visitors, the likes of which this small-town prison had never witnessed before, members of the Scientific Soul Sessions collective in their Asian and African attire arriving before the doors even opened for visiting hours in the morning! The phone calls and letters and press coverage continued, to the point that the prison had to hire a staff member just to deal with my case.

We learned that I'd been transferred to Mahanoy with the intention of starting me on what the Department of Corrections called a Step-Down Program, a long process with the goal of ultimately allowing me back into the general population. But empty words and fickle promises are standard department practice. Sure enough, a few months later I was again shunted off, this time just down the road to the Hole at the State Correctional Institution at Frackville. Again we were told that this was part of the process to release me into the general population, but a month later I was still in isolation, still talking to my visitors from behind bulletproof glass, still shackled everyplace I went. They were playing the long game, counting on my people eventually running out of energy, resources, and steam, the fervor fizzling out, and me going back to pacing my cell and waiting to die.

Broadly speaking there are two kinds of maroons—treaty maroons and fighting maroons. Confederations of treaty maroons signed accords, made deals, reached agreements with their former slave masters. Fighting maroons were soldiers and guerrillas, defending their land and their newfound freedom with firepower and weaponry. Circumstances demanded different tactics and history will judge them differently, yet at their core both groups shared one crucial similarity: they refused to be slaves.

I had spent a big part of my life being a fighting maroon. I took up arms and declared myself to be at war with the forces that had enslaved and were still killing my people. But the world changed. Our oppressors invented new and gruesome ways of silencing us. Prison walls came down, and something much more sinister went up in their place, high-tech surveillance systems and psychological torture. It became so that you couldn't shoot your way out of a situation. You had to find other ways of getting free.

As for me, I had to marshal all my forces, forge alliances, sacrifice relationships, and start from scratch in order to win my freedom. I had to become, in short, a twenty-first-century maroon. It was not the *Shawshank Redemption* story of using a rock hammer to tunnel to freedom. I used a different kind of tool to scratch down the walls. I had to keep the Hydra fed and fighting fit. I had to fuel the struggle with my pen, which was my sword. Long into the night I wrote. I accepted visits from hundreds of people. I took long phones calls and sat in endless deliberations with my lawyers. We battered against the walls from all sides, inside and out, north, south, east, and west. I worked my fingers numb at my typewriter. I tightened every thread in the mosaic of my life.

I entered the general population on February 20, 2014.

Fred Ho died two months later. My sister Akila didn't live to see my release.

There is something eerily flat about the kind of victory that involves a bureaucrat simply signing his name on my release papers. It was, in fact, a victory inside a defeat. I was "freed" from solitary confinement into a regular prison! And not just any prison—the State Correctional Institution at Graterford, the facility from which I launched my very first liberation attempt with Tariq! You have to laugh. You have to force yourself to make sense of it.

Graterford is one of only four "wall" prisons left in Pennsylvania, along with Pittsburgh, Huntingdon, and Rockview. All other facilities are part of the electric fence–surveillance system circuit. My memories of Graterford were of a deadly place where you could get stabbed in the chow hall or jumped in the corridors. As a young, able-bodied, and respected prisoner this hadn't bothered me much, but as an old dude I was on edge. I'd been in total isolation for close to twenty years, and that does things to a person.

For a start, I'd lost my sense of balance. When the leg irons and shackles came off, I found it difficult to steady myself, to walk unencumbered by chains. Stairs were a particular problem. Then there was the matter of adjusting to wide-open spaces after spending so much time in a cage. And finally, the other prisoners.

I don't really use words like *celebrity* or *legend*—but that's how I was perceived. The stories of my exploits had been passed down among generations of prisoners, and the moment I entered the general population I was mobbed. Even when I retired to my cell I received a constant stream of visitors, young guys stopping by to see me, to shake my hand, to ask questions. To see for themselves, with their own eyes, the man behind all the mayhem. Eventually I gave up on the idea of reading and writing; I just couldn't get a moment to myself.

On the other end of that were my visits with people from the outside. My children, whom I hadn't touched in years. My sisters. Those who'd held down the fort and who knew me as an absence, a missing person. Imagine experiencing that for the first time in a visiting room full of other inmates and guards. Full of beeping vending machines and security cameras. On rows of plastic seats that make it impossible to comfortably face your visitors. You are allowed to hug your family only at the beginning and end of the visit. No hand holding, no physical contact in between. It was that kind of victory. The kind that makes you wonder if you've actually won.

They still call me Maroon. It's a title. An honorific awarded to those who never stop fighting. It's not about escaping once, or even twice. To be a maroon is to reclaim your freedom every single day, and create liberated zones where other fugitives can escape to. It won't be over until we tear the prisons down.

The men who built the prisons in Pennsylvania did so under the illusion or fallacy that they were serving God. They contrived a place of such intense isolation that inmates would be forced to meditate on the error of their ways, and "repent" for their "sins." I feel no affinity to the gods who inspired these chapels of misery, these tombs. Nor will

I ever accept that those who fight against the injustices of the world be marked as criminals. The real criminals are the ones who built the plantations and the penitentiaries.

But the prisons did something their architects never intended. They became a place of tremendous revolutionary scholarship and activity. Not a place of "repentance" but of a devastating reckoning with who we were and what we'd done, and why, and for whom. Back in the sixties, a lot of Panthers used to quote the words of Ho Chi Minh: "When the prison doors are opened, the real dragon will fly out."

Think of this book as a little dragon. Make no mistake: it may appear compact, or harmless, but it is a wild thing. Handle it with care, run away from it, dispatch it as a weapon, but whatever you do, don't try to tame it. Dragons aren't meant to be caged. Sooner or later they will breathe fire, and fly.

AFTERWORD

We Are Maroon

I write about Maroon not as a fellow political prisoner, for a political prisoner I was not. Nor do I write about Maroon as an analyst of the struggle for Black liberation. I write as one of many he has been a mentor and father figure to when we were condemned as children to die in prison.

I write as someone who caused harm in my community but whom Maroon saw something worthwhile in, something asleep that needed to be awakened and directed in the service of my people.

I write as one among many living testaments that Maroon was more than the state's monsterfication of him and the people's mystification of him.

I was, like just about everyone who meets Maroon for the first time, already familiar with the sensational aspects of his story, and looking forward to a close encounter with a legend. He was the General, the indomitable military tactician and strategist, the revolutionary theoretician, an escape artist who could think his way out of any trap, and could lead an army to victory. Every time he was in a general prison population, he either escaped or he damned-sure tried. No matter if the prison was state or federal, Maroon never made peace with captivity and never waited for freedom to come to him. That was the reputation that preceded most people's first encounter with Maroon.

As a young 'un being moved from one adult state prison to another, I heard Maroon's lore. It was a feature of every joint I entered.

Rob J, one of my mentors, boxing trainers, and dear friends, was a close comrade of Maroon's. He also became for me a source of more personal and eyewitness accounts of Maroon. Evening after evening in the State Correctional Institution at Huntingdon's prison yard, at some point during our daily talks, without fail, I asked to learn more about Maroon, then hung on Rob's every word as he told me some inspiring and often thrilling story.

"You might get to meet the General one day," I remember Rob saying. "Whenever you do, tell him Sergeant Major sent you."

"That's your title? Sergeant Major?" I remember asking.

"Yes."

An eventual altercation with prison guards landed me in the Hole where I spent months with another legendary prisoner of war, JJ. I learned as much as I could about life and struggle from JJ until my jailers announced the date of my transfer out of Huntingdon.

"You're about to go to Greene County," JJ said to me. "The General is there, in the Hole."

"Maroon?" I asked.

"Yes. He's MY Old Head. He tightened ME up. Get with him. Now, you can't just walk up to him and expect him to take you seriously and trust you. So, you tell him that Field Marshal JJ sent you."

"Alright."

Words cannot describe the level of honor I felt. It was as if my freedom-fighting ancestors had given me their blessings. I felt like a young Luke Skywalker being sent by Obi-Wan Kenobi to planet Dagobah to find grandmaster Yoda to complete my training. I was twenty-three years old. I had already been in prison for eight years.

I did not know what Maroon looked like. I only expected him to be larger than life; certainly larger than me. I am five feet eight inches. When I met Maroon I did not expect him to be shorter than me. Much shorter. But when I witnessed a small, older man running around the dog kennel, commanding much bigger men's attention with political analyses and lessons from history, without breaking stride except to drop down to do one hundred push-ups straight, then repeating the whole routine over again, it was clear that this wasn't just any dude. I surmised that he must be the General.

I asked him "Are you Maroon?"

He replied, while still running, "Yes sir!"

When I told him that I was directed to him by the Sergeant Major and the Field Marshal, he stopped running and faced me with an intense curiosity. He wanted to know what prison I came from and how I came to know the Sergeant Major and the Field Marshal, especially by those titles. After briefly telling my story, I witnessed his curiosity turning into a welcome. He lit up when I shared that I had been reading about the maroons. For the rest of our time in the dog kennels that day, we talked about this subject that clearly was a passion of his. The words he projected from his kennel to mine became, among countless insights I would later receive from him, guideposts on my road to maturity.

"Escaping from slavery doesn't make one a maroon. A lot of people escaped or tried to escape the nightmare. It's when you came back to take others to freedom that you became a maroon."

Maroon and I immediately submitted requests to meet up in the law booth. One meeting led to another, then another, then another. Those meetings were a dream come true for me. Aside from my own readings, Maroon provided me with my most transformative educational experiences in prison. Not once did he offer me military materials to read, only books on African/Black history and world history. Even when I pressed him for books about war, he maintained with me a strict diet of cultural, political, and historical literature. He schooled me not as a general schools a soldier, but as a professor schools a student. As a father to a son.

Maroon understood that young men being brought into prison in droves were suffering from poor self-image that came from a sense of historylessness: the resignation that we had nothing in history with which we could look back and connect ourselves to with pride. In his view, our undeveloped sense of historical continuity became fertile soil for the seeds of self-hate to sprout. Our hatred or despised self-image translated to our disdain for everyone who looked like us, which then led to our maltreatment of each other—the kind of maltreatment that was allowing the state to justify corralling young people of African descent and condemning us to die in prisons. Drug dealing, gang wars, and other levels of intracommunal violence were results of that self-hate and self-destructive behavior. In Maroon's view, Black youth were in need of cultural pride reinforcement as much as political consciousness. He thought that a healthy political consciousness and astuteness needed to be built on a solid cultural foundation.

More than the books Maroon gave me to read by Ivan Van Sertima, Cheikh Anta Diop, John G. Jackson, C. L. R. James, and Frantz Fanon, among others, were his own writings and educational materials he created.

In 1996, I was released from solitary confinement into the general population. I would not see Maroon again over the next eighteen years. Meanwhile, I took all that he had taught me, and the study materials he himself had created, and designed a Cultural Awareness and Self-Enhancement (CASE) program with it for young men of all ethnicities in the general prison population.

Maroon sent word out to let me know how proud he was to learn of CASE. More and more young men who were released from solitary confinement and signed up for CASE expressed that they were referred to the program by Maroon.

From the general population I heard of the cultural and political classes Maroon started for and with the men in the Restricted Housing Unit (RHU). Word also reached me that Maroon and other men in solitary confinement, with the support of family members on the outside, had founded an organization known as the Human Rights Coalition. HRC was founded to organize family and community members against the abuse of imprisoned people.

In one of Maroon's letters, he directed me to connect with one of his daughters about another organization he founded from behind the walls—Families and Communities United. FCU had an after-school program for children of incarcerated parents. It was through FCU that I learned of the ten million children of incarcerated parents who were seven times more susceptible to be incarcerated themselves if no positive intervention was made in their lives.

Maroon was always organizing, always educating, always creating, to have a positive impact on his community, even from within a cage characterized by sensory deprivation and institutional abuse.

In 2014, after spending thirty years in solitary confinement, Maroon was released into the general population and transferred to the State Correctional Institution at Graterford, the same prison I was in at the time. It was the first time we saw each other since I left him in the Hole back in 1996. It was the first time ever that we were able to shake hands and embrace and not be separated by a metal partition between us as was the case in the RHU's law booths. We were able to sit in the prison gym and auditorium together and talk.

Although Maroon was as sharp as ever in his thinking and analyses, something was different. His focus had shifted. He admitted that now as a septuagenarian, his "Kunta Kinte" days were behind him. Time had cut off his feet. It was a realization that seemed sadder to me than to him. He still moved through the prison like a man on a mission; only now, with the world on his head, literally. He had become more preoccupied with something more threatening than anything he had committed himself to fighting against in the past. That threat was ecological collapse and its most glaring manifestation—climate change. He saw this threat not on the horizon, but already tightening its grip around all our throats. He described it not as a political or military threat, but as an existential one. He admitted to a pessimism about it.

Yet, his pessimism did not foster defeatism. In typical Maroon fashion, he incessantly challenged himself and the rest of us to think of ways to make it through what he saw enveloping us all in swift and horrifying fashion.

We read books together, such as *Deep Green Resistance*, *This Changes Everything*, *The Sixth Extinction*, *Extinction Dialogues*, and *Parable of the Sower*, which deepened our understanding of what was afoot. He introduced me to the work of Quincy Saul, whom he had a profound respect for. He then encouraged me to join Ecosocialist Horizons, the organization that Quincy was a part of.

The ecological issue also did not steer his attention away from the carceral matter that had consumed almost all of his adult life. He came up with a concept of mass education over mass incarceration that called for the implementation of massive open online courses (MOOC) in prison as a tool to empower imprisoned people and increase their chances of success once released from prison. Maroon never stopped thinking of ways to educate, enlighten, and empower people who found themselves on the downside of destiny.

All the while, something was different about me, too, in my second encounter with Maroon. I was now in a class of incarcerated people who the US Supreme Court had ruled were eligible to have our life without parole sentences vacated, which meant that we could be resentenced and even released, due to our age at the time of our offense. That Supreme Court decision was *Miller v. Alabama* (2012).

When I first met Maroon at Greene, back in 1995, I was twenty-three years old and on my eighth year in prison. Yes, I was condemned at fifteen. The second time I met him I was a forty-two-year-old man who'd spent twenty-seven years in prison. My sentence had been vacated two years prior to Maroon's release from the Hole and I was embroiled in a battle with Pennsylvania's colonial punishment system over their refusal to recognize *Miller*'s impact on my sentence.

Quite a few people whom Maroon had mentored as youth, whom the colonial punishment system had condemned to death by incarceration, were now on the verge of release. Maroon was so genuinely excited for us, even though the US Supreme Court decision did not apply to him and he would remain behind to, for all intents and purposes, die in prison. He was about to see some of his adopted sons get an opportunity to show the world what he knew to be true about us: that we were more than what we were condemned for. He had faith that we would show the world that we are assets and not liabilities to our communities.

Over the years, Maroon thought it important to bring many of us into closer relationship with his family. He often invited me to joint visits with his children. And it was here that I saw up close and personal what I perceived to be Maroon's greatest achievement—his children. Even with their father not physically present, but in solitary confinement for most of their lives, Maroon's children had grown into revolutionaries and servants of their community, fighting to free others from death-by-incarceration sentences, and leading community empowerment initiatives. They are activists, teachers, and community organizers, much like their dad.

Maroon confessed that family and fatherhood were areas where he did not do as well as he should have. He confided a great regret that he did not know how to be a father. Even though I pushed back on that notion, expressing my admiration for how fine and exemplary his children turned out, and for how many of us, including myself, that he had been a father to, he was not convinced. He insisted that he could and should have done better, and he was determined to try. His children, more than anyone, he said, did the time with him.

Thirty years after I entered prison, I was released. I walked out with a mixture of joy and survivor's guilt. Joy for rejoining my family, survivor's guilt for leaving so many friends who had become like family behind, especially Maroon. Survivor's guilt was a term I heard Maroon use to describe his own feelings when he was released from solitary confinement. "Some dear friends are still in there," he said.

A year after I left Maroon, my own son was born. My wife and I named him Karume, an East African word that translates to "he protects the land and forests" or, more generally, "he defends the earth," a choice that was largely due to my ecological consciousness which had been nourished by Maroon.

In a letter to Maroon, I expressed my misgivings about helping to bring a precious human into our increasingly unstable world. Maroon affirmed my sentiments, then added, "but you might have also helped to bring someone into the world who, with the right upbringing and guidance, can end up saving a lot of lives." That one little nugget continues to inform and influence how I show up in the life of not only Karume, but every young person I come in contact with.

Meanwhile, Maroon's children continued to fight doggedly for his freedom. And free him they did, with the help of the Abolitionist Law Center and many supporters.

In 2020, the campaign to free Maroon reached such a high level of urgency that his legal representation resorted to the state of Pennsylvania's Compassionate Release avenue. In order to receive the state's "compassion," the state had to be certain that Maroon would die very shortly after his release. Even Maroon's diagnosis of stage four cancer was not enough for swift compassion from the state. The battle for compassionate release had become such a long and excruciating one for Maroon, and such an emotional one for his loved ones, that the rallying cry went from Free Maroon to Mercy for Maroon.

After appealing the court's decision to deny him compassionate release, Maroon was called back to court. On that particular day, Maroon was in the throes of such ill health that he had resigned himself to it being his last on earth. He was sure he would not live to see another day. Suddenly, his cell door was opened and someone stepped in, wrapped him in a blanket, then lifted and carried him out while telling Maroon he was wanted for a legal hearing. Maroon was certain he could not physically endure another institutional proceeding, or even a legal visit. He did not want to go. Yet, he did not have the strength to express any objection to the person carrying him. Maroon was taken to a room in the prison and set down in front of a camera and monitor, through which he found himself once again virtually in a courtroom full of people, the majority of whom were his loved ones. His appeal had won reconsideration. Maroon commenced by expressing his regret for being a participant in a cycle of violence and loss and pain. It was a soul-stirring, tear-jerking plea to the people, not to the court.

He was granted compassionate release after nearly fifty years in prison.

After so many attempts, escapes, disappointments, and tortures, the state he had fought against his whole life decided to open the gates.

But what does that mean for a political prisoner, who has always refused to accept the legitimacy of the state?

I saw how Maroon and other political prisoners struggled against the state's judgment of them, and suffered under the people's, especially the movement's, perception of them. As with other POWs the state *monsterfied* Maroon, while we, the people, *mystified* him. To the state he was a cop killer, domestic terrorist, manipulator. To the people he was more than a hero, he was the General, he was the implacable, the invincible, the one true twentieth- to twenty-first-century Maroon. We needed him to be invincible. But, between the state's monsterfication and our mystification of Maroon was a human being as vulnerable as any of us. And here is where I hope we will allow Maroon and all political prisoners, even posthumously, the grace of being more or less (depending on perspective) than what we demand that they be for us.

Redemption from the perspective of a political prisoner might not be about apologizing or repenting for the politics, principles, morals, or worldview that impelled them to act against the state. It may simply be about regret and remorse born out of a deepening consciousness and heightening sensitivity about the effects of the cycle of violence, and their part in that cycle, regardless of the fact that they did not initiate the cycle. It's human to wish things were different, that they hadn't engaged in, or become ensnared in, deadly struggles with other humans, whatever the reasons, and whoever the other humans were, and whatever those other humans represented.

Like anyone else with a beating heart, political prisoners, at least the ones I know, and certainly Maroon, wish they were not shedders of anyone's blood, whether or not they were responding to violence and not initiating violence, and whether or not they had ideological reasons for their actions. Some political prisoners, if not all, have deep feelings of regret about the ramifications and ripple effects of violence that no one can control once set in motion.

Redemption for Maroon became a way to free himself not from his revolutionary convictions and his political and cultural values, but from a past guided by rage, humiliation, testosterone. We both explored redemption as the fulfillment of our obligations to the struggle to be human.

Yeah. We all wanted that action movie ending. After all, Maroon's story, not just what he narrated, but what the FBI files narrated about him, read like a combination of Ho Chi Minh and Jason Bourne. Maroon had become more than an American political prisoner and POW to us behind the walls. He was our brilliant, indomitable General.

I cherish the opportunity I had to spend even a few of Maroon's last minutes with him. And even with his last struggling breaths, he continued to impart wisdom and guidance.

To the state, we can proudly say, you've always been wrong in your judgments of Maroon. He was not a monster. He spent most of his life in your cages as a teacher and redeemer of many of us who acted like monsters in our communities. He helped us to reclaim our humanity and moral rectitude. He utilized art and whatever meager materials he could get his hands on to situate troubled youth like me in the continuum of time. Beginning with the Big Bang and continuing through the birth of planet earth and through all of the eras, periods, and epochs, Maroon connected us to the first single cell life-form and graduated us through the phases of fish, dinosaurs, mammals, hominids, all the way to Homo sapiens. He educated us about plate tectonics, archeology, and anthropology. He took us from the first formations of civilization in Africa to the diffusion of humanity throughout the globe. He brought us through the eras of slavery and colonialism and our resistance to all forms of oppression. He connected us to our heritage of maroonage. He was a father who loved his own children and family dearly and admitted his fallibilities. In every way, Maroon is more human and evolved than the state can ever be.

To the people, when we see that Maroon was just as burdened by life as we all are and he did the best he could with what he had to resist, was honest and humble enough to address his personal flaws, and gave us every bit of himself until he could give no more, we can realize that he was just like the rest of us and that, therefore, We Are Maroon.

Kempis "Ghani" Songster

ACKNOWLEDGMENTS

First, we would like to acknowledge all those whom we have not mentioned. Your efforts and sacrifices shall forever sustain the fight for those who continue the struggle for liberation.

To the patriarch Russell Shoatz Sr. and matriarch Gladys I. Shoatz, the Shoatz siblings, the Inabinettes, Gibsons, and Golstons, thank you, for without you, there would be no Shoatz family clan or legacy.

It is in homage that we pay tribute to our mothers, the women who brought us into existence, nurtured us and fortified us with their knowledge, guided us, and strengthened us, imparting their wisdom, sculpting our personalities, molding our characters, giving and showing courage, forging warriors' hearts while exemplifying love, ensuring we are empathetic and compassionate, and preparing us for whatever shall stand before us in this life.

To the offspring of Russell "Maroon" Shoatz, for they all shared the same fate of not having the opportunity to grow up with their father, thank you for all your contributions and support.

To the dynamic team of lawyers—Dan Kovalik, Bret Grote, Dustin McDaniel, Hal Engel, Glenn R. Mahone, and Reed Smith LLP—thank you for over four decades of legal expertise.

Thank you to Dr. Barbara Zeller and the late Dr. Alan Berkman for your unwavering commitment to applying your medical knowledge as doctors in the struggle for liberation and freedom.

Thank you Kempis "Ghani" Songster, the juvenile lifers, mentees, and scholastic cohorts who were able to benefit from the education and knowledge imparted by Maroon, for he saw in you what the world should have seen.

Thank you Joseph "JoJo" Bowen, who employed his military technical mind with exact precision, for exemplifying the steadfast heart of a warrior and for your dedication to the cause and your never-ending love for the Shoatz family.

To Erick A. Bolden, thank you for your steadfast support and over three decades of commitment to the liberation and freedom of Maroon, and for being that rock and shoulder to cry on.

To the comrades, organizations, artists, musicians, supporters, and the countless nameless individuals who contributed through their works or just through their words and prayers, we thank you for your participation and dedication to the liberation and freedom of Maroon.

Special acknowledgment and recognition to Russell Shoatz III and Sharon and Theresa Shoatz, who spent their adult lives in search of freedom and liberation for their father and numerous other incarcerated individuals and their families. Over the decades each sibling has grabbed the baton and has been instrumental in leading the charge for the freedom and liberation of their father. It can truly be said that teamwork makes the dream work.

By all measures this list is far from complete. If your name has not been mentioned here, know you are forever in our hearts.

Hakeem, Herman and Iylaluua Ferguson, Safiya Bukhari, Dhoruba bin Wahad, Chango Monges, Mama C, Marpessa, Laura Whitehorn, Ali Bey Hassan, Janet and Sala Cyril, Selma and C. L. R. James, Mumia Abu-Jamal, Julia Wright, Max Stanford, Kim and Mark Holder, Mike Africa Sr., Clare Grady, Angola 3, Jerome Coffey, Hamid, and Toby Emmer.

The Futch family, Burton family, Henderson family, Joyner family, and Williams family.

NYC Jericho, Deep Dish Network, People's Video Network, Philly & NYC ABC, the Rosenberg Fund, the ABCF Warchest, MXG, the Freedom Archives, Running Down the Walls, RAPP, NEPPC, San Francisco Bay News, the Committee to Free Russell "Maroon" Shoatz, and the BPP Alumni Association.

Riders Against the Storm, Yungchen Lhamo, Sophia Dawson, Dead Prez, Talib Kweli, Mos Def, Erykah Badu, Chuck D, Riconstruction, Ben Barson, Tongo Eison, Liza Jessie Peterson, DJ Sid Vicious, General Steele, and Smith & Wesson.

Khalid Abdur-Rasheed, Hamid Abdul Aziz, Sifu Alugbala Nkruma, Orie Lumumba, Netdahe and the Stoddard tribe, Jerome Coffey, Kenyatta Funderburk, Juan Mendez, Alina Dollat, DeeDee Halleck, Joel Kovel, Key West, Anne Lamb, Pandora Thomas, Raphael Cohen, Etta Cetera, Dr. Sandra Joy, Dominique Conway, Phoebe Jones, Clarissa Rodgers, Thomas Whitaker, Raymond Neal, Daniel McGowan, Tim Faschnt, Fred Ho, Matt Meyer, Deborah Engel, Steve, Sunny Hate5sxi, Peter Franck, Clare Grady, Paul Sayvetz, PM Press, Angelique Tran Van Sang, Alison Lewis, Francis Goldin, and Bold Type Books.

To all the "children of struggle and resistance" who've lost a parent or parents in the fight for liberation, WE SALUTE YOU!

"In Solidarity and Struggle"
Straight Ahead
Free Them All

—*Shoatz Family*

First, and mostly, and for everything: Fred Ho and Quincy Saul.

Also, and in immense ways: Ben Barson and the Maroon Unit. New York City and Pittsburgh. Scientific Soul Sessions and the Pennsylvania Prison Society. Ayanna and Rahim. The Philadelphia Five and the Angola Three. Bret Grote and the Abolitionist Law Center. Theresa, Sharon, and Russell III. Deb and Hal Engel. Kitty Stapp and Thalif Deen. The Red Rooster and the National Black Theatre. Mama C and Colia Clark. George Rahsaan Brooks-Bey and all the brilliant jailhouse lawyers. My girls, S & R. EH and IPS. Joel Kovel and DeeDee Halleck. Margaret Cerullo and Chris Tinson. The Afro Yaqui Music Collective and the Eco-Music Big Band. Matt Meyer and the War Resisters. Jim Lobe and the Washington Bureau. *TruthOut* and Al Jazeera. Ru Freeman and Leslie Jamison. Hampshire College and SJP. Angelique Tran Van Sang and Alison Lewis. RAPP and No Separate Justice. Francis Goldin and Chuck D. Arabelle and Dawit. Saed and Steve. Ramsey Kanaan and PM Press. Anu Roy-Chaudhury and Bold Type Books. Clarissa and Oscar Lopez. The Schomburg Center for Research in Black Culture and public libraries everywhere. Gizelxanath Rodriguez and the Zapatistas. Spiritchild and the Villalobos Brothers. Maria D'Almeida and Sarah Saul.

Every single person who called the prison, listened to our music, raised hell, read our literature, believed it was time, slept in our home, echoed the demand, held the fury, and drank the wine.

Finally: Peter D'Almeida, for the words of H. Rap Brown. Nejma Nefertiti, for bringing back my voice. Kempis "Ghani" Songster, for getting free. And Khalil James, for whom I was born again.

—*Kanya D'Almeida*

INDEX

RUSSELL "MAROON" SHOATZ was a dedicated community activist, founding member of the Black Unity Council, former member of the Black Panther Party, and soldier in the Black Liberation Army.

KANYA D'ALMEIDA is a writer and winner of the 2021 Commonwealth Short Story Prize. As a journalist, she reported for a decade on global economic apartheid, reproductive justice, and prison abolition. She was awarded the Society of Authors' annual short story award in 2022. Her journalism has appeared in Al Jazeera, *TruthOut*, and *The Margins*, and her fiction has appeared in *Granta*. She holds an MFA from Columbia University.

PublicAffairs is a publishing house founded in 1997. It is a tribute to the standards, values, and flair of three persons who have served as mentors to countless reporters, writers, editors, and book people of all kinds, including me.

I. F. STONE, proprietor of *I. F. Stone's Weekly*, combined a commitment to the First Amendment with entrepreneurial zeal and reporting skill and became one of the great independent journalists in American history. At the age of eighty, Izzy published *The Trial of Socrates*, which was a national bestseller. He wrote the book after he taught himself ancient Greek.

BENJAMIN C. BRADLEE was for nearly thirty years the charismatic editorial leader of *The Washington Post*. It was Ben who gave the *Post* the range and courage to pursue such historic issues as Watergate. He supported his reporters with a tenacity that made them fearless and it is no accident that so many became authors of influential, best-selling books.

ROBERT L. BERNSTEIN, the chief executive of Random House for more than a quarter century, guided one of the nation's premier publishing houses. Bob was personally responsible for many books of political dissent and argument that challenged tyranny around the globe. He is also the founder and longtime chair of Human Rights Watch, one of the most respected human rights organizations in the world.

.   .   .

For fifty years, the banner of Public Affairs Press was carried by its owner Morris B. Schnapper, who published Gandhi, Nasser, Toynbee, Truman, and about 1,500 other authors. In 1983, Schnapper was described by *The Washington Post* as "a redoubtable gadfly." His legacy will endure in the books to come.

Peter Osnos, *Founder*